# In Praise of Poverty

# In Praise of Poverty

*Hannah More
Counters Thomas Paine
and the Radical Threat*

MONA SCHEUERMANN

THE UNIVERSITY PRESS OF KENTUCKY

Publication of this volume was made possible in part
by a grant from the National Endowment for the Humanities.

*Editorial and Sales Offices:* The University Press of Kentucky
663 South Limestone Street, Lexington, Kentucky 40508–4008

06 05 04 03 02     5 4 3 2 1

Library of Congress Cataloging-in-Publication Data

Scheuermann, Mona.
  In praise of poverty : Hannah More counters Thomas Paine and the
radical threat / Mona Scheuermann.
      p. cm.
Includes bibliographical references and index.
  ISBN 0-8131-2222-8 (acid-free paper)
  1. More, Hannah, 1745-1833—Political and social views.
2. Conservatism—England—History—18th century.
3. Conservatism—England—History—19th century. 4. Paine, Thomas,
1737-1809. Rights of man. 5. Radicalism—England—History.
6. Poverty—England—History. 7. Poor—England—History. I. Title.
PR3605.M6 S34 2001
828'.609—dc21                                          2001003181

*For Peter*

To improve the habits and raise the principles of the
mass of the people, at a time when their dangers and
temptations, moral and political, were multiplied
beyond the example of any other period in our
history, was the motive which impelled the writer of
these volumes to devise and prosecute the institution
of the Cheap Repository. . . . As an appetite for
reading had from various causes been increasing
among the inferior ranks, it was judged expedient at
this critical period to supply such wholesome aliment
as might give a new direction to the public taste, and
abate the relish for those corrupt and impious
publications which the consequences of the French
Revolution have been fatally pouring in upon us.

ADVERTISEMENT
*The Works of Hannah More* (1830)

# Contents

# Preface

The premise of this book is that Hannah More's writing represents in an explicit way the beliefs and fears of her peers as they encountered the social order—and the threat of disorder—in the 1790s and the years following. Our understanding of the issues that preoccupied the upper classes is deepened by analyzing not only More's social engineering Tracts and the correspondence in which the social issues she dealt with in these and other works is reflected, but in studying a selection of the documents that emphasize her congruity on these social issues to the thinking of her peers or, in the case of Thomas Paine's *Rights of Man*, the threat that actually precipitated More's entrance into the pamphlet wars. The first chapter of my book, then, analyzes Robert Townsend's *A History of the Poor Laws*, which is an exploration of social policy and its relationship to the poor; the second, focusing on *Rights of Man*, reminds my reader just what it was in *Rights of Man* that was so frightening to the upper classes in England. With these preliminaries for context, my discussion of More herself I hope will have added resonance. Finally, in my conclusion, I bring together the unlikely sisterhood of More and Mary Wollstonecraft to suggest the congruence of much of the late-century's thinking about the poor.

This book is meant to be as much social history as a study of one particular writer. As I hope will become clear, it is only within these contexts that More herself, and the extraordinary respect she inspired in her contemporaries, accurately can be understood. For More in her own time was seen as something very much like a saint; men made pilgrimages to meet this woman whose reputation for good works reached far beyond the boundaries of England. Quite typical is the tone of S.G. Goodrich, an American educator, who describes his journey to meet Hannah More. After several pages of buildup to the interview itself ("I hired a post-coach, and went to Barley-wood—some ten miles distant. Hannah More was still there!), and an account of their conversations ("I

told her of the interest I had taken, when a child, in the story of
the Shepherd of Salisbury Plain, upon which she recounted its
history, remarking that the character of the hero was modeled from
life. . . . Her tract, called 'Village Politics, by Will Chip' was written at the request of the British Ministry"), he concludes

> My interview with this excellent lady was, on the whole, most
> gratifying. Regarding her as one of the greatest benefactors of
> the age—as, indeed, one of the most remarkable women that
> had ever lived—I looked upon her not only with veneration but
> affection. She was one of the chief instruments by which the tor-
> rent of vice and licentiousness, emanating from the French Revo-
> lution and inundating the British Islands, was checked and
> driven back: she was even, to a great extent, the permanent re-
> former of British morals and manners, as well among the high
> as the humble. And besides, I felt that I owed her a special debt,
> and my visit to her was almost like a pilgrimage to the shrine of
> a divinity. . . . I had long entertained [the desire] of making a
> reform—or at least an improvement—in books for youth. . . . In
> this interview with the most successful and most efficient teacher
> of the age, I had the subject still in mind. . . . Hannah More had
> written chiefly for the grown-up masses; her means, however,
> seemed adapted to my purpose. . . . She had discovered that
> truth could be made attractive to simple minds. . . . The great
> charm of these works which had captivated the million was their
> verisimilitude.[1]

The modern reader of More, trying to make sense of a "great benefactor" whose idea of helping the poor is to convince them that a
single blanket and a bowl of hearty gruel should bring them to
ecstasies of thanksgiving ("The Shepherd of Salisbury Plain"), is
perplexed at the gulf between More's contemporaries' perceptions
of her work and our judgments. It was in fact my own discomfort
with More's social prescriptions in the context of what I found to
be the virtually universal praise of her peers that led me to the
explorations that culminated in this study. As so many recent literary critics have found, my answers lay as much in social history
as in the works of a single author; in the case of More, this specifically means a study of upper-class attitudes toward the poor.

# Acknowledgments

The process of exploring an idea until it takes on the substance and form of a book is for me a great pleasure. And this pleasure has been renewed and multiplied at all stages of the process as the insights and the kindnesses of many colleagues have touched this study. My first acknowledgment is to Robert Maccubbin and Adam Potkay, who separately made the same suggestion about the shape of this project; their arguments made this a better book. I enjoyed the benefits of discussions at the various universities where Hannah and I visited: UCLA, Georgetown, The College of William and Mary, Catholic University, the University of Nevada-Las Vegas, and the University of Milan. Thanks especially go to Max and Estelle Novak and to Tim and Clarissa Erwin for their truly gracious hospitality. The liveliness and enthusiasm for the project of the audience at the University of Nevada, an audience that included faculty from at least four disciplines, remains one of the most pleasant memories I accrued in the course of the writing. My thanks as well for their valuable suggestions to the colleagues at the 1999 International Society for Eighteenth-Century Studies meeting in Dublin, the American Society for Eighteenth-Century Studies meetings of 1999 and 2000, the Northeast Society for Eighteenth-Century Studies meeting in 1997, and the 1996 conference of the Gesellschaft Für Englische Romantik where I presented aspects of this work. I am indebted to Richard Schwartz for arranging my year as Visiting Scholar at Georgetown University for 1997 -98 .

During the year when much of the writing was done, Robert Mahony seemed to have an unerring instinct about when I needed an encouraging word. As well, Paul Korshin's support has buoyed my spirits on the personal level and shaped my scholarship on the professional. As I write these lines of acknowledgment I feel very rich indeed, for I have yet to thank J. Paul Hunter and Howard Weinbrot for the interest they have shown in my work over many years; conversations with them have enriched my readings of the eighteenth century immeasurably. Sean Shesgreen responded within hours to my excited questions about Hogarth, enabling me to get the material into the manuscript just under the press' deadline.

I appreciate the help I received from the Folger Shakespeare library and the Newberry library. And especially I appreciate the extraordinary generosity of the Northwestern University library, specifically from Carol Turner, who allowed me to borrow the relevant volumes of the 1830 edition of *The Works of Hannah More* for extended periods. The generosity of the several libraries that have allowed me virtually unlimited access to their books brings me to one of the debts that a line here barely can recognize. Nancy Sherman and Judy Kroll, our interlibrary-loan specialists, spoiled me utterly and then thanked me for appreciating them. I simply cannot say what their work has meant to my own. And our research librarians, Judy Mayzel and Joan Cichon, also deserve acknowledgment.

The reader for the press contributed many helpful suggestions and caught a number of slips, both large and small. I thank him most gratefully for all the care he took with the manuscript.

Parts of this study were published in *Eighteenth-Century Life* and in *The Age of Johnson*, and I appreciate the editors' permission to use this material here.

And finally, as is a most pleasurable habit in each of my books, I get to thank my husband Peter for being everything that any woman could ask of a spouse. Your kindness, your interest, your patience in listening to long explanations of what I'd just found out about Hannah More, are only part of what make you my best friend.

One

# Introduction

HANNAH MORE had an extraordinarily successful life. She apparently had many physical illnesses, that is true, and we certainly would not envy her that part of her existence. But in all other respects, it seems to me that if one wanted to wish someone well, it would be a considerable kindness to wish her—or him—an existence so replete with personal and public satisfactions as More experienced. She was an intellectual prodigy as a child, and her gifts were appreciated and nurtured by wise and capable parents. Her young girlhood was full of accomplishment and recognition for her poetry and her charm, and by the time she reached earliest adulthood she was the intimate of the greatest artistic and intellectual figures of her day, among them David Garrick and Samuel Johnson. Her values, deeply felt and steadfastly adhered to throughout her long life, happened to be the very values that were the bedrock of the middle and upper classes whose spokesman she became, so that her proselytizing at all levels was as a voice speaking into receptive and appreciative ears. She had extraordinary support from every angle, from her close-knit family, first her parents, especially her father, and then her sisters, and from circles beyond circles of male and female friends who were unfailingly supportive of their dear Hannah. Her accomplishments were obvious to all: books that sold in numbers ranging from the respectable to the almost unimaginable (and that brought her very considerable sums) and community works that stood as physical, real-world monuments to her efforts. This was a woman who sent off her first poems to be published with the comment that she was not going to be put off with a piddling sum, and who was answered with the promise that if she could learn what Goldsmith had earned for "The Deserted Village," she would get a matching amount. Keep in mind that her proposed publisher, Cadell, apparently had not yet even seen the poems under discussion. She could not find out what Goldsmith had been paid—so she and Cadell settled on £40. Cadell remained her publisher for more than fifty years.

Biographical information about More essentially comes from four major sources. By far the most important sources are letters from and to More, and these break down effectively into two sets, those that appear in Roberts, where they often are linked by various degrees of commentary, and those that we have from other manuscript and printed sources, such as the Walpole and Thrale letters. Patti More's *Mendip Annals* provides a great deal of information about the sisters' school projects. Finally, the 1838 biography by Henry Thompson is the first major biography, and, in light of my own studies of other sources, it seems scrupulously accurate, though never without a patina of loving devotion to its subject. I emphasize the tight circle of sources—although together with More's various works themselves it seems to me that they present a complete and satisfying picture of their subject—because all other discussions of More come back to them, often with a less than scrupulous confession of where the information comes from. The *Dictionary of National Biography* entry, for example, which has become the thumbnail sketch of choice for many modern scholars, put its material together from these sources.[1]

For Hannah More perhaps more than for some other writers the biography is important because, as will become a central theme of my study, More herself, as well as her friends, saw her as a public spokesman in the trying and dangerous political atmosphere of the late-eighteenth and early-nineteenth centuries. More wrote about, and wrote to, the concerns of her peers, and these concerns took on a moral, that is, religious, dimension that not only coexisted with the political and social movements of the time that were of deep concern to More and her circle but in fact to them seemed to define these events. To take one very obvious example of such a conjunction, the revolutionary events in France horrified More's circle not only in their political and social implications but on the most basic of moral levels. More's initial foray into the pamphlet wars of the 1790s is instigated by her friend the bishop of London and, as we will see, the tie between religious commitment and social activism, while totally sincere, is grounded in the interests of a class-defined allegiance; this synergy gives extraordinary power to More's writing. By this I do not mean, of course, that More was a good writer in the sense that she produced great art as, for example, did Austen. But because More wrote with the complete support of the powerful classes and not only gave voice to their concerns but used her writing—always in the honest belief that she was doing God's work—to uphold that class's interests, she had the full support of those powers to spread her influence. As we will see a bit later, many of her political works were markedly aided by a distribution network that included the government itself at the highest levels.

For More and her circle God's work very conveniently supported the status quo; in fact, any suggestion of changing that status quo—"equality" in the terms of the revolutionary rhetoric in France, for example—was to go directly against God's plan and thus to insult the Divinity himself. To fight in any way possible against what they saw as French godlessness was not considered merely expedient in terms of preserving society as they knew it but as a basic moral duty. The problem perceived by the upper classes in England at the latter part of the eighteenth century and in the early decades of the nineteenth was that the poor, although decidedly part of God's plan, did not always seem to accept their place in the grand scheme of things with quite as much grace as might be wished; in other words, especially as the ideas first of the American Revolution but much more dangerously the concepts of the French Revolution were bruited about more and more in England, the poor showed signs of becoming increasingly restive.

Tom Paine and his *Rights of Man* are seen by Church and King as a very real threat, and, as we shall see, although Paine's was the most widely disseminated work and without doubt the most effective single "pamphlet" in the radicals' attempt to stir up social change in England, his was only part of a large-scale pamphlet war. Along with the political unrest so feared by the entrenched elites of England, there was, too, the ever-growing financial burden of the poor rates, which even in the years before the poor came to be perceived as a political threat was a significant presence in the minds, and the pockets, of the upper classes. In this book, I explore these various contexts—that is, the upper class's sense of itself vis-à-vis the poor and laboring classes, the frustration with the Poor Laws and their effect on the economy, and the political and social upheavals set off by the home-grown radical rhetoric that attempts to plant French ideals in English soil. I look at all of these issues to present a slice of social history that provides the context for someone like More, especially in her Tracts directed specifically to the poor, to suggest that the images we derive from her involvement in social issues are extraordinarily representative of the perceptions of the upper classes in this period of intense political and social turmoil. More's amazingly successful career as a writer and as a social activist is directly attributable to the fact that her perceptions are so remarkably typical of the thought of her peers. She repays our study in many ways more than some writers who were much better craftsmen, for her talent is to distill through her writing the thought of the powerful of her time, while through her active participation in the lives of the poor we see that thought made manifest in action. She exerted tremendous influence in both spheres. This must, then, be a book not just about Hannah More but about the contexts for her work. We cannot fully understand what she says about the poor, to whom so much of her work was directed, without understanding the ubiquitous discomfort that the poor evoked for More and her friends. The upper classes in short were quite terrified that what had happened in France was going to happen in England. We must look, then, in detail at Paine's *Rights of Man* to see what all the fuss was about. More's first venture into the political pamphlet wars of the 1790s is *Village Politics*, a piece she essentially was commissioned to write by Bishop Porteus, bishop of London, to counter Paine. Her Cheap Repository Tracts, which so often have been misinterpreted by modern critics in a variety of contexts, follow quite simply from this initial foray, as any reader coming upon repeated references to Tom Paine in the Tracts might realize.

In addition to Paine's *Rights of Man,* I examine Henry Townsend's *A Dissertation on the Poor Laws,* a book-length tract entirely representative of the basic thinking of More's contemporaries about the poor and about social responsibility for poor relief. One of the fascinating things about many of the social issues we will see raised in More's works is that responses to these issues are remarkably similar from the political Right to the Left. Townsend and More, it would seem clear, are thinking from a conservative perspective; when we look at Josiah Wedgwood, whose politics as a dissenter and "new industrialist" we would assume to be considerably more liberal, we find the persona he adopts as he attempts to control his workforce very much the same as the stance taken by Townsend or More. And thus, to suggest some of the breadth of these approaches to the poor, I look also in some detail at Wedgwood's rather Gothic (!) *Address to the Workmen in the Pottery on the Subject of Entering into the Service of Foreign Manufacturers* (1783). Similarly, as part of my argument that More's general stance is typical of the thought of her time, I will discuss the remarkable similarities between the conservative More and that "hyena in petticoats," Mary Wollstonecraft, on education. I wish that I could claim to have discovered this last parallel, but the similarities between More's and Wollstonecraft's advice books on education were already being remarked on by their contemporaries.

Henry Thompson, More's first biographer, comes to Wrington just six months after More has retired from Barley Wood; he tells us that "he could not become minister of a parish in which she had resided nearly half a century, without constantly associating with many who had known her intimately."[2] In the course of his ten years' ministry there, he also has "become well acquainted with several more of the privileged class in Bath, Bristol, and Clifton." This personal acquaintance with those who themselves knew Hannah More forms the "ample nucleus" for beginning his work as biographer. And the place itself is redolent with the spirit of More: "Nor was the 'relligio loci' altogether to be disregarded. Insensate indeed must be the heart which could encounter daily . . . some memorial of the greatness and goodness of a human mind, and yet feel no interest in its history. In almost all the neighbouring parishes there exist schools or clubs, instituted or suggested by Hannah More." Her writings, "which are the property of an admiring world," were created here; physical mementos, "the frequent Bible, Prayer-book, or other religious work, found on the peasant's shelf, bearing his name in her writing, 'from Hannah More,'" all these call upon him, Thompson says, to write his biography. What we need to note is Thompson's tone of intense admiration and affectionate respect. He is writing about a greatly good person, Hannah More, whose legacy permeates both the physical surroundings and the intellectual ambience of the neighborhood and of the time. "That [the writer] entertains a very high admiration for the character of Hannah More, he has no where concealed; but his object has not been to write a panegyric, but a fair and accurate record of facts." The overweening "fact" is, as "those who knew Mrs. More best . . . attested[,] they never had seen so near an approach to perfection." Rather remarkably, this is the attitude of virtually everyone with whom More came in contact. When at the end of his first volume Thompson comes to the years of the Blagdon controversy, it is clear that he regards the attacks she suffered in this episode as a kind of moral imperfection in the grand scheme: she is a woman who "had drawn the chain of truth and virtue around the whole frame of society; and the applause of an admiring world was but the echo of a pure conscience. Like the wisest of men, she had dared to prefer wisdom to riches and honour; and like him, too, she had received the object of her desire, while riches and honour were superadded. Blest with the love of many friends, and, above all, with the peace of God, she might seem to be the happiest of human kind; but such periods of unqualified serenity suit not long our probationary condition. The cloud was gathering" (I, 194).

Before we look at the events of More's life, it is worth pausing to remark on Thompson's sources, since, as I mentioned, his biography still constitutes the major documentation of her life. He is very precise in his acknowledgments. The materials, he says, are derived principally from private letters and from "living memories." Cadell's family loans him more than one hundred sixty letters; since More published for over fifty years with Cadell, these letters illuminate virtually her entire career. Eighty letters come from R. Lovell Gwatkin, Esq., an early friend of More's; one hundred come from the children of J.H. Addington. Ninety additional letters from More and her sisters are contributed by the Rev. Hill Dawe Wickham, and so on and on. Thompson's list of donors and sources comprises three pages of exceedingly small print. These names, except for Cadell's, are not familiar ones; Thompson left it for more modern scholars to explore the correspondence between More and such friends as the Garricks and Walpole. But it is clear that Thompson is making every effort to document the life of More while she is alive in the memories of his contemporaries; nothing in modern scholarship that I have found proves him inaccurate in any factual detail. And Thompson's own attitude toward More itself serves as yet another source, like Roberts' commentary in his collection of More's letters, for modern scholars to get a sense of More's extraordinary place in her own community.

Thompson begins his impartial biography by insisting that in "whatever sense the appellation GREAT can be legitimately applied to any human being, history perhaps will not furnish one name more truly deserving the appendage than hers who is the subject of these pages" (I, 3). More, he tells us, raised herself "by her own industry and merit" (I, 3) to be the equal of the most distinguished of her contemporaries; she did great good, and that good was widely recognized as well as widely disseminated. Her influence was far-reaching during the fifty years that she worked, and it will spread into the future as generations to come are taught by her example and her writing. Her writings "have already effected a moral revolution, not merely on the surface, but in the inmost vitals of aristocratic and middle life. They were extensively influential in calming the passions and correcting the delusions of a misguided populace in times of turbulence and discontent." She has, in fact, "altogether changed the moral conduct of the labouring classes" (I, 18). For Thompson, no little part of More's greatness lies in the efficacy of her molding of the poor, a point to which her contemporaries reverted repeatedly.

More was born about four miles from Bristol in February 1745. Her father, whose expectations of a large estate were ended in a legal contest with a cousin, earned his living as master of the free school at Fishponds, the hamlet where his five daughters were born. Hannah, the fourth child, was precocious in her reading, even apparently beginning to write poems by the age of four.[3] At eight, Thompson tells us, Hannah began to learn Latin from her father, who apparently could accept her abilities in language but was a bit taken aback by her talent for mathematics. Nonetheless, Mr. More gave Hannah and her sisters good access to learning, and in 1757 the oldest daughter, with her sisters, opened a school for young women that was quite successful. Hannah's talents only increased as she grew up, and she began to attract the attention of people outside her immediate circle of students and friends.

One Mr. Turner proposed, although he was more than twenty years older than the twenty-two-year-old Hannah, but then kept putting off the wedding. In the meantime, having sold her share in the school in preparation for her marriage, More had suffered a real financial loss, and when, after six years, the engagement was broken off entirely, Turner insisted that she be compensated with an annuity for the expenses she had incurred. More at first declined this offer, but eventually her friends convinced her to accept it. This episode has been remarkably distorted by a number of contemporary critics who present a situation of callous disregard in which a horribly wronged female is victimized by the usual cruelty of man.[4] Actually, the situation really was neither so simple nor so vicious. Poor Turner genuinely admired More; he simply could not bring himself to marry her (or anybody else), at least not during the period that her patience held out. Thompson draws Turner and the whole courtship sympathetically: Turner, after his offer of an annuity had been rejected by More, "then sought an interview with Sir James Stonhouse, to whom he renewed the offer of the annuity, saying, at the same time, that he would marry Miss More at any hour the doctor would call upon him to do so, if only her consent could be obtained" (I, 34). Stonhouse without More's knowledge accepts the offer of an annual sum of two hundred pounds. More finally consents to the arrangement when it seems that "farther resistance might be thought ungracious and resentful. Mr. Turner, indeed, always entertained the most respectful friendship for Miss More"; twenty years later, the "long suspended intercourse" (I, 35) is renewed accidentally, and he and More remain friends until his death. She presents him with copies of every work she publishes; she invites him to the last of the Mendip feasts. At his death, he leaves her one thousand pounds. Thompson insists that he has been very careful in presenting this episode because it "has been so grossly misrepresented by some, and so libellously characterized by others" (I, 35). All his care, however, has not prevented these events from being misrepresented from his time to ours. More apparently had two other offers of marriage, both of which she declined.

In 1773 More visited London, where she saw Garrick playing Lear. This was the beginning of the young Hannah's introduction to the world of the brightest intellectual and artistic circles, for a letter that she wrote to a friend about Garrick's performance made its way to the great actor himself and piqued his interest in its author. "Garrick was delighted with his new acquaintance," Thompson notes, "and took pride and pleasure in introducing her in the splendid circle of genius in which he moved: to the Royal Family, who inquired of him concerning her, he spoke in terms of the most ardent commendation: Mrs. Montagu, Sir Joshua Reynolds, Dr. Johnson, rapidly succeeded in her acquaintance; and in the course of six weeks (for such was the limit of this visit) she had become intimate with the greatest names in intellect and taste" (I, 39–40). By 1774 she also knows Edmund Burke, with whom she remained friendly until his death many years later. One of the interesting things about More's friendships, in fact, is the permanence of her relationships. Very early in her life she makes the acquaintance of many of the people who would be her friends, and whether they are her own contemporaries or older, they remain within her circle until they die. Should the question of Ann Yearsley come up here, it must be noted that she and More were never friends. More was Yearsley's patron and mentor, but it never would have occurred to More, largely for reasons of class, that they would be friends. As I will discuss in the chapter on More's correspondence and her correspondents, her friendships were one of More's greatest assets, both personally and professionally. In 1775 she initiates what will turn out to be one of the great relationships of her life. Her "Search after Happiness" had reached a sixth edition; a Philadelphia imprint had netted one hundred pounds. According to Thompson, these successes prompted her to offer Cadell two poems to be brought out in a small quarto: the rest of this story is the famous one of Cadell offering her whatever Goldsmith had earned for his "Deserted Village."

The year 1789 marks the earliest involvement in the Cheddar communities, as well as the move to Cowslip Green. This, and a residence in Great Pulteney Street, Bath, was the common property of all the sisters. Their "ample competence . . . [allowed them to retire] from the labour of tuition" (I, 103) by January 1790. And thus could the Misses More afford to devote themselves to this new project of civilizing the natives, first in the Cheddar hills and then in the surrounding communities. Patti More's *Mendip Annals*[5] emphasizes the savagery of the inhabitants, as do Hannah More's many letters describing the project. In terms of how the sisters viewed their mission, Thompson's comment that the women's work "has produced a material alteration in the condition of the Cheddar peasantry" although "some traces of their former barbarism are still in existence" (I, 101) catches the flavor of Hannah and Patti's perspective.[6] The Cheap Repository Tracts come at this time too, largely to satisfy More's belief that if the poor are to be taught to read, they must be supplied with safe reading materials. More writes in a famous letter that "To teach the poor to *read*, without providing them with safe books, has always appeared to me a dangerous measure. This induced me to the laborious undertaking of the Cheap Repository Tracts, which had such great success, that above two millions were sold in one year, in the height of our domestic troubles."[7] That comment about "the height of our domestic troubles" is remarkably important: More, as I will show in detail later on, is writing the Tracts precisely with this intent of keeping the poor from the kind of actions that had had such dire consequences in France. She is honest in her desire to help them, but always within this context of social order.

More's idea of charity schools for the poor was not new. Thompson notes that Sunday schools had been opened in Old Brentford three years earlier, in 1786: "They were connected with the church, through a private charity; and even then reclaimed from vice, idleness, and savage ignorance, many hundreds of poor children. . . . These schools had been followed up by the institution of schools of industry; and their success must have been known to Mrs. More, as they were not only in high repute through the patronage of the Queen, but they were described, together with many others of like character, in Mrs. Trimmer's admirable manual of practical benevolence, 'The Economy of Charity'; a work addressed to ladies, with which it is impossible to suppose Mrs. More unacquainted" (I, 106). More herself probably had inspected these schools since her friend Bishop Porteus was also a friend of Trimmer's, "as well as a warm promoter of [Trimmer's] schools" (I, 106). It is worth noting the closeness of these circles, a point to which I shall be returning repeatedly.

More and her sister set out to convince the local farmers that educating the poor would not make them "lazy and useless" but that their "little plan . . . would secure [the farmers'] orchards from being robbed, their rabbits from being shot, their game from being stolen, and . . . might lower the poor-rates."[8] This is More writing to Wilberforce, explaining how she managed to obtain the cooperation of the farmers, and her point is that these were the arguments that worked with *them*. Nonetheless, as we will see in the Tracts themselves, as well as in many of the letters that circulated among More's circle, although More to some degree is mocking these arguments to Wilberforce, this suspicion of the poor and fear of the harm—petty or serious—that the poor can do if they are not somehow reined in runs through much of the period's thinking about them. Certainly the Poor Rates are a major concern of the time, as is evident in document after document across the political spectrum from More to Thomas Paine.

More's work with the poor of Cheddar and the surrounding villages brings her much respect in her own social circle; all of More's social activism finds support among her friends on all levels from financial contribution to moral encouragement. It is not only this large-scale work in the villages but also such examples as the Ann Yearsley episode that reflect virtually unwavering backing. Partly this is because the proper application of benevolent impulse is one of the major topics of thoughtful people in More's period. Wilberforce, whose financial support began the project— "If *you* will be at the trouble, *I* will be at the expense"[9]—later writes to More, "Your accounts have afforded me the utmost pleasure. . . . I trust you will speak freely when the money is exhausted; indeed, I conceive it must be all spent already. Not to do so would be to give way either to pride or to false delicacy."[10] Compare his comment with the heroine Anna St. Ives' injunction to her friend Frank Henley in Thomas Holcroft's radical novel *Anna St. Ives*, when she sends the brave and wise, but financially impoverished, hero out into the world to do good. Frank does not want to take money from Anna, but she insists, in words very like Wilberforce's, that his refusal can only be false pride; indeed, soon after he accepts the money, Frank saves a deserving young couple from prison and certain ruin because he happens to have the twenty pounds from Anna.[11] Here again, social thought often is oddly congruent on both sides of the political spectrum. Coming back from fiction to the historical account, we find that fifty years after More's exertions "the good work has never been suffered wholly to decline. Close to the rude hut which formerly contained the whole establishment, has arisen a noble building, containing two school-rooms, and apartments for the master and mistress erected at a cost of upwards of 500£; of which 50 pounds were bequeathed by Mrs. More" (I, 111).

Of course, one issue on which conservative and radical found little if any common ground was the revolutionary spirit about in the time. As early as 1780 we already find More publicly antagonistic to any manifestation of support for revolution. In the election of 1774 More had supported one of the candidates, a Mr. Cruger, but in the election of 1780 she was "altogether opposed to him." Why? Thompson explains that "In the first instance he impugned the policy of the American war; in the second he openly advocated the rebellion, and his mob marched under the thirteen stripes" (I, 41). The French Revolution and its aftermath shocked More and her friends enormously; the fear that the events in France would be reproduced in England seemed to them a real and present danger. Thompson talks of the "pestilence that was desolating the mind of France. . . . The doctrines of the French Revolution were not left to make their way in England by their simple accommodation to the depravity of nature everywhere. They had preachers and propagators who were disseminating the poison with Satanic diligence. Tracts of the most anarchical and blasphemous character were dispersed in the manufactury, the cottage, the workshop, and the mine" (I, 149).

Thompson's introduction to the work More did in counteracting the well-orchestrated pamphlet campaign of Tom Paine and his followers precisely places More in terms of the political and social contexts that gave shape first to *Village Politics* and then to the Cheap Repository Tracts. To those in More's circle the attempt to change the status quo by preaching insurrection to the lower classes indeed did seem satanic: the good Christian, for More and her friends, simply is not a revolutionary. Early on, as Thompson points out, there might have been some sympathy for the oppressed in France: "How little soever it was possible for the Christian to approve of rebellion[,] . . . still it was scarcely possible, at the time, not to entertain some hopes that these excesses [the violence that opened the Bastille] might subside at length in orderly obedience to a form of government less unworthy of an intelligent people" (I, 150). But More does not labor long under this "delusion. . . . [A]nd long before the darkest features of the revolution had attained their full proportion, England did not number among her sons or her daughters a more ardent antagonist of the revolutionary party than Hannah More" (I, 151). By 1792, as "the peasantry of England" is courted by the forces of "atheism and blasphemy[,] . . . universal, almost, became the call on Mrs. More to arm in the most holy cause of religion and order" (I, 151). Thus is the call to liberty and equality perceived by the upper classes, and thus is Hannah More designated the spokesman for, essentially, God and country. As this conjunction of events is the central matter of my book, I shall leave further discussion of these issues for later chapters. But it is important to understand just how grave the threat seemed to More and her friends and how seriously she took this duty conferred on her by Bishop Porteus and others to battle Paine and company.

More's printed work always seems to have been in high demand. When in 1793 she published "Remarks on the Speech of M. Dupont," the profits—intended for the relief of the French emigrant clergy—reached £240. But More, although she could show a most astute business sense,[12] is not particularly interested in profiting from her work. Much of it seems to have been given away in various social causes; this is especially true of the Cheap Repository Tracts. What she wants to do in almost all of her writing is to change the behavior of her intended readers, whether higher or lower class. The stories for the Cheap Repository are filled with lessons, directions, even recipes, all designed to make the poor better poor people. This naturally first and foremost means making them good Christians; More uses Christianity as a means of social control. In the Tracts, as we shall see, she may be answering Paine's *Age of Reason,* as Thompson suggests (and as most modern scholars repeat), but her primary aim, as in *Village Politics,* is social control. While Thompson thinks of the Tracts as a "Village Christianity" (I, 166), he also notes that "Songs and tracts had been to a great extent influential in the corruption of the lower orders of France, and the same machinery was now worked by the revolutionists of England" (I, 167). More in fact apparently discussed the shape of her project with the Bishop of Dol.[13] Thompson quotes Dol's comment that "'[p]enny papers . . . might have saved France, and so I told the king,'" and states that this "at once decided and encouraged her. Penny papers unquestionably contributed to the salvation of England; and none were more blessed to that object than those of Hannah More" (I, 168).

More continued writing into her eighties and was eightyeight when she died. One of the best known of her later works is written in her sixties: *Coelebs in Search of a Wife,* her courtship novel, as Demers notes is "a curious alternation" of the pattern in that it is the male Coelebs who wishes to marry.[14] In light of More's other works, it does not surprise a reader to find that Coelebs' major problem is finding a suitably moral partner. In addition to *Coelebs,* More produced a number of works that were directed to the moral improvement of the upper class such as her *Estimate of the Religion of the Fashionable World, Thoughts on the Importance of the Manners of the Great,* and, of course, *Strictures on the Modern System of Education.* Within our context, one of the most interesting of these works is the *Hints Towards Forming the Character of a Young Princess* because its genesis and development reflect the same pattern of response to the express request of the Establishment that we see in the overtly political works that occupy the central focus of my book. Thompson notes that the idea of such a work was suggested to More by "the Rev. Dr. Gray, then prebendary of Durham, and afterwards Bishop of Bristol, who earnestly urged her to undertake it. Several persons of rank afterwards seconded the call" (ll, 61).

His discussion of the *Hints* is preceded by an analysis of the contemporary political crisis, with England "threatened with French principles, no longer in French pamphlets, but at the muzzle of French artillery. Persuasions, however, were not neglected; the foolish and mischievous sophism that 'the poor have nothing to lose' was sedulously rung in the ears of those who were intended to be the dupes of it; and no means were left unemployed to seduce the people of Britain from those religious and political attachments which were the pledge and essence of their safety and happiness. Mrs. More had now had proof enough of the efficiency of spirited songs and ballads," and, Thompson tells us, More goes on to produce not only patriotic songs but, "solicited by the committee of Lloyd's to compose the address for the Patriotic Fund" ll, 58–59), she fulfills this request too. Good King George held the nation together in that time of crisis, and it seems obvious to all responsible citizens that the future of the monarchy needs to be in equally firm hands. "In the right guidance of the infant mind of the Princess Charlotte of Wales appeared then to centre the hopes of the nation for a very distant period; and certainly the King's dominions did not contain one mind more capable of advising her soberly, rightly, and liberally than that of Hannah More" (ll, 60–61). And thus the idea of a work that should educate a princess was brought to More: further, Dr. Gray "throughout assisted her with his advice and information on the subject" (ll, 61). The bishop of Exeter transmits copies of the *Hints* to the king and queen; not only is the book dear to the princess (it is the last book she reads both before her marriage and before her death, Thompson reports) but apparently to many others too; it goes through six printings of one thousand copies each. For Thompson, the link between More's patriotism and her morality, as for More herself, is inevitable. And Thompson's perspective on More is entirely accurate. More works throughout her life, both in her writing and in her charities, to support the state in what she sees as a moral imperative.

Two

# Conservative Contexts

## Joseph Townsend's *A Dissertation on the Poor Laws*

IT IS THE NATURE OF eighteenth-century English fiction to be remarkably mimetic of the real world it purports to fictionalize. The scholar of the novel, looking at the historical record, is forcibly struck by a sense of the familiar. Fanny Burney's letters, for example, reflect the details of a social world no different from that of her novels; John Howard's accounts of the horrors of the contemporary prison system record the same details William Godwin depicts in *Caleb Williams.* The evolution of the Poor Laws in England and the attitudes of the upper classes toward the poor provide one of the major cultural contexts for the situations of the stories in Hannah More's Cheap Repository Tracts. Looking back from eighteenth-century fictions to their contexts, one must wonder why a particular theme might become a virtually ubiquitous presence in that fiction. In More's case, as we have seen, her writing is always a response to specific social issues that seem to her to require her intervention; the writing directed at the upper classes comes out of her own concerns about the moral development of those who may or (in the case of the royal princess) will have the ability to shape society, and the writing to the poor arises out of specific political and social issues seen by More and her friends to be so pressing that those friends, Bishop Porteus for example, actually enlist her in their campaigns.

Modern critics find it difficult to deal with Hannah More because her conservative, patriarchal, "whatever is, is right" perspective disturbs, even offends us. More's recent biographer tries hard to sympathize with her subject, but repeatedly finds that she must apologize for her. Other critics simply rewrite More, making her a feminist, or a daddy's victim. We find it much easier to deal with writers like Paine whose ideas either truly are liberal or writers who, at the least, had the grace to present essentially conservative ideas in less aggressive packaging, like Austen. But if we dismiss Hannah More because of the unadorned nature of her philosophical stance, we miss an excellent opportunity to see clearly into her age. For what modern critics often look away from, perhaps because it does not appeal to our own sensibilities, is the very conservative nature of much of the age's thought. Like many eighteenth-century women writers, More has been inching her way into modern critical attention. The problem, however, is that while she is a most interesting figure, her ideas largely are repugnant to modern sensibilities. Critics often seem to deal with this inconvenient state of affairs either by apologizing for their subject or by changing what she says so that More seems closer in spirit with our own times. In this book I will look in detail at a selection of More's stories and treatises to see what she in fact does say, and I will show that More's position on social issues is entirely representative of her own times. Her full welcome into the most influential circles points to this acceptance by her peers; the extraordinary sales of her Tracts attest to the chord she struck in her own society. And when we look at eighteenth-century laws regarding the poor, and contemporary commentary on those Poor Laws, we understand just how accurately More reflects much of the spirit of her time.

More's most recent biographer, Patricia Demers, makes a quite charmingly earnest effort "to deal justly with Hannah More," although that "means admitting both the expansiveness and the limitations of her charity, methodology, and vision."[1] She worries about "how to accord justice" to this woman "who is—and, as some would argue, always was—so devastatingly out of step. . . . More's central belief in a natural hierarchical social order . . . is now angering in its condescension and immobility" (3). More's work "is now widely assumed to have been a narrow exercise of knowing and keeping one's place"; this line is particularly irritating to feminists: "Feminist criticism has been understandably and rightly severe about More's dedication to the doctrine of the two spheres and her solemn discourses on submission" (21). Gamely, Demers insists that More "is altogether more complex and conflicted than most detracting comments or piecemeal excerpts indicate" (22). Less scrupulously, Mitzi Myers, delighted to have found a female eighteenth-century writer who was clearly successful, largely rewrites More so that "didactic" works like hers "scarcely stand second to the canonical novel in interest and importance" in terms of "what they reveal about women."[2] More becomes "a pioneer social novelist" (267), although we are talking about short tales. Ignoring entirely the form More used for the Tracts, Myers insists that "[t]ranscribing her society's exigent problems into fiction, More helped give the novel a new seriousness, relevance, and direction" (267). More's tales, designed to teach the poor to be satisfied with their lot in life and those better off how to help the poor without raising them too much, become in Myers' reading "fresh literary analogues of urgent social awareness; her thematic message of domestic heroism occasions a new domestic realism, ideas and aesthetics are generated from the woman novelist's characteristic stance. In its complex mix of literary and cultural innovation, More's Repository illustrates how women's educative and caretaking role fed into new strains of social fiction, and her work exemplifies how women could translate female ideology's didactic imperative into an authoritative voice capable of documenting and interpreting historical realities" (268). Other recent readers fall somewhere between Myers' and Demers' readings; Elizabeth Kowaleski-Wallace, for example, presents a rather strange More who, along with sister Patti, has a morbid response to the physical nature of the poor; much of Kowaleski-Wallace's discussion centers on "the 'grotesque' body" and More's presumed need to tame it, especially in the poor. In other words, Kowaleski-Wallace, like Myers, reshapes a More who fits her own interests. The title of her book, in fact, itself suggests a biased reading: *Their Fathers' Daughters: Hannah More, Maria Edgeworth, and Patriarchal Complicity.*[3] So the More that contemporary critics discuss is troubling and, in Kowaleski-Wallace's case, troubled. What we don't get is much of an eighteenth-century More, and before I get to my own discussion of More's work—with my own discomfort with More's perspectives apparent at many points—I want to try to present part of the context for her ideas by looking first at some aspects of the eighteenth-century's Poor Laws.

As we shall see when we look at More's Tracts, the stories

largely are directed at keeping the poor working. This connection between relief and labor goes back in English history at least to the Middle Ages, as does More's insistence that only the laboring poor (with perhaps the addition of the truly disabled) should be helped.[4] In comparison to Anglo-Saxon times, when poor relief was almost entirely under the control of the church, although also apparently consistently attended to by kings and noblemen, by the thirteenth century secular authorities had become much more involved in matters of poor relief. After the middle of the fourteenth century, that is, after the Black Death of 1348 and the attendant scarcity of able-bodied men, statutes concerning beggars were closely connected with statutes regulating laborers. E. M. Leonard notes that these laws "were designed to force every able-bodied man to work, and to keep wages at the old level. . . . In the first regulation of this kind, the Ordinance of Labourers of 1349, the first step is taken towards the national control of poor relief" (3). This ordinance forbids the private individual from giving relief to able-bodied beggars so that "they may be compelled to labour for their necessary living" (4).

We will see repeatedly in More's stories what seems to a modern reader a relatively cruel stress that poor people must—and should—work unremittingly to survive, and that it is almost immoral for a well-off person to help any but the "deserving" poor. The roots of these ideas, as we see from this very early legislation, go far back in English history. Because of the suppression of wages effected by the 1349 ordinance, laborers tried to evade the law by moving to areas where it was not being enforced. Leonard tells us that some of these laborers pretended to be crippled so that they could "beg with impunity" (4); others, joining bands of pilgrims, simply would stop in some area where they still could make good wages. In 1388, to inhibit this evasion of the law, regulations were made restricting the movement of all laborers and of all beggars, able-bodied or not. Henceforth, any laborer, servant, or beggar found away from the district where he lived, unless he had a letter from a local official stating the cause of his journey and the time he would return, would be placed in the stocks until he found a way to return home. Thus, from the fourteenth century, freedom of movement was severely restricted in order to manipulate the labor market. Our interest here is the definition of the poor simply as a source of labor, without regard to their human needs or desires. With some sentimental overlay, this is More's view.

Leonard's analysis of the implications of this ordinance explain its importance: this law is in effect the first English poor law.

> This statute is often regarded as the first English poor law, because it recognizes that the impotent poor had a right to relief, and because it carefully distinguishes between them and the ablebodied beggars. The provisions also imply the responsibility of every neighborhood for the support of its own poor. Moreover, this enactment may be regarded as a law of settlement. Not only were the impotent poor confined to their own district, but all unlicensed labourers were likewise forbidden to migrate. Probably the Act had little effect because it was too stringent to have been enforced.
>
> Not only Parliament, but the municipal rulers also, made regulations for the restraint of vagabonds. The authorities of the City of London, in 1359 and in 1375, forbade any able-bodied person to beg, and at the end of the fifteenth century the constables were ordered to search, not only for the vagabonds themselves, but for the people who harboured them. (5)

The concept of poor relief thus is integral to English culture from the Middle Ages. By the eighteenth century, however, poor relief had come to be perceived as a significant burden by many of those taxed to support it. The debate about how much relief to give, and to whom, colors not just discussion about the poor rates but also about all aspects of interaction with the poor. The distinction between the worthy poor and those seen as merely lazy, or worse, criminal, is the focus of much discussion. More's stories repeat and in fact shape these themes, but they are part of a continuing discourse. As Mark Neuman reminds us in his discussion of Joseph Townsend's *A Dissertation on the Poor Laws, By a Well-Wisher to Mankind,*

> The preoccupation of Townsend's contemporaries with that code is not surprising. The Poor Law intruded into the lives and pocketbooks of ordinary men more directly and persistently than did any other instrument of government. By far the greater part of

the sums that the subject paid for the security and maintenance of his kingdom normally went to the relief of its poor. Although national statistics pertaining to the number of persons on relief at any one time are unreliable for this period, it is certainly true that many Englishmen, particularly in years of shortages and high prices, could find a third or even more of their neighbors wholly or in part dependent on the support the Poor Law provided. In brief, the Poor Law and its implementation were a major component of life in Joseph Townsend's England, and no understanding of the author or his nation is possible without an appreciation of this fact.[5]

Townsend begins by expressing compassion for the poor, especially for those "suffering objects [who] have been distinguished for industry, honesty, and sobriety." There are indeed laws that make "provision for their relief," and the sums collected are "more than liberal," but "the laws being inadequate to the purposes for which they were designed, and the money universally misapplied, the provision, which was originally made for industry in distress, does little more than give encouragement to idleness and vice" (17).[6] The problem is that these laws "promote the evils they were meant to remedy, and aggravate the distress they were intended to relieve" (17). He notes that no other nation has adopted such a scheme, and if nothing is done to change the laws, he sees the burden they place on the economy as likely to destroy the nation. In addition to a crippling debt, these laws "multiply the poor" (18). The problem began, he says, when "At the dissolution of the monasteries, the lazy and the indigent, who were deprived of their accustomed food, became clamourous, and having long since forgot to work, were not only ready to join in every scheme for the disturbance of the state, but, as vagrants, by their numbers, by their impostures, and by their thefts, they rendered themselves a public and most intolerable nuisance" (18). At the same time, those with legitimate needs also were protected by law. But by making poor relief a matter of law rather than private compassion, the whole situation has been distorted even more. Townsend complains that in his own time those who produce in society are taxed so much that they themselves often fall into poverty, while normal human compassion shrivels in the heat of resentment against such a system. For, in the face of an assured living, "the most worthless are the most unreasonable in their expectations, and the most importunate in their solicitation for relief" (19). We shall see these concepts illustrated repeatedly in More's Tracts, as in the story of Black Giles, for example.

Townsend's analysis of the effect of the Poor Laws is reminiscent of our own contemporary debate about welfare.

> There never was greater distress among the poor: there never was more money collected for their relief. But what is most perplexing is, that poverty and wretchedness have increased in exact proportion to the efforts which have been made for the comfortable subsistence of the poor; and that wherever most is expended for their support, there objects of distress are most abundant; whilst in those countries or provincial districts where the least provision has been made for their supply, we hear the fewest groans. Among the former we see drunkenness and idleness cloathed in rags; among the latter we hear the chearful songs of industry and virtue. (19–20)

This distinction between "idleness and rags" and "chearful . . . industry and virtue" we will meet as a steady theme in More: in fact, as in "The Shepherd of Salisbury Plain," one way to know if a man is of the "deserving" poor is to note whether his clothes are properly mended. Rags, reflecting idleness, indicate lack of good character. Townsend's words describing the poor are sharp: "poverty and vice prevail, and the most vicious have access to the common stock," he laments. He goes on, "If a man has squandered the inheritance of his fathers; if by his improvidence, by his prodigality, by his drunkenness and vices, he has dissipated all his substance; if by his debaucheries he has ruined his constitution and reduced himself to such a deplorable condition that he hath neither inclination nor ability to work; yet must he be maintained by the sweat and labour of the sober and of the industrious farmer, and eat the bread which should be given only to virtue in distress" (20). The implication here, that many of the poor have become impoverished through their own lack of character, underscores that careful distinction between deserving and undeserving poor. The hardworking farmer himself "is oprest with poverty . . . [and] with all his labour and care he can scarce provide subsistence for his numerous family." Yet he must first contribute to feeding "the prodigal"; he must first clothe "the children of the prostitute" (20–21). Since the poor for whom he must contribute are continually increasing, it is not impossible that this burden may drive our hard-working farmer himself into poverty:

> when he considers, that all the efforts, which have been made in his own parish or in others, have been vain, and that the evil is constantly increasing, he is driven to despair of help, and fears that he shall be himself reduced to work for daily hire. It will be evident that his fears are not altogether groundless, if we consider, that even in parishes, where no manufactures have been established, the poor rates have been doubling, some every fourteen years, and others nearly every seven years; whilst in some districts, where the manufactures are carried on to a considerable extent, the poor rates are more than ten shillings in the pound upon the improved rents. (21)

Townsend finds that the numbers of the poor increase rather than decrease the more poor relief the state mandates. The "natural tendency" of these laws "is to increase the number of the poor, and greatly to extend the bounds of human misery" (22).

Townsend says, in what to our ears sounds like an ironic reversal of Scott Fitzgerald, that the poor are different from you and me: "The poor know little of the motives which stimulate the higher ranks to action—pride, honour, and ambition. In general it is only hunger which can spur and goad them on to labour" (23). In other words, while the "higher ranks" work because of responsibility and ambition, the poor only work from the physical necessity of surviving. But if that goad is removed, they degenerate to what is for them an inevitable state of debauched profligacy. The problem with laws that guarantee the poor a living is that such a guarantee takes away the necessity, and therefore the will, to work: "For what encouragement have the poor to be industrious and frugal, when they know for certain . . . that if by their indolence and extravagance, by their drunkenness and vices, they should be reduced to want, they shall be abundantly supplied, not only with food and raiment, but with their accustomed luxuries, at the expence of others?" (23). But while hunger is the only spur that will lead the poor to work, "our laws have said, they shall never hunger" (Townsend, 23).

We might note that while More does not quite so nakedly discuss hunger as the incentive of the poor to work, this concept is also central to her view of the poor: More repeatedly shows her reader that hard and never-ending work by the poor is never to be pitied, but rather is to be praised as being precisely the virtuous way of life for them. Townsend comments that while hunger is not the only thing that will get the poor to work—laws also can force them to labor—hunger is by far the most efficient and least dangerous incentive. For "legal constraint is attended with too much trouble, violence, and noise; creates ill will, and never can be productive of good and acceptable service: whereas hunger is not only a peaceable, silent, unremitted pressure, but, as the most natural motive to industry and labour, it calls forth the most powerful exertions; and, when satisfied by the free bounty of another, lays a lasting and sure foundation for good will and gratitude" (23–24). Townsend assumes, essentially, that idleness leads to poverty and thence to vice. We shall see precisely this dynamic in More's stories: Black Giles could serve as Townsend's poster boy. Townsend's axiom, "that where bread can be obtained without care or labour, it leads through poverty to vice" (24), would not be out of place in any of More's Tracts.

Townsend's argument is that the poor multiply in direct response to the amount of relief available—guaranteed aid, he says, is the same as "imaginary wealth" (24). This principle is the same for individuals and for nations. The Spanish nation fell apart morally and then economically after Spain discovered gold and silver in Peru and Mexico, and therefore the Spanish had the illusion that they did not need to work any longer. The Italians, whose religious houses provide charity without questions, are overrun with poor: "in Naples six thousand Lazaroni are daily fed by the monastic orders, under the specious name of charity, not upon a sudden emergency, but stately, and as the only means of their subsistence. As a peace offering this may be politic and wise, well calculated to conciliate the good opinion of the unthinking mind, and to command the admiration of the vulgar; but at the same time it is inconsistent with the most established principles of political economy: for as industry and frugality are the only foundation of national prosperity; so temperance and labour are the only source of happiness and wealth to individuals" (25).

Widespread, unmediated charity ruins societies; not only is the general economy destroyed, but so too are the individual objects of the charity. Townsend insists that the poor must help themselves through their own efforts—that, in fact, help from outside is no help at all. Labor must be the center of the poor man's existence; the only useful help to give the poor is to give them work. "He, who statedly employs the poor in useful labour, is their only friend; he, who only feeds them, is their greatest enemy. Their hopes and fears should centre in themselves: they should have no hope but from their own sobriety, diligence, fidelity, and from the well-earnt friendship of their employers" (26). Note the emphasis on the "well-earnt friendship" of the employer. More, too, repeatedly shows us that the well-off are a source of aid, especially in emergencies, but only to those poor people who have earned such aid through diligent, even health-shattering attention to the interests of their "employers." The poor have security, then, as long as they are careful not to "forfeit . . . by their misconduct, that favour and protection which wuld be their principal resource in times of sickness and distress" (26).

Central to both More and Townsend is the concept of social hierarchy. Servants are not the same as masters, and social policies that blur social distinctions are harmful. Townsend finds that the Poor Laws, by removing the essential link between performance, that is, satisfactory work, and reward, have in fact destroyed what should be the "natural obligations" implicit in the "various relations which [heretofore] connected man to man" (26). For Townsend the truth of these connections is so obvious that it requires neither hedging about nor embellishment: "Among the first of these relations stands the relation of a servant to his master; and the first duty required from a servant is prompt, chearful, and hearty obedience" (26). The Poor Laws "tend to weaken these bonds, and to destroy their subordination." Once the poor need not fear going hungry if they are thrown out of their jobs for whatever reasons of insufficiency, there is nothing to make them work seriously. The master, then, essentially "is at the mercy of his servants; he must connive at their neglects, and bear their impertinence with patience." It is either this, or "to maintain them without work" (27). Society should require the lower class to be obedient to those above them; the Poor Laws interfere where

> the natural sanctions [otherwise] are sufficient to secure obedience without disturbing the peace and good order of society. . . . The wisest legislator will never be able to devise a more equitable, a more effectual, or in any respect a more suitable punishment, than hunger is for a disobedient servant. Hunger will tame the fiercest animals, it will teach decency and civility, obedience and subjection, to the most brutish, the most obstinate, and the most perverse. A good servant need not be afraid of wanting work. If one master should dismiss him from his service, others will be happy to receive him. But should a man be notorious for a thief, and for spoiling or neglecting work; should he be either so false, so vicious, or so ill-tempered, that no master would be willing to employ him; it would certainly be just that he should suffer hunger till he had learnt to reform his conduct. (27)

The images of taming, breaking, and punishing seem remarkably harsh, but they are not harsh within the context of laws regarding the poor. Going back to Elizabethan times, the law provided for the punishment of "'rogues, vagabonds, or sturdy beggars'"; such a man or woman "was to be stripped to the waist and whipped 'until his or her body be bloody.'"[7] And near the beginning of the eighteenth century we have the notorious Black Act (1723), about which E.P. Thompson rather wryly notes, "At no stage in its passage does there appear to have been debate or serious division; a House prepared to debate for hours a disputed election could find unanimity in creating at a blow some fifty new capital offences."[8] Thompson's famous study of the social environment surrounding the extraordinarily harsh set of laws known as the Black Acts describes a society that sees the lower class as a threat to property and sees the safety of property itself as the highest priority. Townsend and More, writing later in the century, write precisely in this tradition.

For Townsend as for More, the poor are a part of nature, God-ordained; their function in the natural economy, as Ashley Montague remarks, "is to cooperate with nature in making its

wealth available by extracting it from the soil so that it can then
be converted into consumable form" (7). Townsend finds that

> It seems to be a law of nature, that the poor should be to a cer-
> tain degree improvident, that there may always be some to ful-
> fil the most servile, the most sordid, and the most ignoble offices
> in the community. The stock of human happiness is thereby much
> increased, whilst the more delicate are not only relieved from
> drudgery, and freed from those occasional employments which
> would make them miserable, but are left at liberty, without in-
> terruption, to pursue those callings which are suited to their
> various dispositions, and most useful to the state. As for the low-
> est of the poor, by custom they are reconciled to the meanest
> occupations, to the most laborious works, and to the most haz-
> ardous pursuits; whilst the hope of their reward makes them
> chearful in the midst of all their dangers and their toils.
> (Townsend, 35)

To try to change these natural laws, this natural hierarchy, is to go
against the intention of God himself. Further, if God created these
differences among men, it actually would be evil to try to revise
his plan. A popular English hymn concisely presents the context
for these arguments: "The rich man in his castle / The poor man
at his gate, / God made them, high or lowly, / And ordered their
estate."[9] The Poor Laws, and the attendant laws limiting the free
movement of beggars and laborers, for Townsend seem directed
precisely at undermining this order. Not only are the "industrious poor" prevented from seeking work where they are needed,
but they are required to remain in place where they are not. Because healthy competition is not allowed to operate, labor prices
go up.

"Now it is evident," he states, "that by raising the price of
labour you must directly check the progress of the manufactures;
and by experience it is found, that the same effect arises indirectly
to a more considerable extent; for in proportion as you advance
the wages of the poor, you diminish the quality of their work. All
manufacturers complain of this, and universally agree, that the
poor are seldom diligent, except when labour is cheap, and corn
is dear" (29). In other words, as More shows in story after story,
the poor should get just enough but never more than they need to

stay at a sustainable level of subsistence. For as soon as they get more, Townsend says, they stop working. Specifically, Townsend makes the assumption that extra money immediately will be spent on drink. A day of drunkenness is followed by a day to recover, thus costing two days lost from work. With fewer days actually worked, the cost per day of labor goes up. This increase, which must happen because the labor pool is fixed due to the antivagrancy laws, is very harmful to farmers and manufacturers. Notice the statement of fact: Townsend has no doubt that "[d]runkenness is the common vice of poverty; not perhaps of poverty as such, but of the uncultivated mind; for it is the characteristic of unpolished nations to be fond of intoxicating liquors. Whatever be the cause, it is notorious, that with the common people the appetite for strong drink is their prevailing appetite. When therefore, by the advance in wages, they obtain more than is sufficient for their bare subsistence, they spend the surplus at the alehouse, and neglect their business" (30). This cycle goes on because such workers have nothing to fear—if they eventually cannot find work, they will be supported anyway.

And what of the "sober" and the "industrious?" The high wages are detrimental to them too, for "Where the price of labour is advanced, the industrious and sober will by degrees acquire a taste for luxury. They will not be contented with bare subsistence, with a sufficient quantity of coarse yet wholesome food, with warm but homespun garments, and with healthy but unfurnished cottages: they will contract habits of refinement" (30). Contrast such workers to the good poor people in More's "Shepherd of Salisbury Plain" who refuse to take more than a pittance even when it is offered, or to those who contentedly are instructed in managing with what they have in "The Cottage Cook." The assumption that in order to be virtuous the poor must reject anything that will raise them beyond what God ordained for them is a major theme of eighteenth-century social commentary.

Dorothy Marshall notes that in our period it was generally argued "that higher wages would lead to a falling off of industry, and that high prices for the necessaries of life were no bad things since they forced the poor to labour steadily if they would not want. In evidence of this viewpoint it was widely averred that workmen were more regular and steadier in their conduct when the price of food was high."[10] She quotes contemporary commentators: "'Everyone but an idiot knows that the lower classes must be kept poor or they will never be industrious'" and "'It is observed . . . by Clothiers and others, who employ great numbers of poor people, that when Corn is extremely plentiful, that the Labour of the poor is proportionately dear: And scarce to be had at all so licentious are they who labour only to eat, or rather to drink'" (180). Marshall argues that the poor worked extraordinarily long hours when they did work, and that a major problem was that the work itself could be very irregular in its availability. Such irregularity was especially a feature of some of the trades with the highest hourly or weekly wages, or in work where the weather played a large part (miners, she notes, would be laid off if the roads were not passable and the coal therefore could not be transported), as well as, of course, in seasonal work. This irregularity of income, she suggests, created an attitude of "eat, drink and be merry, for tomorrow we die." Since in any case the poor could not possibly hope to save enough to support themselves in old age, or in case of sickness, but would have no alternative but to turn to the parish, they would have no reason to save. And drink, she suggests, would ease some of the burden of those intolerably long days. Drinking beer, porter, and gin, she notes, "was part of the ordinary routine of the workman's life"; the beer and porter, if not the gin, "may have helped to balance an inadequate diet" (182–83).

For many eighteenth-century commentators, there was a kind of moral distaste for the idea that the poor somehow should avail themselves of "luxury" goods. Like More, Townsend argues against the idea that "private vices are public benefits"—that is, that consumption of luxury goods, even by the poor, forwards the economy. Mr. Fantom's servant William in More's story "The History of Mr. Fantom" absurdly explains that, having heard this concept of private vice as public benefit discussed repeatedly by Mr. Fantom and his friends, he chose, for the public good, to indulge his vices. Townsend similarly, but without irony, explains that the poor indeed have acquired the taste for luxury, which he defines for the poor as such nonnecessities as shoes and stockings, "By the present system of our poor laws . . . the benefits which arise from luxury, in promoting industry among the labouring poor, are lost" because the poor are assured of money to buy these things whether they work or not—in fact, the poor man knows that "in times of scarcity his wants shall be the *first* supplied" (33–34). Notice too the insistence here, as in More, that luxury means quite different things for the poor than for others. Townsend finds it offensive that the poor feel entitled to these "luxuries"; the poor should be happy to attain the most basic level of subsistence and should work during the interstices of their labor at providing some of these things they desire—such as stockings. When we look at the model family in "The Shepherd of Salisbury Plain," we will recognize Townsend's formula of appropriate behavior for the poor, as here:

> When they return from threshing or from plough, they might card, they might spin, or they might knit. We are told, that one thousand pair of Shetland stockings are annually imported into Leith, of which the price is from five to seven pence a pair: yet labour at Learwick, the capital of Shetland islands, is ten pence a day. These stockings are made at leisure hours. In these islands they have no dependance but upon their industry and frugality. They consume neither tea, nor sugar, nor spices, because they cannot afford to purchase useless articles; neither do they wear stockings or shoes, till by their diligence they have acquired such affluence as to bear this expence. How different is theirs from the dress and diet of our common people, who have lost all ideas of economy! (62)

If in "the colder regions of the North" (62) people can be happy without stockings, he sums up, surely here in the South they can make do also. In More's tale, this is precisely how the shepherd's family manages, with even the boys knitting their coarse stockings (the fine ones knit by the women are sold) as they guard the animals. But these good folk are fictional models. Unfortunately, Townsend finds that in the real world these people "work too little, they spend too much, and what they spend is seldom laid out to the best advantage" (62).

These comments seem, to a modern reader, supercilious, even unfeeling. Does not the poor man feel cold, or fatigue, or the rough quality of coarse fabric against his skin just as the rich man does? For many, perhaps most people in the eighteenth century, apparently the self-understood answer was no, the poor man does not have the same feelings or needs as the rich.[11] When More shows in story after story that the good poor man does not even desire more than he has, she objectifies Townsend's theory. As we have noted earlier, for Townsend, it "seems to be a law of nature, that the poor should be to a certain degree improvident, that there may always be some to fulfil the most servile, the most sordid, and the most ignoble offices in the community." His assumption is that there must be an under class, for there must be people to do the dirty work. And the "more delicate" people would be most unhappy if they had to do these unpleasant chores (note the not-very-subtle characterizing of the poor as of somehow less fine sensibility than those above them), while the poor are "chearful" in the midst of their labor because they essentially are working to keep themselves alive.

It is the simple pressure of hunger that motivates the poor to work, and because this motivation is, as it were, internal, its spur is not resented; the poor respond cheerfully to its goad. "There must be a degree of pressure" for the poor to work, Townsend says, "and that which is attended with the least violence will be the best. When hunger is either felt or feared, the desire of obtaining bread will quietly dispose the mind to undergo the greatest hardships, and will sweeten the severest labours" (35). Surely, Townsend insists, this natural system is better than any external force in terms of social harmony. In fact, "The peasant with a sickle in his hand is happier than the prince upon his throne!" (35–36). We will recognize all those happy, ever-working poor people in More's stories—it is an unkindness that no good man would inflict to raise the poor from their contented state. Indeed, Mr. Johnson tells the shepherd in "The Shepherd of Salisbury Plain" that he would not change the shepherd's state if he could.[12]

Thus society would be in a state of balance, with the poor driven by their need for food just hard enough to keep them working and content with their work, if the Poor Laws did not disturb this balance by creating a situation in which the poor have a fixed provision whether they work or not. The Poor Laws "[do] not promote that chearful compliance with those demands, which the community is obliged to make on the most indigent of its members" (36). As Pope had enunciated in his *Essay on Man,* as More repeats in so many contexts, Townsend sees in the relation of the rich to the poor a pattern imposed by an infallible God. The Poor Laws "destroy the harmony and beauty, the symmetry and order of that system, which God and nature have established in the world" (36).

If the society makes support a right, then there is no social structure: "nothing will remain but to cast lots, who among the active and virtuous shall perform the vilest offices for the indolent and vicious" (36). Note the equation of "indolent" and "vicious." Not wanting to work and evil character are closely connected. In "The History of Mr. Fantom," as the servant William slips further into indolence, he slips further into moral dissolution as well, ending as a murderer on the gallows. Note too the derogatory vocabulary of Townsend for those poor who do not measure up. We will see such language used for discussing even the children of the poor in More's stories, as when she refers to the children of Black Giles as "ragged brats," "little scarecrows," and "little idle creatures." Townsend insists that it is the unalterable nature of society that some must have less than others, and that some will suffer want. If the poor are provided for, it is inescapable that some of those who are taxed for their support will themselves suffer, so that what these laws in effect do is punish the "diligent" and the "virtuous."

If society could wipe out all inequalities and start off all men on an even plane, "the improvident, the lazy, and the vicious, would dissipate their substance; the prudent, the active, and the virtuous, would again increase their wealth" (40). More makes precisely these points in *Village Politics*. For both writers, inequality is a natural product of the differences among men. Townsend argues that the Poor Laws, by burdening the "provident," prevent them from prospering. The "provident" wait to marry until they think that they can afford the burdens of marriage, a time that inevitably must be put off because of the additional burden they bear supporting the poor. The poor have no such worries since they are assured of support. And so the poor increase constantly, in such numbers that no matter how much society puts forth for their support, it can never be enough: "For more than a century the struggles have been obstinate and unremitted, yet for more than a century the poor's rates have been constantly increasing" (48). Townsend notes that "two millions [are] annually expended on the poor without relieving their distress" (50). While social conditions add to the problem—like More, Townsend sees the "alehouses . . . [as] the principal nurseries for drunkenness, idleness, and vice" (65)—the major problem is that the Poor Laws create an unnatural world in which larger numbers of poor people can survive than is justified by what the land can support. It has been pointed out that Townsend first enunciates the ideas on population and survival of the fittest that Malthus and Darwin would later make so famous.[13] With guaranteed support, Townsend argues, the poor simply multiply without concern for finding adequate resources to sustain themselves and their families.

Townsend ends his analysis of the Poor Laws by suggesting that the laboring poor themselves be forced to contribute to a fund for their own maintenance in times of trouble—as, for example, times when their particular kind of manufacture hits a low period (should such a period continue overlong, the particular kind of manufacture would cease altogether, since the owners would not be able to keep them going, and these workers would need to find other work). Should more help be needed, Townsend is sure that those better off in the community would gladly and adequately contribute because "To relieve the poor by voluntary donations is not only most wise, politic, and just; is not only most agreeable both to reason and to revelation; but it is most effectual in preventing misery, and most excellent in itself, as cherishing, instead of rancour, malice and contention, the opposite and most amiable affections of the human breast, pity, compassion, and benevolence in the rich, love reverence, and gratitude in the poor" (68–69). We see here a theme that goes across the eighteenth century through Wordsworth's "Old Cumberland Beggar": the better off are both improved and pleasured by their own acts of charity. The relationship between the poor and their betters is necessary for both, for while the poor receive charity and can feel those "amiable" affections of love and reverence and gratitude, the rich get to experience benevolence. Note that, again, this exchange rests entirely on the assumption that one group is subordinate to the other, and indeed this is an explicit base of Townsend's argument. "It is evident," he says, "that no system can be good which does not . . . encourage industry, economy, and subordination" (61–62). The legal right to subsistence does not do this; individual, voluntary charity does:

> Nothing in nature can be more disgusting than a parish pay-table, attendant upon which, in the same objects of misery, are

too often found combined, snuff, gin, rags, vermin, insolence, and abusive language; nor in nature can any thing be more beautiful than the mild complacency of benevolence, hastening to the humble cottage to relieve the wants of industry and virtue, to feed the hungry, to cloath the naked, and to sooth the sorrows of the widow with her tender orphans; nothing can be more pleasing, unless it be their sparkling eyes, their bursting tears, and their uplifted hands, the artless expressions of unfeigned gratitude for unexpected favours. Such scenes will frequently occur whenever men shall have power to dispose of their own property. When the poor are obliged to cultivate the friendship of the rich, the rich will never want inclination to relieve the distresses of the poor. (69)

There are many answers to be made to Townsend's argument, of course. As we shall see in the next chapter, in the 1790s there were a great many voices arguing that the whole distribution of wealth in England was unfair, and that philanthropy, public or private, was not the point at all. The most well known of these voices, and without doubt the most dangerous in the eyes of Church and King, was Thomas Paine.

Three

# Radical Contexts

## Thomas Paine's *Rights of Man*

HANNAH MORE'S POOR PEOPLE, except for a scurvy few, are lovely folks. They respect their betters. They work hard all day and then continue to work by the light of one candle at night. They are heart-warmingly grateful for any help their superiors give them, but they never would demand any aid—and, in fact, should they (unlikely case) ever be offered more than a modicum of help, they would turn it down, for they are totally content with what they have and appreciate their "blessings." They are, in short, the upper class's ideal, fantasy poor. Modern readers, as we have seen in the preceding chapter, sometimes fail to look carefully at the political, social, and economic context of More's writing on the poor, specifically when they discuss the stories of the Cheap Repository Tracts. Commentators on More sometimes drop the hint that More's tracts and pamphlets "were attempts to reform popular culture and defuse radical social protest in England"[1] or were written "to advocate quiet obedience,"[2] but these are general formulations that do little to place More firmly in a political milieu that will allow us to understand just what she was doing. What follows in the next two chapters has just this goal.

We have seen that Bishop Porteus asked More to produce some sort of response to the revolutionary pamphlets in circulation in the early 1790s. It was, More writes, to be "some little thing, tending to open [the lower order of people's] eyes under their present wild impressions of liberty and equality." Jonathan Wordsworth, retelling the story, comments that More "was an effective propagandist."[3] But Wordsworth's account, like that of most critics whose focus is on the stories themselves, somehow misses the urgency of the social warfare played out in the 1790s. For this, we must turn to the historians. Anyone who wants to understand what Hannah More was doing in her stories for the poor must first read E. P. Thompson's classic *The Making of the English Working Class*, and much of the following discussion is based on Thompson's extraordinary work. Complementary to Thompson's study is Isaac Kramnick's *Republicanism and Bourgeois Radicalism*.[4] It needs to be emphasized that those sweet, malleable poor and laboring people whom we meet in More's stories are rather far from the poor and laboring classes that More's class actually perceived. For there was real fear among "Church and King" (Thompson takes this label from Burke via Paine) that, sufficiently incited, the lower classes might rise up with formidable power. In this context, the following anecdote is instructive. In 1795, in response to the passage of the Two Acts,[5] many demonstrations were held. In Yorkshire a massive meeting was called to protest against these sedition bills. "Wilberforce, on his way to church in London, . . . was intercepted by an express message from Yorkshire. Overcoming, without difficulty, his scruples against travelling on the Sabbath, he drove to see Pitt. Pitt said he must attend the county meeting. But Wilberforce's carriage was not ready. 'Mine,' said Pitt, 'is ready, set off in that.' In Pitt's borrowed carriage, he made the 'forced march' up to the north" (Thompson, 146). This incident indicates just how seriously Pitt and his party viewed the situation. Two months earlier, on October 26, 1795, John Thelwall was among the speakers at a demonstration in Copenhagen Fields, Islington, where the crowd apparently numbered more than 100,000, and 150,000 was claimed (Thompson, 144). The situation for the poor was at this time especially severe. In Spitalfields, Thelwall lamented, "you will find the poor [out of work silk] weavers and their families crowded together in vile, filthy and unwholesome chambers, destitute of the most common comforts, and even of the common necessaries of life"; Thompson reminds us that "there was actual starvation in London" (Thompson, 143).[6]

People talk about taking away aristocratic land holdings. Thomas Spence, author of "another *Rights of Man* . . . that goes farther than Paine's," explicitly wants to expropriate the lands of the aristocrats: "'Do you think Mankind will ever enjoy any tolerable degree of Liberty and Felicity, by having a Reform in Parliament, if Landlords were still suffered to remain? . . . A Convention or Parliament of the People would be at eternal War with the Aristocracy'" (Thompson, 138). A pamphlet of 1794 called *Revolutions without Bloodshed* demanded, among other things, reform of the Poor Laws and of the Game Laws and work for the unemployed.

The most dangerous pamphlet was Tom Paine's 1791 *Rights of Man*. One Christopher Wyvill, whom Thompson characterizes as a "moderate Yorkshire reformer," nonetheless wrote in 1792, "'If Mr Paine should be able to rouze up the lower classes, their interference will probably be marked by wild work, and all we now possess, whether in private property or public liberty, will be at the mercy of a lawless and furious rabble'" (24). If these were the sentiments of a "moderate" reformer, it is not hard to guess the responses of the more conservative. Paine's of course was not the only voice espousing the radical cause, nor had the radical movement erupted suddenly with the appearance of *Rights of Man*. As early as 1776 Richard Price's *Observations on Civil Liberty* had "achieved the remarkable sale of 60,000 within a few months" (Thompson, 27). (These and other "remarkable" figures should be kept in mind to bring a bit of wholesome scepticism to the "millions" in sales universally claimed for More's Cheap Repository Tracts.) But it was in the 1790s that the perceived threat came to seem so very alarming. A large part of upper-class discomfort centered on the fear that if the poor once noticed that they had human, or spiritual, value just as their "betters," social order might become too difficult to maintain. An older cousin of Joseph Priestley (who obviously did not share Priestley's more radical social perspective) seems to feel quite self-satisfied that he had "determined to give four or five loads of wheat to Christ's poor," and, again, some days later, "[o]rdered brother Obadiah to give a load of wheat among Christ's poor" (Thompson, 26). Thompson notes rather wryly that "[i]f Christ's poor came to believe that their souls were as good as aristocratic or bourgeois souls then it might lead them on to the arguments of the *Rights of Man*," as the Duchess of Buckingham seems to have noticed: "'It is monstrous to be told you have a heart as sinful as the common wretches that crawl on the earth'" (Thompson, 42-43).

There were, proportional to the upper classes, huge numbers of these "common wretches." But their numbers traditionally had been harnessed by Church and King, so that "rioting" very often was a government-planned, government-controlled activity; the best known of the mob actions are perhaps the Birmingham Riots of 1791, among the victims of which was Joseph Priestley. But this sort of mob action is seen as more and more dangerous as the nineties go on. If earlier Fox could declare that he would "'much rather be governed by a mob than a standing army,'" as Thompson comments, "after the French Revolution no Whig politician would have risked, no City father condoned, the tampering with such dangerous energies" (Thompson, 72). By the nineties "the deliberate use of a crowd as an instrument of pressure, by persons 'above' or apart from the crowd" (Thompson, 63) comes to seem quite risky.

What we need to understand from Thompson's analysis of mob behavior as an instrument of protest, as in the many food "riots" from the 1760s on, is that the laboring classes and the poor were active in masses working together. When in the nineties the laboring poor seemed increasingly vulnerable to radicalization, a radicalization fueled to a large extent by a deliberate campaign to distribute to the lower classes the writings of Tom Paine, the upper classes perceived that they had to fight back. Hannah More was the weapon of choice. Her first story directed to this lower-class audience, *Village Politics*, essentially is commissioned just for this purpose of counter-propaganda. But before we look at *Village Politics*, we need to see just what it was that More and her friends were afraid of.

Tom Paine and his *Rights of Man* are extraordinarily prominent in the political scene of the 1790s. Paine's earlier *Common Sense* had been an important catalyst in bringing the American colonists from anger to action, essentially helping to bring the as yet undecided colonists to the point of revolution. In England in the 1790s among the upper classes there was a real sense that *Rights of Man* and those who distributed it presented a direct threat to the upper classes and to the government whose job it was, as Mary Wollstonecraft put it, to safeguard the property of those classes. *Rights of Man*, Paine's response to Edmund Burke's attack on the French Revolution in his *Reflections on the Revolution in France*, followed Burke's *Reflections* by one year. Paine's projected audience was the mass of Englishmen and, as Kramnick comments, "Paine's uncomplicated, unscholarly, and unsophisticated rhetoric brought him unprecedented popular success. He was an instant hero in England, not only to the intellectual radicals among whom he moved, such as Blake, Holcroft, Horne Tooke, Godwin, and Wollstonecraft, but to hundreds of thousands of artisans and journeymen who bought *The Rights of Man* for sixpense or read it reprinted by their provincial radical association" (Kramnick, 141–42). In the context of More's pamphlets, we should note the modus operandus: cheap pamphlets distributed in huge numbers to the lower-class men who were Paine's objects. And what were they being told? "'If universal peace, civilization and commerce are ever to be the happy lot of man, it cannot be accomplished but by a revolution in the system of governments'" (Kramnick, 142). England's governing class was less than enthusiastic about Paine's message; William Pitt the Younger, George III's prime minister, acted almost immediately: "in 1792 charges of seditious writings were lodged against Paine, and a trial was scheduled" (Kramnick, 142).

More and her friends had good reason to be horrified by *Rights of Man*. Paine's book (although *Rights of Man* usually is referred to as a "pamphlet," both parts together run to 246 pages in a recent edition)[7] essentially is an economic treatise that argues for an entire change in the distribution of the wealth of the nation. *Rights of Man* is an extraordinary work: it is as if Paine simply reinvents everything in the English system of government that had been taken as given, or perhaps even God-ordained.[8] This last is not merely a figure of speech, for the Church and King party, including Burke and More, insist that the standing paradigm of English society in fact *is* God-ordained. Paine leaves God entirely out of the question, thus seeing hereditary monarchy as no more than a laughably inadequate—but highly expensive—system of handing on power, primogeniture as a corrupt and, again, socially expensive system for handing on property, and the current system of taxation as one that produces, and ensures, the continuance of a large class of poverty-stricken, powerless men.

Paine's argument is based on what he perceives as "the natural rights of man." The first part of *Rights of Man*, published in 1791, largely is a response to and refutation of Burke's *Reflections*. Paine begins by asserting that Burke has undertaken to prove that the people of England have "no . . . rights [to determine their own government], and that such rights do not now exist in the nation" because "the persons, or the generation of persons, in whom they did exist, are dead, and with them the right is dead also" (90). To prove this, Burke quotes a declaration made by Parliament a hundred years earlier to William and Mary: "'The Lords Spiritual and Temporal, and Commons, do, in the name of the people aforesaid,—(meaning the people of England then living)—most humbly and faithfully *submit* themselves, their *heirs* and *posterities*, for EVER'" (90). But Paine argues that no generation has the right to decide what a future generation shall do.

> There never did, there never will, and there never can exist a parliament, or any description of men, or any generation of men, in any country, possessed of the right or the power of binding and controuling [sic] posterity to the "*end of time*," or of commanding for ever how the world shall be governed, or who shall govern it; and therefore, all such clauses, acts or declarations, by which the makers of them attempt to do what they have neither the right nor the power to do, nor the power to execute, are in themselves null and void.—Every age and generation must be as free to act for itself, *in all cases,* as the ages and generations which preceded it. The vanity and presumption of governing beyond the grave, is the most ridiculous and insolent of all tyrannies. Man has no property in man; neither has any generation property in the generations which are to follow. (90–91)

The argument that no previous generation has the right to make determinations for succeeding generations, as we shall see, results down the road in refuting entirely the idea of a hereditary monarchy, for Paine will insist that monarchy essentially passes down a nation as individual inheritance passes down estates and their farm animals. But before discussing Paine on monarchy, we must first understand his analysis of the roots and effects of the rights of man.

If no one generation has the right to decide for all succeeding generations what laws and governments shall rule them, from whence do come man's rights? Paine argues that men always base their systems on "antiquity"—that which came before. But, he asks, which antiquity should we use, that of a hundred years ago, a thousand years ago? The problem, he says, is that any one of these is arbitrary. We must go back to the beginning:

Why then not trace the rights of man to the creation of man? . . .
If any generation of men ever possessed the right of dictating
the mode by which the world should be governed for ever, it
was the first generation that existed; and if that generation did
it not, no succeeding generation can shew any authority for doing it, nor can set any up. The illuminating and divine principle
of the equal rights of man, (for it has its origin from the Maker of
man) relates, not only to the living individuals, but to generations of men succeeding each other. Every generation is equal in
rights to the generation which preceded it, by the same rule that
every individual is born equal in rights with his contemporary.
(117)

This extraordinary paragraph shimmers with power. Never mind
that the American and French Revolutions already had enunciated such principles; here they are being set forth for England.
Paine, as further analysis of *Rights of Man* makes clear, means what
he says literally: "every individual is born equal in rights with his
contemporary." Not just men of a particular class are equal, but
*all* men. The concept of class, then, not to mention the concept of
kingship, must be void. No wonder that More and her friends
were so troubled; no wonder that the government felt so threatened that it put Paine on trial.
    This equality is the source of the natural rights of man. Paine
insists that the "Mosaic account of the creation" states "*the unity
or equality of man*"; there is male and female, "but no other distinction is even implied." Thus "the equality of man, so far from being a modern doctrine, is the oldest on record" (118). There is no
room in this picture for class or other distinction; since all men
are equal, power only can be delegated, never assumed. Since all
men have these natural rights to equality, when men enter into
social compacts, it only can be "to have those rights better secured," for "Man did not enter into society to become *worse* than
before, nor to have fewer rights than he had before. . . . His natural rights are the foundation of all his civil rights" (119). What is
the distinction between natural rights and civil rights? Civil rights
are preceded by natural rights, and in fact civil rights exist to protect natural rights. It stands to reason that, this being so, no government has any authority to abridge rights that, Paine insists,
are universal. It also stands to reason that government does not

have the authority—say by taxation—to change this condition of equality. Society does not *give* man rights; when he enters into society, a person in effect exchanges some of his natural rights for civil rights: "every civil right grows out of a natural right; or, in other words, is a natural right exchanged" (120). In joining society, man puts some of his rights into that society, becoming "a proprietor in society" from which he has the right to "draw . . . on the capital."

Governments have been founded upon three bases, superstition, power, and "the common interest of society, and the common rights of man" (120). The first is a kind of primitive power that lasts as long as men believe in consulting oracles, as long as men bow under superstition. The second, unfortunately, remains longer imposed, for although it begins in force (that is, conquest), it allies this conquest to a species of superstition, to a "fraud" called "Divine Right," which, "in imitation of the Pope, who affects to be spiritual and temporal, and in contradiction to the Founder of the Christian religion, twisted itself afterwards into an idol of another shape, called *Church and State*. The key of St Peter, and the key of the Treasury, became quartered on one another, and the wondering cheated multitude worshipped the invention" (121). One only can imagine the force with which this argument must have hit Paine's contemporaries. In Anglican England it would not have been seen amiss to attack the pope in this way, but the king would be a different matter. Paine's paralleling here of iniquity between pope and king has the logical force of using the socially acceptable distaste for the pomp and power of the Catholic Church to support his assertion that the king's power is equally invalid.

Paine's very unsubtle argument is that royal rule in general, and specifically in England, is rule by usurpation. That is, someone comes into power by conquering the country, sets himself over it—in effect stealing the nation—and then simply passes down the goods he has taken by force in the first case to his descendants. For Paine, kingly rule is rule by brigand. William the Conqueror founded his rule in force, "and the sword assumed the name of a sceptor" (121). Nothing, in Paine's view, has changed since. Kings, it is clear, have no valid right to form or head governments, for only the people of the nation themselves have such rights.

The only legitimate government for Paine is one in which

individuals enter into compacts *"with each other* to produce a government: and this is the only mode in which governments have a right to arise, and the only principle on which they have a right to exist." The distinction is that government either arises *"out* of the people, or *over* the people" (122). The current government of England is of the latter sort and is therefore invalid. For there to be a legitimate government, he says, there first must be a constitution that calls it into being and that then regulates its forms and functions. Where, he challenges Burke, is the English constitution? A constitution

> has not an ideal, but a real existence; and wherever it cannot be produced in a visible form, there is none. A constitution is a thing *antecedent* to a government, and a government is only the creature of a constitution. The constitution of a country is not the act of its government, but of the people constituting a government. It is the body of elements, to which you can refer, and quote article by article; and which contains the principles on which the government shall be established, the manner in which it shall be organized, the powers it shall have, the mode of elections, the duration of parliaments, or by what other name such bodies may be called; the powers which the executive part of the government shall have; and, in fine, every thing that relates to the compleat organization of a civil government, and the principles on which it shall act, and by which it shall be bound. A constitution, therefore, is to a government, what the laws made afterwards by that government are to a court of judicature. The court of judicature does not make the laws, neither can it alter them; it only acts in conformity to the laws made: and the government is in like manner governed by the constitution. (122–23)

Paine's definition is direct and lucid. England simply has no constitution; it has, instead, laws that, since they are not based on a legal constitution, are themselves not valid. They are, however, though not legitimate, often damaging in the extreme. Parish laws, for example, derive from the fact that "each chartered town is an aristocratical monopoly in itself." Anyone coming from another part of the country "is hunted from them as if he were a foreign enemy. An Englishman is not free of his own country: every one of those places presents a barrier in his way, and tells him he is not a freeman—that he has no rights" (122).[9] Most people are disenfranchised; in Bath, a city of twenty to thirty thousand inhabitants, "the right of electing representatives to parliament is monopolized by about thirty-one persons" (126). The lack of a constitution touches negatively on everyone at every step of the social scale and at every stage of an individual's existence because in the absence of a constitution bad laws take over.

Among the most damaging of these laws are those of primogeniture, a social system that Paine sees as simply unnatural. Primogeniture preserves an aristocratic line at the expense of all younger members of a family. First of all, Paine urges the dismantling of the whole idea of "aristocracy." Concepts like "*Duke,* or *Count,* or *Earl* [are] rattle[s]" (132), words without meaning. The words "Judge" or "General," he says, are associated with functions or characters; but what is a "Duke"? We need only to ignore these distinctions, he says, and they will disappear. As long as we respect the concept of aristocracy, on the other hand, we support the damage that it does to society and to individuals, since in order to keep up aristocratic succession, in any aristocratic family, there is "never more than *one* child. The rest are begotten to be devoured. They are thrown to the cannibal for prey, and the natural parent prepares the unnatural repast" (133).

The damage does not stop with the individuals, for all those children that the aristocracy disowns are cast upon society for support, but, unlike lower-class orphans on the parish roll, these men come at enormous expense: "Unnecessary offices and places in governments and courts are created at the expense of the public, to maintain them" (133). The monarchy is useless, expensive, and illegal; the aristocracy is a corruption. It should come as no surprise that the church, too, is corrupt, its corruption closely connected to its ties to government, for when religion is made a legal constraint and connected into, as Burke calls it, "Church and State" (Paine, 138), persecution, intolerance, and social waste are inevitable. We can imagine the fury with which this particular argument would have been met by More and her friends. We also should remember the social context for this argument: the question of what to do with the Dissenters in the 1790s is especially pressing as they accrue ever greater financial wealth through their central role as the engines of the industrial revolution.[10]

One of the many aspects of Paine's argument that is incendiary is that at virtually every point where he discusses what is wrong with England, he contrasts the English system with the French—which always is better. The French have dispensed with titles; the French have learned that character, not rank, makes the man. Even before the Revolution, the French did not make of their aristocracy "a body of hereditary legislators. It was not 'a corporation of aristocracy'" (134), as Paine quotes M. de la Fayette describing an English House of Peers. And after the Revolution, France rid itself of all the features of corruption and inequity that characterize the British system. Not only have secular distinctions of rank and class been erased, but religion too has been reformed. Most important, "Church" has been severed from "State."

Persecution and intolerance only come when religion is made legal constraint: "By engendering the church with the state, a sort of mule-animal, capable only of destroying, and not of breeding up, is produced, called *The Church established by Law*" (138). All evils associated with religion—the "Inquisition in Spain," for example—come from making a state religion. Paine argues that parceling out "tolerance" is not the same as the "Universal Right of Conscience" (137) that the French constitution guarantees. Under the French system, no one needs a special dispensation to be part of society while adhering to other than the state religion. Only in such circumstances, Paine insists, can religions be what by their nature they should be: "kind and benign, and united with principles of morality" (138). For More and the many of her friends whose view of self as well as of society centered on religious identity, such attacks on the privileging of their own Anglicanism would be discomfiting not only on a political but surely on an emotional level as well, so that the negative response would be doubly loaded. Further, since in England religion and monarch are linked, to attack the monarchy is to attack religion itself.

Toward the end of part I of *Rights of Man* Paine prints a full translation of the "Declaration of the Rights of Man and of Citizens, By the National Assembly of France," following it with some "Observations." His comments are incendiary, his enthusiasm unbounded: "The three first articles are the basis of Liberty, as well individual as national; nor can any country be called free, whose government does not take its beginning from the principles they contain, and continue to preserve them pure; and the whole of the Declaration of Rights is of more value to the world, and will do more good, than all the laws and statutes that have yet been promulgated" (165). The principles of the Declaration are discussed throughout Paine's essay, but the baldness of his statement here emphasizes the uncompromising nature of his challenge to the established government of England. Paine ends with a "Miscellaneous Chapter" that drives home this challenge, returning first to a personal attack on Burke and then, more significantly, to an attack on the monarchy itself. Burke's argument in favor of monarchy essentially is that of heredity. Paine's argument against it is economic. Kings cost too much; the fact that they are mostly idiots ("it is impossible to make wisdom hereditary"), only makes things worse. It is the "enormous expence of governments [that] have [sic] provoked people to think (167). Even "the humblest individual in the country" (169) pays for the waste that supporting a king requires: "part of [each man's] daily labour goes towards making up the million sterling a year, which the country gives the person it stiles a king" (171). A hereditary crown, Paine says, certainly is not natural and probably not even legal. If a given generation wants to live under a certain government, that is its prerogative, but it has no right to make these decisions for future generations.

As to what is owed the king, Paine dismisses entirely the demands of the monarchy. Monarchy is merely "human craft to obtain money from a nation under specious pretences." America's government "extend[s] over a country ten times as large as England" and is conducted "for a fortieth part of the expence which government costs in England. If I ask a man in America if he wants a king? he retorts, and asks me if I take him for an ideot?" (175–76). So begins the final section of the essay; the rest of the chapter piles up reason upon reason why England should follow France's model and rid itself of its king. The only arguments to be made in favor of monarchy are made by those who directly profit from the institution. The arguments against, and these are overwhelming, deal with the monarchy's lack of usefulness and its cost.

Paine mocks the "Placemen, Pensioners, Lords of the bedchamber, Lords of the kitchen, Lords of the necessary-house, and the Lord knows what besides [who] can find as many reasons for monarchy as their salaries, paid at the expence of the country, amount to" (177). People who produce, that is, farmers, merchants, and "down through all the occupations of life to the common labourer," know that monarchy is "a sinecure." Although the taxes of England amount to almost £17 million a year, the real governing—that of magistrates and juries, what Paine calls "all the internal government" (177), essentially comes without charge to the nation. Yet England's taxes are so high. As the cost is not in the civil government, Paine concludes, it must be in the monarchy. Yet "the people of England submit to taxation without enquiry" (187). The clear implication is that in this situation the (poor) people of England are fools to impoverish themselves to pay the expenses of the monarchy.

Nation and government are not the same: the former may be solvent while the latter is in debt; it is absolutely necessary that the nation, not the government, be seen "as the real paymaster" (188), for under this condition the significant power resides in the nation itself because creditors must look to it rather than to the monarch for repayment: "this precedent [France, where the government's insolvency was not allowed to affect creditors] is fatal to the policy by which governments have supposed themselves secure" (188). And this is precisely Paine's point. The French economy, by ridding itself of the expenses of corruption, is in a position all European nations should envy. Its political situation has "every court in Europe . . . dreading the same fate" (189). Mixed government, of the sort that England has, is virtually as bad as absolute monarchy. As long as one branch, the king, can do no wrong, responsibility always can be shifted and the moving power becomes, "of necessity, Corruption. However imperfect election and representation may be in mixed Governments, they still give exercise to a greater portion of reason than is convenient to the hereditary Part; and therefore it becomes necessary to buy the reason up" (191).

Reason, not corruption, should be at the center of government. In the face of the events in France, reason soon shall take its rightful place in England too. *Rights of Man* part I ends on a note of limitless optimism: "From what we now see, nothing of reform in the political world ought to be held improbable. It is an age of Revolutions, in which every thing may be looked for" (197). By the following year, when he brought out part II, the optimism is perhaps a bit more measured, the economic arguments even more central. Part II, in fact, is almost entirely an economic treatise.

Part I of *Rights of Man* we know is intended as an answer to

Burke's *Reflections*. John Keane suggests that the *Reflections* are themselves a response to a letter Burke received from his friend Paine describing the happenings in France. That letter, full of the triumphs of the revolution, in addition to Richard Price's *A Discourse on the Love of Our Country*, point as much to flaws in British government as to triumphs of the new French regime. Burke's position hardens in the face of these attacks.[11] Paine, aware that Burke's book is in the works, waits for it to appear and makes part I of *Rights of Man* into a public reply to Burke. In line with my emphasis that More in writing *her* Tracts is engaging in conscious and direct battle with Paine, it is helpful to note that direct response to other people's published attempts to determine public opinion is part of the established method of discourse for More's contemporaries. So, too, as we will see shortly, is the careful strategizing of publisher, author, and author's friends to get the word out—literally. Keane notes that Paine, hearing that *Reflections* finally was about to appear, crossed back from France during the last week of October, in time to buy a copy when it appeared in London bookshops on November 1. *Reflections* sold fifty-five hundred copies during the first seventeen days, twelve thousand by the end of the month, and within a year nineteen thousand. Within three months of its appearance in a French translation, sixteen thousand copies sold in that language.[12] These figures were to be dwarfed by the sales of Paine's pamphlet.

*Rights of Man* part I was a matter of governmental interest even before it reached publication. Paine's plan had been to bring out the book in time for the opening of Parliament—and Washington's birthday—on February 22. The publisher, Joseph Johnson, "was visited repeatedly by government agents," as Keane notes, even as the unbound sheets piled up in his shop.[13] Johnson, who already had published critiques of the *Reflections* by Wollstonecraft, Thomas Christie, and Capel Lofft, somehow became aware that Paine's book was more dangerous than the others, and he stopped sales within four hours; over a hundred copies already had been sold.[14] J. S. Jordan agreed to publish the book, and Paine, having scrambled to borrow forty pounds to pay these unexpected costs to Jordan, delivered to him the already printed sheets from Johnson's shop. Having literally carted the pages from one publisher to the next with a wagon and a horse, Paine left the actual publication in the hands of three friends, Thomas Brand,

William Godwin, and Thomas Holcroft, and apparently left for France.[15] Although there were rumors that the book had been toned down as it crossed from one publisher to the next, Holcroft was ecstatic to find that there had not been "a single castration."[16]

*Rights of Man* sold as no book had before. A new edition was brought out by Jordan three days after the first; it sold out in hours. By May a sixth edition was published, and fifty thousand copies had been sold. The relatively high price of three shillings—precisely the same price as Burke's *Reflections*—clearly did not deter sales.[17] Although the government had considered whether to prosecute, it decided against taking any action; perhaps they felt that they could not make good a charge of sedition, although surely a packed jury would have solved this problem.[18] The book reached an extraordinary proportion of the reading public. Keane posits four million readers out of a ten million population in Britain: "Based on those figures, one reader in ten purchased a copy of *Rights of Man*. Even that figure is misleadingly low if pirated and serialized editions are taken into account and if it is considered that in a society with a wretched standard of living, books were for most readers still occasional luxuries. . . . *Rights of Man* was read aloud and talked about to the illiterate on an unheard-of scale."[19]

The three-shilling price of *Rights of Man* probably was one of the reasons the government decided not to prosecute: its price, as Paine himself understood, would put it out of reach of most people. Within weeks of the appearance of Jordan's edition, Paine had authorized requests from all over Britain to print cheap, popular editions. By April 1791 he had decided "to print a very numerous edition in London, under my own direction, by which means the work would be more perfect, and the price be reduced lower than it could be by *printing* small editions in the country, of only a few thousands each."[20] Thus the campaign to reach enormous numbers of people was consciously planned. As with *Common Sense*, Paine understood that getting his message out was as important as the message itself. And in this he was, as we have seen, amazingly successful. Given the message, and his unprecedented success in spreading it, we can understand the urgency of the response of More's class. Part I of *Rights of Man* would have posed enough of a threat; part II turned the heat up even higher.

Neither Jordan nor Johnson would put his name on *Rights of Man, part the second*. Thomas Chapman agreed to publish it, offer-

ing Paine the incredible sum of one thousand guineas for the copyright, but Paine refused to give up the copyright, fearing that he
would lose control of the manuscript. Chapman, before the book
appeared, got cold feet. Paine renegotiated publication of the already printed sheets with both Jordan and Johnson; they would
"sell" the book, but he, Paine, was the "publisher."[21] Within two
weeks, five editions had come from Jordan's press. Knowing that
the government now had decided to prosecute, Paine went ahead
in the planning of cheap editions for part II. Keane notes that
"Paine's six-penny book was held in the hands of crofters in Scotland, tin miners in Cornwall, shepherds in Cumbria, and shoemakers in Norwich. It was reported that in the Staffordshire
potteries of Newcastle 'almost every hand' and in Sheffield 'every cutler' owned a copy. . . . [It was reported in Dundee, Scotland
that] a single person has sold here more than 1,000 copies of T.
Payne's pamphlet [and in Glasgow] '10,000 copies per week are
being sold.'" It is clear that the pamphlet was directed to just such
an audience as these workingmen.

Paine's language, in contrast to Burke's, is simple and direct. It is the language of plain people, as Boulton reminds us.
Paine "claims, for instance that by requiring wisdom as an attribute of kingship Burke has, 'To use a sailor's phrase . . . *swabbed
the deck*'; Court [*sic*] popularity, he says, 'sprung up like a mush-
room in a night'; a State-Church is 'a sort of mule-animal, capable
only of destroying, and not of breeding up.'"[22] Boulton's analysis
of Paine's language, as of Burke's, remains one of the most useful
discussions of their respective styles and the aims to which each
man directed his prose. But Boulton is in some degree unfair to
Paine, or, perhaps more accurately, he has trouble accepting Paine's
language in its own terms. Boulton argues that Paine uses "vulgar phraseology" and then goes on rather elaborately to explain
that in the context of Paine's intentions, "vulgar" does not really
carry its usual pejorative meaning. "But when the term is applied
to Paine and his style the pejorative is completely out of place;
'vulgar' is necessary as a critical word, but it should be descrip-
tive, meaning, not boorish or debased, but plain, of the people,
*vulgus*." Yet Boulton had begun this paragraph describing Paine's
style by saying that *Rights of Man* "is 'clear,' but it is also inelegant
and occasionally ungrammatical; Paine can certainly be said to
use 'vulgar phraseology.'"[23]

Because Boulton's analysis is so authoritative, this lukewarm view of Paine's style has come to be the accepted one in modern criticism, but it is not an accurate assessment. Paine's style actually is remarkably good: his prose is readable, unpretentious, and direct. It indeed lacks the convolutions of Burke's prose, and in the absence of that ornament Paine's ideas glow with undispersed energy. Paine makes fun of Burke's style, puncturing its pomposity, satirizing its classical allusions. Upper-class readers were outraged by the inappropriateness of Paine's style, although, ironically, Burke also was taken to task for what seemed to many of *his* readers an inappropriate informality. What is perhaps most interesting is that when More answered Paine, she chose to take her own style down several additional notches. While Paine's language is straightforward and relatively unornamented, More's is almost childlike, as we will see in discussing *Village Politics* and the Tracts of the Cheap Repository. The battle among More's contemporaries for men's minds is consciously waged on the level of diction.

But if Paine's language is simple, his argument is not. Especially in part II, *Rights of Man* sets out detailed economic analyses, including itemized budgets, to explain why England's political system has created the current economic problems and what changes need to be implemented to reform the system. These passages of *Rights of Man* make for somewhat heavy reading (and for rather slow explication, I'm afraid), but they are important in delineating Paine's faith in the principle that political reform inevitably would produce economic reform. Even more directly than in part I, the second part of *Rights of Man* insists that no aspect of the current hierarchy in England is worth having. In part I Paine says that monarchy is useless and expensive and that the aristocratic practice of primogeniture is harmful not only to younger sons but to society in general. In part II he focuses his argument on the social costs of monarchy and aristocracy, concluding that paying for these institutions, especially paying for the monarchy, causes all the economic dislocations in society. Paine announces his thesis immediately in his preface: "I do not believe that the people of England have ever been fairly and candidly dealt by. . . . It is time to dismiss that inattention which has so long been the encouraging cause of stretching taxation to excess" (208). It is overtaxation, especially taxation of commodities, that tips so many from an adequate maintenance into poverty. Paine argues that this economic dislocation is a result of political decisions: "To say that any people are not fit for freedom, is to make poverty their choice" (208).

*Rights of Man* is one of the most extraordinary documents to come out of this period; its challenge in part I to the centuries-old political organization of England is remarkable enough, but the total rethinking of the relationship between power and poverty set out with such clarity and simplicity in part II is breathtaking. Surely many of these ideas were in circulation at the time, but Paine's fearless and marvelously lucid analysis as surely is unique. Paine tears down with reasoned exposition the walls of respect and obedience that custom had erected around the upper orders; he believes that such argument will change people's thought and, inevitably, the social and political shape of the nation. All this will happen through the power of the written word. As we shall see in my chapter on More and Wollstonecraft, such belief in the enormous power of the written word is typical of those on both sides of the political divide. Paine's celebration of the power of print is also a challenge and a warning.

Try to limit what people can read, Paine says, and you will incite revolution! "Mankind are not now to be told they shall not think, or they shall not read; and publications that go no farther than to investigate principles of government, to invite men to reason and to reflect, and to shew the errors and excellences of different systems, have a right to appear. If they do not excite attention, they are not worth the trouble of a prosecution; and if they do, the prosecution will amount to nothing, since it cannot amount to a prohibition of reading. This would be a sentence on the public, instead of the author, and would also be the most effectual mode of making or hastening revolutions" (207). Those in government, then, have no way to prevent Paine's arguments from being made. Surely they wished to and, as we know, they did indeed attempt to silence him. It is not hard to understand the upper class's panic in the face of the challenge that Paine sets.

For he says simply that the poor are a "direct consequence of what . . . is called government," of "the greedy hand of government thrusting itself into every corner and crevice of industry, and grasping the spoil of the multitude" (211). It will become clear as part II goes on that Paine means this literally. Paine argues that in order to support the monarch and his hangers-on, taxes must be so high that they suck the life from the individual and from society as a whole, for by interfering with the free development of commerce, the very potential of the nation is cut off: "The amazing and still increasing expences with which old governments are conducted, the numerous wars they engage in or provoke, the embarrassments they throw in the way of universal civilization and commerce, and the oppression and usurpation they act at home, have wearied out the patience, and exhausted the property of the world" (212). One of the ways that governments siphon off revenue is by waging war; wars are pursued only to enrich the monarch and his friends. "All the monarchical governments are military," he says. "War is their trade, plunder and revenue their objects" (212).

Government essentially is irrelevant to the functioning of society; society performs for itself those functions that government claims to support. No one man can supply all his own needs, and it is the supplying of "those wants, [that] act upon every individual" (214) that creates the need for each man to be part of society. Most of what men do arises from mutual interest, which, if unregulated, will develop civilization. "All the great laws of society are laws of nature," Paine asserts. "Those of trade and commerce, whether with respect to the intercourse of individuals, or of nations, are laws of mutual and reciprocal interest. They are followed and obeyed, because it is the interest of the parties so to do, and not on account of any formal laws their governments may impose or interpose" (216). But these natural interactions too often are "destroyed by the operations of government" (216). Civil disturbances most often are caused by government itself: "instead of consolidating society, it divided it" (217). In a comment to which More essentially replies with all of the Cheap Repository Tracts, Paine says, "Whatever the apparent cause of any riots may be, the real one is always want of happiness. It shews that something is wrong in the system of government, that injures the felicity by which society is to be preserved" (217). More, in all her writing to the poor, simply tells them that they are happy. Paine insists that the solution to the unrest that repeatedly breaks out in England is an equitable social system, like America's, that shares out the goods of society fairly. In America, "the poor are not oppressed, the rich are not privileged. Industry is not mortified by the splendid extravagance of a court rioting at its expence. Their taxes are few, because their government is just; and as there is nothing to render them wretched, there is nothing to engender riots and tumults" (218). He sets out first to show the origins of the current system of government in England and then, in extraordinary detail, how to improve that system.

The current government, like all monarchies, is founded on the theft of the nation, and, from its beginnings, has been nothing but "a continual system of war and extortion" (221). It is too corrupt for reform; the only remedy is to begin anew: "All hereditary government is in its nature tyranny" because "[t]o inherit a government, is to inherit the people, as if they were flocks and herds" (224). Equally absurd, those who so inherit do it not on the basis of talent "but as animals" without regard to mental or moral characteristics. In fact, "the mental characters of successors, in all countries, are below the average of human understanding; that one is a tyrant, another an ideot, a third insane, and some all three together" (224–25). To be a mechanic, Paine notes, requires some talents; to be a king, requires only "a sort of breathing automation" (226). Hereditary monarchy is the worst form of government because a "permanent family-interest is created, whose constant objects are dominion and revenue" (227). Procuring money becomes the only goal of such a government. Monarchy in itself has no value; it is "a deception" (236), a kind of pretense behind a curtain.

Government itself ought not to be very expensive. The whole cost of the federal government of America is one-eighth what the civil list in England for the support of the king costs. There is no explanation for this discrepancy, Paine insists, except that the English are kept ignorant and therefore can be duped into allowing the collection of such excessive revenues, whereas in America, "the representative system diffuses such a body of knowledge throughout a nation, on the subject of government, as to explode ignorance and preclude imposition. . . . In the representative system, the reason for every thing must publicly appear. Every man . . . examines the cost, and compares it with the advantages" (236). Those who govern by law do so by the choice of the people "while they chuse to employ them" (242); government is "a trust," and, as such, it is delegated—that is, it functions only by the consent of the governed. Because England has no constitution, this power has been usurped by those who use government as an unearned—but virtually bottomless—source of income. In England, he remarks ironically, "every thing has a constitution, except the nation" (244).

Because no law limits English government, government has run away with the country. And Paine has the figures to prove it. The taxes in France under its new government "are not quite thirteen shillings per head, and the taxes in England, under what is called its present constitution, are forty-eight shillings and sixpence per head, men, women, and children, amounting to nearly seventeen millions sterling, besides the expence of collection, which is upwards of a million more" (247). He reminds us that in England the entire civil government (magistrates, courts, and so on) is supported locally; it is, then, "astonishing how such a mass of taxes can be employed" (247)—and yet new taxes are forever being levied. All of this money goes to pay for the king. Paine argues that no matter who the man, no matter what his service to society, he can only do so much: his service "can never exceed the value of ten thousand pounds per year. . . . It is inhuman to talk of a million sterling a year, paid out of the public taxes of any country, for the support of any individual, whilst thousands who are forced to contribute thereto, are pining with want, and struggling with misery" (256).

In giving "extraordinary power and extraordinary pay" to one man, that man becomes the center of inevitable corruption" (256). A "master fraud," monarchy protects itself by surrounding the monarch with a huge and powerful group of people whose source of power and wealth is the king himself—whose interests they zealously guard to the detriment of the larger society. In America, the far better system provides for decent but not extravagant pay for those in the government. Monarchical governments require huge sums of money; we have seen that they foment wars to have the excuse to levy ever more taxes—war "affords . . . pretences for power, and revenue, for which there would be neither occasion nor apology, if the circle of civilization were rendered compleat" (264). The burden is especially hard on the poor, from whom a relatively greater proportion of their earnings is taken. "Apart from all reflections of morality and philosophy, it is a melancholy fact, that more than one-fourth of the labour of mankind is annually consumed by this barbarous system" (264). This waste can be halted through revolution; in fact, revolutions "have for their object, a change in the moral condition of governments, and with

this change the burthen of public taxes will lessen, and civilization will be left to the enjoyment of that abundance, of which it is
now deprived" (265). This is the core of his economic argument.

If not distorted by such an unnatural burden, society would
blossom. Like so many of the other Dissenters, Paine is sure that
unfettered commerce would cure all economic ills—and in the
natural course of events, once poverty and want had been dis-
patched, other social problems would disappear as well. But government gets in the way of the natural workings of commerce in
two ways: by levying unfair and burdensome taxes and by waging wars, for war not only is expensive but disrupts commerce.
Because "[c]ommerce is no other than the traffic of two individuals, multiplied on a scale of numbers; and by the same rule that
nature intended the intercourse of two, she intended that of all"
(266), every disruption of the natural intercourse between nations
takes away from commerce. "Like blood, it cannot be taken from
any of the parts, without being taken from the whole mass in circulation, and all partake of the loss. When the ability in any nation to buy is destroyed, it equally involves the seller. Could the
government of England destroy the commerce of all other nations,
she would most effectually ruin her own" (266). Nations cannot
be both buyer and seller of their own goods; for commerce, they
need partners. Any nation's prosperity "is regulated by the prosperity of the rest" (266). Obviously, the corrupt pursuit of war by
governments intent on enriching themselves is diametrically opposed to the commercial good of society at large. Almost as bad
for commerce and therefore for the nation is "foreign dominion"
because the "expence of maintaining dominion more than absorbs
the profits of any trade. It does not increase the general quantity
in the world, but operates to lessen it" (269). Thus all the functions by which governments justify their existence and their costs,
the waging of war and the policing of empire, not only are useless
but actually are harmful to the nation.

The British system of government distorts every aspect of
social interaction. The parish system, effectively preventing population movement, has dire consequences for society as well as for
the individual because these laws not only prevent the individual
from pursuing his own best interests but also destroy the towns
themselves. The value of property is determined by what it produces, but without labor it cannot be productive and so its value

decreases. If newcomers are not welcome, or must pay "premi-ums" to enter a community, the labor pool is restricted, with the inevitable result that the "generality of corporation towns are in a state of solitary decay" (275).

But by far the greatest cause of social decay is the corruption of government that allows the tax structure entirely to be con-structed for the benefit of the rich to the detriment of the poor. It seems to Paine that his is the generation that has the extraordi-nary opportunity to choose "whether man shall inherit his rights, and universal civilization [shall] take place? Whether the fruits of his labours shall be enjoyed by himself, or consumed by the prof-ligacy of governments? Whether robbery shall be banished from courts, and wretchedness from countries?" (271). These are re-markable words, remarkable both for the optimism they express for the future and for their total rejection of the past. This sense of a new moment is common among the radicals in 1792; the hero of Thomas Holcroft's novel *Anna St. Ives* exclaims, "I live in an age when light begins to appear even in regions that have hitherto been thick darkness . . . and I myself am so highly fortunate as to be able to contribute to the great the universal cause; the progress of truth, the extirpation of error, and the general perfection of mind,"[24] and everything in Holcroft's novel supports that view.

But in order for the light to triumph, the grit in the old sys-tem must be exposed and swept away. To do this, things must be labeled clearly and openly: proud monarchy, Paine says, is prop-erly named "robbery." Civil government ought to make "provi-sion for the instruction of youth, and the support of age, [so] as to exclude, as much as possible, profligacy from the one, and de-spair from the other." But this is not what happens in England: "Instead of this, the resources of the country are lavished upon kings, upon courts, upon hirelings, imposters, and prostitutes; and even the poor themselves, with all their wants upon them, are compelled to support the fraud that oppresses them" (271). In words remarkably reminiscent of our own contemporary social discourse, Paine demands to know, "Why is it, that scarcely any are executed but the poor?" (271). His answer is that the poor are "bred up" without morals and without prospects, the "exposed sacrifice of vice and legal barbarity" (271).

The remedy, however, lies close at hand: the millions wasted on government could easily pay for the reform of society. But, as

Paine goes on to show in a carefully reasoned economic essay of
more than fifty pages within his larger pamphlet, it is not so much
a matter of reforming social ills as of not causing them in the first
place. For it is the tax burden that pushes so many into poverty.

The those who make the laws, that is, the aristocracy, create a
tax system that forces everyone else to pay to support the rich.
The House of Peers, he says, "amounts to a combination of persons in one common interest" (277). If men whose occupation is
in renting property compose an entire house of legislation, why
are there no houses of brewers, bakers, and so on? While all other
taxes have increased and multiplied, the land tax actually has di-
minished: "In 1788, the amount of the land-tax was 1,950,000£.
Which is half a million less than it produced almost an hundred
years ago, notwithstanding the rentals are in many instances
doubled since that period." Paine elaborates: "Before the coming
of the Hanoverians, the taxes were divided in nearly equal pro-
portions between the land and articles of consumption, the land
bearing rather the largest share: but since that aera, nearly thirteen millions annually of new taxes have been thrown upon consumption." This increase in consumption taxes is responsible for
the increase in the "number and wretchedness of the poor" (277).
This burden does not affect the rich, who live apart from the poor
and apart, too, from the expense of relieving them. It is in the
manufacturing towns and villages where most of the poor are to
be found, and often, there, "it is one class of poor supporting another" (278).

The taxes are "contrived" so that they do not fall on the rich.
One of the most lucrative taxes is that on beer, but the rich, who
have the means to brew their own, do not pay it. This tax alone is
equal to the whole of the land tax. Paine comments, "That a single
article, thus partially consumed, and that chiefly by the working
part, should be subject to a tax, equal to that on the whole rental
of a nation, is, perhaps, a fact not to be paralleled in the histories
of revenues (278). The aristocracy exempt themselves from paying taxes simply because they have the power to do so. A house of
farmers would not permit game laws; a house of merchants would
hold down taxes. Inequity exists because one interest controls the
law. And because the body is hereditary, it cannot be held account-
able. Its members indulge themselves of public monies through
all sorts of pretend jobs like "candle-holder" or "groom of the

stole," thus allowing them to be paid and yet avoid "the direct appearance of consumption" (280). In addition, all those disinherited through primogeniture wind up on the public expense, most often in these pretend jobs. The "charge of aristocracy to a nation . . . [is] nearly equal to that of supporting the poor" (281). Paine's example seems unanswerable: "The Duke of Richmond alone (and there are cases similar to his) takes away as much for himself as would maintain two thousand poor and aged persons. Is it, then, any wonder, that under such a system of government, taxes and rates have multiplied to their present extent?" (281). At the top of the obscene pyramid sits the Crown: "It signifies a nominal office of a million sterling a year, the business of which consists in receiving the money" (282). The Crown, he says, "means nothing"—neither judge nor general, neither law-keeper nor law-giver, the office and the man function solely to eat up the tax revenues that otherwise could support a large proportion of the populace.

Paine supplies extraordinary sets of figures to prove that the history of taxes in England has not always been one of ever-increasing burdens. Citing "Sir John Sinclair's History of the Revenue," Paine shows that in the four hundred years after the Norman conquest, taxes decreased substantially in each succeeding hundred years until by 1466 they were £100,000, or one quarter of the £400,000 levied by William the Conqueror in 1066. But by 1566 taxes were at £500,000; 1666 saw a burden of £1.8 million and by 1791 taxes had enlarged by the greatest degree to £17,00,000! Paine notes that the expense of government—pay for the army and navy, and so on—"is the same now as it was above a hundred years ago, when the taxes were not above a tenth part of what they are at present" (284). Where then does the money go? "With the revolution of 1688, and more so since the Hanover succession" (285), the European powers have engaged in a series of continental wars that allowed them to claim vast expenses without needing to produce accounts. Much of this money goes not for its purported use of supporting the war effort but to enrich corrupt officials, especially the king.

But what has happened in the past can happen again: the English can throw off an onerous burden of taxation and reduce their taxes through a national reconsideration of the tax structure. Paine breaks down the taxes for the recent year of 1788 into five categories, with a total of £15,572,970; since 1788, he notes, more than a million pounds in new taxes have been added, bringing the sum to £17,000,000. Merely by declaring peace with France, and thus dismantling part of the fleets and armies, this load immediately could be lessened significantly to the amount necessary before England and France were at war, say, prior to 1688!

The excessive taxation in England has a single cause: the unlimited greed of king and aristocracy. "To read the history of kings, a man would be almost inclined to suppose that government consisted in stag-hunting, and that every nation paid a million a year to a huntsman" (289). He repeats that no man, whatever his contribution to society, should be paid more than ten thousand pounds a year—there is no possible service to the nation that can be worth more—"and as no man should be paid beyond his services, so every man of a proper heart will not accept more" (289). Paine's language reaches real eloquence here: "Public money ought to be touched with the most scrupulous consciousness of honour. It is not the produce of riches only, but of the hard earnings of labour and poverty. It is drawn even from the bitterness of want and misery. Not a beggar passes, or perishes in the streets, whose mite is not in that mass" (289). But it has cost an obscene 70 millions sterling to support this royal family—even their doctors' bills are put to the public account. No wonder, he says, "that jails are crowded, and taxes and poor-rates encreased" (290). Reform will not come from the government. It must come from the nation.

And so Paine sets out a reform budget. He finds a total tax of £1,500,000 million more than sufficient to support an honest government; there then will be six million left over above current expenses. These additional revenues cannot simply be scaled back because most of them are in commodity taxes on articles already taxed; also, since commodity taxes are reflected in such small amounts at the consumer levels, to remove them individually would not much relieve the consumer. These commodity taxes as a whole, however, have dire effects on the laboring classes, taking from such families seven or eight pounds a year, or at least a quarter of their income, thus in many cases, especially if illness or some other affliction strikes, pushing the family into poverty. Fully one fifth of Englishmen are of that class that needs support. But the Poor Rates, while putting a great tax burden on those who pay them (very often those laboring just beyond poverty who ironically themselves can be nudged over the edge into poverty by this additional burden, a point we have seen made by Townsend as well), do not adequately help the poor. In fact, "a considerable part of [the money] is expended in litigations, in which the poor, instead of being relieved, are tormented. The expence, however, is the same to the parish from whatever cause it arises" (292).

The Poor Rates should be done away with. The extra money available once the poor rates are discontinued can be distributed directly to the poor. Most poverty comes either from the burden of supporting children or age, which first diminishes and then ends a worker's ability to earn a living. Paine would contribute to each poor family four pounds per child each year; such children must then be sent to school so that "not only the poverty of the parents will be relieved, but ignorance will be banished from the rising generation, and the number of poor will hereafter become less, because their abilities, by the aid of education, will be greater" (294). The aged, from fifty to sixty years old, should get a supplement of six pounds per year; those over sixty should get ten pounds. "This support . . . is not of the nature of a charity, but of a right" (296). So much at least has each person paid over his lifetime in taxes, so this return is only each laborer's due. Since inevitably there will be some who fall through the cracks, workhouses should be erected where men can get back on their feet by earning enough to keep themselves in the workhouse while also putting aside some share of these earnings to allow them a stake when they leave. Paine sums up:

> By the operation of this plan, the poor laws, those instruments of civil torture, will be superceded, and the wasteful expence of litigation prevented. The hearts of the humane will not be shocked by ragged and hungry children, and persons of seventy and eighty years of age begging for bread. The dying poor will not be dragged from place to place to breathe their last, as a reprisal of parish upon parish. Widows will have a maintenance for their children, and not be carted away, on the death of their husbands, like culprits and criminals; and children will no longer be considered as encreasing the distresses of their parents. . . . The poor, as well as the rich, will then be interested in the support of government, and the cause and apprehension of riots and tumults will cease. (300–301)

And if this last sounds like a threat—it is.

Paine is setting out a society with a much more equitable allocation of resources than has been customary. He even outlines a system of progressive taxation of estates, so that if rich land-holders do not voluntarily break up their estates among their re-lations (we remember his discussion of primogeniture), their estates slowly will erode through taxation. Even further, laws regu-lating wages must be eliminated. Why, he asks, should men be allowed to sell anything freely but their own labor? And if all these reforms are not made? "The poor, in all countries, are natu-rally both peaceable and grateful in all reforms in which their in-terest and happiness is included. It is only by neglecting and rejecting them that they become tumultuous" (319). In fact, how-ever, it is unlikely that such reforms will come from government because "reforms of this kind are not those which old govern-ments wish to promote" (319).

Paine's clear implication, then, is that these reforms must come when "the nation," that is, the people, take over. This im-plied threat becomes ever more explicit as part II of *Rights of Man* draws to a close. "Will any man say" (322)—will any man dare to say—that helping the poor and making society more equitable is not a good idea? Paine's conclusion is essentially an ultimatum: the government has but two options, to enact reform or to endure revolution. The government responded, as we know, by among other things making it illegal to sell *Rights of Man*.

It is no wonder that the dissemination of Paine's ideas was seen as a serious threat to the status quo, for he was advocating no less than a redistribution of property. The lower classes come to be seen as really dangerous; large numbers of them, often meet-ing in places of religion, talk serious politics. Thompson finds in various groups labels connecting them to Paine: "all who have embraced the sentiments of Paine" or the "Tom Paine Method-ists." He notes that "In Halifax, at the Bradshaw chapel, a reading club and debating society was formed. The people of this weav-ing village discussed in their class meetings . . . Paine's *Rights of Man*" (Thompson, 45). The danger was that these ordinary people, the weavers, miners, potters, and other laboring men would be persuaded that they were not getting a fair deal in their England. These are precisely the audience for whose loyalty More contends. Frances, Lady Shelley, in her diary notes that "the awakening of the labouring classes, after the first shock of the French Revolu-

tion, made the upper classes tremble. Every man felt the necessity for putting his house in order." As Thompson wryly points
out, the house she really means is that of the poor. "The message
to be given to the labouring poor was simple, and was summarised
by Burke in the famine year of 1795: 'Patience, labour, sobriety,
frugality and religion, should be recommended to them; all the
rest is downright fraud'" (Thompson, 56). These are the lessons
More serves up in all of her Tracts.

Thompson reminds us that "the agitation of the 1790s, although it lasted only five years (1792–96), was extraordinarily in-
tensive and far-reaching. It altered the sub-political attitudes of
the people [and] affected class alignments." One observer in the
summer of 1792 "found that the seditious doctrines of Paine and
the factious people who are endeavouring to disturb the peace of
the country had extended to a degree very much beyond [his]
conception" (Thompson, 102–3). Sheffield was "a centre of all their
seditious machinations. . . . Here [in the Constitutional Society]
they read the most violent publications, and comment on them, as
well as on their correspondence not only with the dependent Societies in the towns and villages in the vicinity, but with those . . .
in other parts of the kingdom" (Thompson, 103). Another report
noted that "[c]onsiderable numbers in Bernard Castle have manifested disaffection to the constitution, and the words, 'No King,'
'Liberty,' and 'Equality,' have been written there upon the Market
Cross. During the late disturbances amongst the keelmen at Shields
and Sunderland, General Lambton was thus addressed: 'Have you
read this little work of Tom Paine's?' 'No.' 'Then read it—we like
it much. You have a great estate, General; we shall soon divide it
amongst us'" (Thompson, 103). Thompson cautions that "the depth
and intensity of the democratic agitation in England . . . is commonly underestimated." His analysis of the response to the second
part of Rights of Man, published in 1793, is worth quoting at length.
The response was, he says, "phenomenal."

> The estimate (in a pamphlet of 1793) that sales totalled 200,000
> by that year has been widely accepted: this in a population of
> ten millions. The Second Part went immediately into a 6d. edi-
> tion, sponsored by the Constitutional Society and by local soci-
> eties. Hannah More [!] complained that "the friends of
> insurrection, infidelity and vice, carried their exertions so far as

to load asses with their pernicious pamphlets and to get them dropped, not only in cottages, and in highways, but into mines and coal-pits". . . . At Newcastle (Staffs.) Paine's publications were said to be "in almost every hand," and in particular those of the journeymen potters: "more than Two Thirds of this populous Neighborhood are ripe for a Revolt, especially the lower class of Inhabitants." Paine's book was found in Cornish tinmines, in Mendip villages, in the Scottish Highlands, and, a little later, in most parts of Ireland. "The Northern parts of Wales," a correspondent complained, "are infested by itinerant Methodist preachers who descant on the Rights of Man and attack Kingly Government." "The book," wrote an English correspondent, "is now made as much a Standard book in this Country as Robinson Crusoe & the Pilgrim's Progress." (Thompson, 108)

The government's reaction to Paine and other radicals was heavy-handed: he was put on trial (in absentia) and the book outlawed. Men were imprisoned for various political acts, often on the pretext of a "disloyal" comment. "A printer named Holt, at Newark, was jailed for four years for reprinting an early address of the Constitutional Society. At Leicester, the bookseller, Richard Phillips, who published the pro-reform *Leicester Herald*, was imprisoned for eighteen months, ostensibly for selling *Rights of Man*" (Thompson, 114). Thompson notes that "at least one illiterate bill-sticker was imprisoned for posting bills in favor of reform" (Thompson, 114). And, of course, there was the pamphlet war. Paine himself writes in the summer of 1792 that "As we have now got the stone to roll, it must be kept going by cheap publications. This will embarrass the Court gentry more than anything else, because it is a ground they are not used to" (Thompson, 111).

But no one was to latch on to the formula of the cheap publication used for political purposes so well as Hannah More. That these publications of More *were* political, despite her claims for them as educational, is clear from her very first venture, the aptly named *Village Politics*, which was published in 1793. It was no less than the bishop of London who gave her the burden of opening the eyes of "the lower order of people . . . under their present wild impressions of liberty and equality," More writes to Mrs. Boscawen in January 1793. She goes on, "It must be something level to their apprehension, or it would be of no use."[25]

*Village Politics* is set up in the form of a dialogue between the rational, right-thinking Jack Anvil the Blacksmith and the flighty, radical Tom Hod the Mason. Its message could not be more direct. Jack asks Tom why he looks so unhappy—can't find work, maybe? Tom says that "work's plenty enough, if a man had but the heart to go to it." Jack notices Tom's book.

> *Jack.* What book art reading? . . .
> *Tom.* (looking on his book.) Cause enough. Why I find here that I'm very unhappy, and very miserable; which I should never have known if I had not had the good luck to meet with this book. O 'tis a precious book!
> *Jack.* A good sign, though, that you can't find out you're unhappy without looking into a book for it! What is the matter?
> *Tom.* Matter? Why I want liberty.
> *Jack.* Liberty! That's bad, indeed. What! has any one fetched a warrant for thee? Come, man, cheer up, I'll be bound for thee. . . .
> *Tom.* No, no, I want a new Constitution.
> *Jack.* Indeed! Why I thought thou hadst been a desperate healthy fellow. Send for the doctor directly.
> *Tom.* I'm not sick; I want Liberty and Equality, and the Rights of Man.[26]

More goes on in this way, taunting good Englishmen who would want to follow the French—the English system is as good as government can be, and as for equality, there can be no such thing, since men by nature differ in their talents. By the end of *Village Politics* good Tom has been thoroughly reeducated; after a round of singing "O the Roast Beef of Old England," he is off to the local tavern to put a stop to the "mischief" of those unpatriotic troublemakers who would challenge good old English ways.

Four

# "The Pen that Might
# Work Wonders"

## The Correspondence of Hannah More

IT HELPS TO HAVE A TIME LINE. More was only thirty-one years old in 1776; perhaps her relative youth explains the general lack of commentary about political issues, especially about the American Revolution. She was forty-four in 1789, certainly of an age to be seriously involved not just with social issues but with their philosophical underpinnings; in her forties, she also was actively involved in the antislavery movement. By 1795, when the first of the Cheap Repository Tracts appeared, she was fifty. This chapter examines the ephemera that precedes and chronologically parallels the creation of the Cheap Repository Tracts, focusing for the most part on More's correspondence. The record of More's letters, along with those of her correspondents, is fascinating but incomplete, since the largest source, William Roberts' four volume *Memoirs of the Life and Correspondence of Mrs. Hannah More* is a selection rather than a complete transcription of the "mass of letters and papers" that Roberts received.[1] Nonetheless, it affords us a remarkable view not only into More's thought but into the social world that helped to shape her perceptions.

As we will explore in more detail in the next chapter, More begins her political tract-writing career with *Village Politics*, her response to Tom Paine's *Rights of Man*; she had been asked by Bishop Porteus to produce a piece of writing to counter Paine. Why would the Bishop of London come to More with this request? More was a well-known writer. Her politics were in line with the bishop's own, and they were good friends. More was good friends with Mrs. Montagu, with Soame Jenyns, with Samuel Johnson. She was, in fact, part of a close circle of generally like-minded people who socialized often and for long periods at a time, and who, when not actually visiting with one another, kept track of each other through regular correspondence. Perhaps the most fascinating aspect for a modern reader of seeing the letters More sent and received is the tightness of More's social circle. We are all familiar with More's meetings with Samuel Johnson, but that nice man Soame Jenyns whom we know only from Johnson's furious review of Jenyns' *A Free Enquiry into the Nature and Origin of Evil?* Johnson and Jenyns clearly disagreed here, but More loved them both. And this disagreement within her circle was the exception rather than the rule. More usual was the complete agreement she experienced with Walpole as they discussed the horrors of the French Revolution, a correspondence that forms such a coherent whole that it will be accorded separate discussion later on in this chapter. Equally worth commenting upon is the exclusivity of the circle; it is both social and intellectual, including Garrick and Burke, Mackenzie, Chapone, and Cowper. Those on the other side of the political line, though, no matter how accomplished or famous, never seem to cross paths with More's set. The closest we come to a meeting across party lines is a greatly comical "marriage" in the newspapers of More and Joseph Priestley of which More ruefully reports, "the papers soon afterwards married me to Priestley, though I reprobate his opinions. I never saw him but once in my life, and he had been married above twenty years" (*Memoirs*, II, 186)[2]

Within our context, the first volume of the *Memoirs*, divided into the periods 1745–76 and 1776–85, is interesting mostly for the social circle it defines. Roberts tells us that More met Garrick "in 1773 or 4. . . . Garrick had seen a letter from Miss More to a person known to them both, so well describing the effect produced upon her mind by his performance of the character of Lear, as to inflame his curiosity to see and converse with her" (I, 47). The next day, she meets Mrs. Montagu at Garrick's house; she meets Samuel Johnson at the house of Sir Josuah Reynolds. Her older sister Sally More writes in 1774 that "Hannah has been introduced by Miss Reynolds to Baretti, to Edmund Burke, (the sublime and beautiful Edmund Burke!). From a large party of literary persons, assembled at Sir Joshua's, she received the most encouraging compliments. . . . Miss R. repeats her little poem by heart, with which, also, the great Johnson is much pleased" (I, 48). Soon after, another visit to Miss Reynolds turns into a visit "to Dr. Johnson's *very own house; yes, Abysinnia's Johnson! Dictionary Johnson! Rambler's, Idler's, and Irene's Johnson!* Can you picture to yourselves the palpitation of our hearts as we approached his mansion" (I, 49). Hannah herself writes of a visit "to Sir Joshua's, where we were received with all the friendship imaginable" (I, 51). Soon after she writes again to her sister to say, "I had yesterday the pleasure of dining in Hill Street, Berkeley Square, *at a certain Mrs. Montagu's, a name not totally obscure.*" This letter is so full of names, and of charmed wonder at being a welcome member of the circle, that it bears quoting at length:

> The party consisted of [Mrs. Montagu], Mrs. Carter, Dr. Johnson, Solander, and Matty, Mrs. Boscawen, Miss Reynolds, and Sir Joshua, (the idol of every company;) some other persons of high rank and less wit, and your humble servant,—a party that would not have disgraced the table of Lelius, or of Atticus. I felt myself a worm, the more a worm for the consequence which was given me, by mixing me with such a society. . . .
>
> Mrs. Montagu received me with the most encouraging kindness; she is not only the finest genius, but the finest lady I ever saw: she lives in the highest style of magnificence; . . . her form (for she has no *body*) is delicate even to fragility; . . . the sprightly vivacity of fifteen, with the judgment and experience of a Nestor. . . . I do not like one of them better than Mrs. Boscawen; she is at once polite, learned, judicious, and humble, and Mrs. Palk tells me her letters are not thought inferior to Mrs. Montagu's. She regretted (so did I) that so many suns could not possibly shine at one time; but we are to have a smaller party, where, from fewer luminaries, there may emanate a clearer, steadier, and more beneficial light. Dr. Johnson asked me how I liked the new tragedy of Braganza. I was afraid to speak before them all, as I knew a diversity of opinion prevailed among the company: however, . . . I ventured to give my sentiments; and was satisfied with Johnson's answering, "You are right, madam." (I, 52-54)

By December 1775 such praises had convinced the young woman that she should "venture to try what is my real value, by writing a slight poem, and offering it to Cadell myself." The poem was "Sir Eldred of the Bower"; the agreement between More and Cadell, Roberts notes, "was the beginning of a connection with Mr. Cadell, which was carried on through an intercourse of nearly forty years, with a reciprocity of esteem and regard which suffered no interruption" (I, 58–59).

The esteem and regard pass continually from one member of the circle to another. Henry Mackenzie writes to More that before he knew the author herself, he knew her *Percy:* "I could not resist the desire I felt of giving my warmest suffrage in its favour, to somebody who had an interest in it; so, for want of a nearer relation, I communicated my sentiments to Mr. Cadell." Perhaps, Mackenzie notes, Cadell had not mentioned these praises to More, for everyone "judged as I did." Mackenzie begs More to write more in the same vein. After all, they share the same opinion of "the *pleasure* of the *pains* of sensibility; I may therefore say, without trespassing against the accuracy of a compliment, that I am proud of having had it in my power to confer that pleasure on you; but you are less in my debt than you imagine; though a man, and a man of business, I too can shed tears and feel the luxury of shedding them; your *Percy* has cleared scores between us in that respect" (I, 134–35). So Mackenzie knows Cadell, and afterward, he knows More personally too.

The Burneys also are part of the circle. More writes to her sister that she had been invited to meet Dr. Burney and Evelina [*sic*] at Mrs. Reynold's (Sir Joshua's sister) but couldn't make it. "This Evelina is an extraordinary girl; she is not more than twenty [in 1779], of a very retired disposition; and how she picked up her knowledge of nature and low life, her *Brangtons*, and her *St. Giles's* gentry, is astonishing!" (I, 161).

From London in 1780 More writes the famous account of Johnson's angry response to her praise of Fielding; interesting in itself, the account within our context underscores the religiously conservative bias of More's circle:

> I never saw Johnson really angry with me but once; and his displeasure did him so much honour that I loved him the better for it. I alluded rather flippantly, I fear, to some witty passage in "Tom Jones:" he replied, "I am shocked to hear you quote from so vicious a book. I am sorry to hear you have read it: a confes-

sion which no modest lady should ever make. I scarcely know a more corrupt work." I thanked him for his correction; assured him I thought full as ill of it now as he did, and had only read it at an age when I was more subject to be caught by the wit, than able to discern the mischief. Of Joseph Andrews I declared my decided abhorrence. He went so far as to refuse to Fielding the great talents which are ascribed to him, and broke out into a noble panegyric on his competitor, Richardson; who, he said, was as superior to him in talents as in virtue; and whom he pronounced to be the greatest genius that had shed its lustre on this path of literature. (I, 169)

More herself, not surprisingly, often refers to the cohesion of the company she keeps. She mentions, for example, being dressed by Mrs. Garrick for a gathering where there "was all the old set, the Johnsons, the Burneys, the Chapones, the Thrales, the Smelts, the Pepyses, the Ramsays, and so on ad infinitum" (I, 171).

Although More occasionally comments on domestic politics—"out of the small number of friends and acquaintance I had the honour to boast of in the British senate, hardly any remain" (I, 187)—in these early years she does not seem much interested in foreign affairs, although it is certainly possible that some such references were edited out of the record by Roberts. The first extended reference in the *Memoirs* to the revolutionary spirit abroad comes in a letter to More from Dean J. Tucker in February 1781. He clearly expects More to be conversant with the events in America, and, as well, he assumes that her displeasure with the American situation matches his own. Some years later all discussions of the happenings in France will take precisely Tucker's tone of sceptical disgust. He writes, "You must have, by every post, fresher accounts from Bristol than any that I can send. If mine are to be depended on, the American government, alias the *Mob-cracy*, is already set up in that place, and will extend itself more and more, if not checked in time. Surely a spirit of insanity and infatuation hath broken loose, and spread itself all over our *enlightened world*, as it is improperly called" (I, 196). We do not, unfortunately, get More's response.

In general the letters of this early period are interesting for what they show us of More's social circle. These men and women met constantly, mostly at each other's houses, though occasionally at more public gatherings. Soame Jenyns, for example, turns up at a little gathering with Lady Edgecombe, the York family, and the bishop of Exeter (I, 200); next we see him at the bishop of Chester's. More has quite a crush on him: "Mr. and Mrs. Soame Jenyns, gay, gallant, and young as ever, are really delectable to behold, so fond of each other, and so free from characteristic infirmities; I do not know such another pair. I think they make up between them about 165 years. There is this peculiarity in Mr. Jenyns' character, that though he has the worst opinion of human nature, he has the greatest kindness for the individuals who compose it," she writes (I, 309). That was March 1784. In April, More has dinner with "the Abbe Grant from Rome, Sir William Hamilton, Sir Josuah, Mrs. Montagu, Mrs. Vesey, Mrs. Carter, Miss Hamilton, and young Montagu. . . . [I]n the evening we had Mrs. Walsingham, the Jenynses, the Pepyses, the Shipleys, Lady Rothes, Mrs. Ord, the Burneys, Mr. Walpole,—in short I think we had above thirty, all as agreeable people as one would wish to see" (I, 318). In addition to the Jenynses, the other names in these lists also of course are familiar ones. As More gets older, and as she becomes increasingly interested in social causes and in political issues, her correspondence reflects a social environment that is absolutely in line with her views. Thus when the "Lactilla" problem comes, More's friends rally round with universal support.

The outlines of the story of the Bristol milkmaid turned poet are so well known that we need here sketch only the briefest outline. More helped Ann Yearsley to become a published poet. Yearsley, unhappy that she did not control the money she earned, accused More of mismanagement and worse. The details spill from the letters More sent to her friends and from their condoling and supportive replies. Again, our focus is on the universality of the view of poverty and of social responsibility held by everyone in More's social circle. An early reference to the Milkmaid project comes in an exceedingly long letter from More to Mrs. Boscawen in 1784. After recounting her recent travels to various friends, with comments upon their health, situation ("I am grieved to find that [Johnson's] mind is still a prey to melancholy, and that the fear of death operates on him to the destruction of his peace"), and current uplifting reading, she devotes a paragraph to a common interest:

> It is now time to thank you, my dear madam, for your very handsome list of subscribers. Do you know that my poor Milkwoman

has been sent for to Stoke, to visit the Duchess of Beaufort and the Duchess of Rutland; and to Bath, to Lady Spencer, Mrs. Montagu, &c. I hope all these honours will not turn her head, and indispose her for her humble occupations. I would rather have her *served* than *flattered*. Your noble and munificent friend, the Duchess Dowager of Portland, had sent me a twenty pound bank note for her; so as I take it, she will soon be the richest poetess, certainly the richest milkwoman in Great Britain. (I, 332)

There are several levels of allusion here that repay our attention. First, note the list of subscribers. Everybody seems to be in on the act. All of More's friends have become patrons of her protégée. Twenty pounds is quite a sum; for comparison, we might remember that forty pounds is considered a reasonably good annual salary for a worker.[3] But it is More's comment on all this good fortune for Yearsley that is most significant, for More is committed to the policy that Yearsley's success shall not change her station in life. It is important that Yearsley not be spoiled for her real occupation, that is, for being a milkmaid. She should never be anything but a milkwoman who happens to write poetry; for More, she cannot become a poet first. The poor, with very specific exceptions,[4] must never aspire to any significant change in their lifestyle or their work. A poor person who wishes to change his station, or a rich person who wants to help the poor to change, is misguided and dangerous. We see this lesson over and over in the Cheap Repository Tracts, and we see it here in the case of Yearsley. The horror of More and her friends at the ensuing chapters of the story is most readily comprehended within this context.

Roberts, who intermittently throughout the four volumes of memoirs sums up periods of More's life, tells the story of the discovery of Yearsley and her starving family. When More was presented with "several scraps of . . . poetry," it

immediately occurred to Miss H. More that this talent might be made the means of exciting a general interest in her behalf, and raising a fund to set her up in some creditable way of earning her subsistence. She accordingly took a great deal of pains in furnishing her with some of the common rules of writing, spelling, and composition; and while the object of her charity was preparing, under her inspection, a small collection of poems, she was employing herself in writing statements of the case to all her friends of rank and fortune, to bespeak subscriptions to this work, setting forth the probability of being enabled, after allowing the woman a certain portion of the sum raised, to apprentice out the children with the remainder. The generous zeal with which Miss H. More's friends seconded her wishes, soon produced a sum exceeding £600. which was placed in the funds under the trusteeship of Mrs. Montagu and herself. (I, 361–62)

More calculated that between letters in Yearsley's behalf and transcriptions of the poems, she had written "more than a thousand pages."

The generosity of More and her friends is large and disinterested. But it never occurs to them, as it obviously does occur to Yearsley herself, that their help should make her independent. It should earn her a "subsistence," not a fortune, and whatever it earns her, More and her friends should be making the financial decisions. This help in setting up Yearsley as a poet is no different from any other charity doled out to the unfortunate; in this case, given Yearsley's unquestioned talents, it simply makes sense to sell the poetry. Yearsley is not a fellow writer, certainly. She is an "object of charity." It is More's right to determine how much of the proceeds of Yearsley's work will go to the poet and how much will be held back to support the future of the children. These assumptions are so natural to those in More's circle that when Yearsley bitterly argues against such usage, More and her friends are truly shocked. Yearsley, much to her discredit, fails to act as the good folks will in More's "Shepherd of Salisbury Plain" and other Tracts. Instead of insisting that she couldn't possibly want anything more than what she has, Yearsley actually demands control of her money.

And so she goes from being "one of nature's miracles" (363), as Mrs. Montagu calls her early in the game, to "that odious woman" (I, 370) that Mrs. Boscawen and others attack for her incredible lack of gratitude. Not that the shock should have been quite so unexpected, for even before "Lactilla" showed signs of bad character, Mrs. Montagu was asking More "to inform yourself, as much as you can, of her temper, disposition, and moral character. I speak not this out of an apprehension of merely wasting a few guineas, but lest I should do harm where I intend to confer benefit. It has sometimes happened to me, that, by an endeavour to encourage talents and cherish virtue, by driving from them the terrifying spectre of pale poverty, I have introduced a legion of little demons: vanity, luxury, idleness, and pride, have entered the cottage the moment poverty vanished." Mrs. Montagu is indeed soft-hearted, however. She earnestly adds, "I am sure despair is never a good counsellor, and I desire you to be so good as to tell her; that I entreat her, in any distress, to apply to me, and she may be assured of immediate assistance" (I, 369). The responsible rich feel a real danger in doing too much for the needy: they perceive that too much aid—that is, enough to change the person's situation significantly—truly has the potential of harming the object of charity. This is a caution that More, in her stories, emphasizes repeatedly. Certainly, given the outcome, the milkwoman seems to More's friends to be a proof of the dangers of doing too much. Roberts tells the story:

> The person alluded to in the preceding letter, was equally a stranger to gratitude and prudence; and inflated by the notice she had attracted, soon began to express, in the coarsest terms, her rage and disappointment, at not having the sum subscribed immediately put into her hands. Neither could she bear, as it seems, to be represented to the public, in Miss More's preface to her works, as an object of their charity. Not being able to gain her point, she soon broke out into the bitterest invectives, and scrupled at no calumnies however absurd and ferocious. We will produce a specimen. The late Duchess of Devonshire having presented her with "Bell's Edition of the Poets," Miss H. More kept them for her till she should be able to find a few second-hand shelves to place them on. Mrs. Yearsley immediately wrote to her Grace, complaining that they were kept back from her, at the same time spreading a report in the neighborhood, that her patroness was purchasing an estate with the sum she had pretended to raise for her benefit. Mrs. Montagu and Miss More resisted with great patience her violent importunities to be put in possession of the principal, as well as interest, of her little fortune; fearing it would be consumed in those vices, to which it now began to be apparent that she was addicted. (I, 370)

Finally, they put the money in the hands of a lawyer, who gives it to a merchant, who "was soon harassed into the relinquishment of the whole concern." Miss More, Roberts comments, never manifested "any resentment towards this unfortunate creature, with respect to whom she had no other feeling than Christian sorrow for her depravity" (I, 370).

Yearsley's resentment at being portrayed as an object of charity is incomprehensible to those in More's circle. Equally puzzling is her determination to get control of her funds. In fact, her very attitude is proof of her unworthiness: a properly moral poor woman would not make such demands. She is "a stranger to gratitude and prudence," "inflated," "coarse," full of bitter "invectives" and "absurd and ferocious" lies. More cannot imagine that it is not her right to keep the books until Yearsley has some proper place to put them; Yearsley resents More's assumption of the responsibility for the books. In large matters and small, More and her friends feel sure that they should manage Yearsley's affairs; they resist with "great patience" her demands, and Roberts' clear implication is that in resisting Yearsley's attempts to wrest control from them, More is doing her duty to one who needs guidance but repays attention with bile. If More does not manifest resentment, Roberts and all of More's friends certainly do attack Yearsley.

Mrs. Boscawen writes to More, "I am in a little care about you, my dear friend: I cannot be sure that you are not vexed, hurt, and made uneasy by that odious woman; the trouble she had given you of another kind, little prognosticated what she would give you now. I really think this passes common depravity" (I, 370–71). Mrs. Montagu writes, "I rejoice with you that we are soon to be free from any connection with the milkwoman.[5] I have the same opinion about favours to the ungrateful-minded, as the common people have in regard to witches, that bestowing a gift on such wretches gives them power over one." Nonetheless, she will not be discouraged from giving to people of talent, even if once in a while it seems a mistake. In any case, her contribution is less than More's, for she "can only assist the woman," while More "can help the poet; your patronage is therefore worth infinitely more than my alms, and I grieve that you have given her so much precious thought and precious time." The great irony is that Yearsley thinks More is professionally jealous of her: "Mrs. Yearsley's conceit that you can envy her talents gives me comfort, for as it convinces me she is mad, I build upon it a hope that she is not guilty in the all-seeing eye" (I, 373–74).

Although More can joke about the incident (trading verses with Pepys, she warns that "you must correct me now, for your own credit, or I will serve you as the milkwoman did me, and declare that all the bad lines are yours" [1, 382]), she is clearly hurt. Had the milkwoman "turned out well I should have had my *reward*; as it is, I have my *trial*," she writes to Mrs. Carter. "Perhaps I was too vain of my success; and, in counting over the money (almost £500), might be elated, and think—'Is not this great Babylon that *I* have built?'" The problem, she finds, is that "[p]rosperity is a great trial, and she could not stand it. I was afraid it would turn her *head*, but I did not expect it would harden her *heart*" (I, 390–91). It was the change in Yearsley's condition, then, that soured her. The experience has not turned More from her perceived duties, however; she is bringing out a second edition of the poems, for the sake of the children. She is still supervising the affair, and she clearly intends, even after all the drama, to retain control of any money that comes in from this second edition. Prosperity may have ruined Lactilla, but More guards against allowing this disappointment to keep her from further charitable work when the occasion for such action arises. Yearsley's bad behavior remains part of the conversation months later, when at a dinner party a somewhat disheartened Burke comments that "he is only fit to be a milk-woman . . . ; but he declares he will not be a *Bristol milk-woman*. [More notes that she had been] obliged to recount to him all that odious tale" (II, 15).[6]

Burke, like Soame Jenyns, is often part of More's company, and, as she does with Jenyns, More finds herself totally in sympathy with Burke. For the forty-year-old More these older men are charming, witty, and, most of all, morally correct, their thought on various social issues precisely in tune with hers. On February 17, 1786, for example, More is "at a small party . . . of which Mr. Burke was one. He appeared to be very low in health and spirits; he talked to me with a kindness which revived my old affection for him" (II, 12). In March, she is going to see Mrs. Vesey; Mrs. Vesey, afraid that her gathering might not be entertaining enough for More, "immediately sent for Mr. Burke to meet me" (II, 13). Burke unfortunately was engaged, but he sent his son. The same letter mentions Walpole as well. In April More goes again to see Mrs. Vesey; "there are a little set who generally go to her in turn every day." More meets Mrs. Carter there, and Walpole, and "likewise Mr.

Burke. The vivacity of this wonderfully great man is much dimin-
ished; business and politics have impaired his agreeableness; but
neither years nor sufferings can abate the entertaining powers of
the pleasant Horace, which rather improve than decay" (II, 14–15).

This letter, by the way, includes a fascinating comment about
Mrs. Piozzi's book, which "is indeed entertaining; but there are
two or three passages exceedingly unkind to Garrick, which filled
me with indignation." More refers to negative remarks Johnson
made about Garrick. She is aware that Johnson didn't appreciate
Garrick's acting and was envious of his riches, but it does not
seem to her that it was necessary or appropriate for Mrs. Piozzi to
record all this. "The speaker, perhaps, had forgotten [the com-
ments], or was sorry for them, or did not mean them; but this
new-fashioned biography seems to value itself upon perpetuat-
ing every thing that is injurious and detracting" (II, 15–16).

In another letter of the same month More talks of one "snug"
little party consisting of her friends Walpole, Mrs. Montagu, and
the Burneys; still in April, More mentions that "the Bishop of
Chester brought me home from Soame Jenyns's the other night.
We had there almost all I know that is wise, learned, and witty;
but there were too many, and we all complained of a superfluity
of good things" (II, 17–18). In May, there is "a great but pleasant
dinner at the Bishop of Salisbury's" (II, 19). That same month More
meets the Turkish ambassador; she finds him handsome and com-
municative as he explains his own religion to her. The same letter
talks about "Mr. and Mrs. Swinburne the travellers, with whom I
am lately become much acquainted." The interesting thing about
them is that "they are people who have been a good deal distinguished in different courts. . . . They live chiefly abroad, and are
great bigots to Popery. She is the great friend of the Queen of
Naples, and not less a favourite of the Queen of France—a singu-
lar pair of friendships for an Englishwoman of no rank" (II, 23–
24). More's rather snide comment, somewhat out of character for
her, suggests that she is offended by the Englishwoman's "friendships" at a number of levels here.

Much more to her liking is Sarah Trimmer, a proper Englishwoman of proper values. More delights in Trimmer's *Fabulous Histories* (II, 41). Trimmer herself seems hardly able to contain her
hero-worship when she writes to More. Remarkably, her tone of
almost awed respect is quite typical of More's correspondents. Note,

too, not only Trimmer's extravagant appreciation for More's support of her work, but Trimmer's comments about More's forthcoming writing. The claim made so often by contemporary feminist critics that women of the eighteenth century were marginalized and powerless surely is made less tenable when we see the remarkable influence of someone like More. Trimmer's letter to More on May 10, 1787, brings together many of the issues I have been discussing. Trimmer tells More

> I feel myself inexpressibly obliged by your kind attention. It would appear like flattery to say how much I value your good opinion, but indeed it has long been the secret wish of my heart to obtain it. Your kind mention of my works to the Bishop of Salisbury I esteem a high obligation. I cannot but be proud of his approbation. . . .
>
> I have been favoured with a most friendly letter from Dr. Stonehouse, and a present of all his Tracts, &c. My best thanks are due to you, madam, for the obliging representations which have procured me the notice of this venerable gentleman, who would otherwise have overlooked me and my humble performances. I need not say that it is a great satisfaction to me to be regarded in so favourable a light by the good and the wise; for you have had such full experience of this kind of pleasure, that you can easily conceive what I enjoy from this circumstance.
>
> When I see new editions of your publications advertised, I sincerely rejoice that there is so much taste remaining in the world. I hope your useful pen does not lie idle. Surely you mean to favour the public with something more shortly. I have long been in hopes of seeing another volume of "Sacred Dramas." Indeed, my dear madam, you should go on with them; they are so extremely engaging to young minds, and the sentiments so agreeable to scripture, that they cannot fail of producing the happiest effects. You know that I read the sacred volume frequently; I may truly say it is my highest *entertainment* to do so. . . .
>
> I avail myself of your kind permission to submit the beginning of my new edition of "Sacred Histories" to your inspection, and should esteem myself greatly obliged, if you would favor me with your sincere opinion whether I have improved upon the former one, or not. . . .
>
> In conformity with your friendly counsel, I wrote to my pub-

lisher, about three weeks ago, desiring that he would settle my account in the course of this month, which he has *promised* to do without fail. At present I am a mere bookseller's fag, but hope to have resolution enough to disentangle myself.

When, my dear madam, may I hope for the favour of your company? I long to introduce my family to you; they are impatient to see a lady whose character and writings they so highly esteem. I wish to show you the spinning wheel; it is really a most interesting sight, to see twelve little girls so usefully and so agreeably employed. I shall experience so great a disappointment, if I should chance to be out when you come, that I hope you will be able to fix the time. I cannot be satisfied with a mere *call*—surely you can spare me a day. I have a bed at your service, if you can be prevailed upon to accept it. (II, 59–61)

It is quite clear that More's approbation brings Trimmer the attention of other important figures; More, then, acts as a patron not just to someone like Ann Yearsley but to those of her own class. Trimmer's praise of More's work is effusive, not to mention fawning, but in the context of the collected letters it does not stand out at all. As I mentioned earlier, More constantly is being asked by her correspondents to publish yet another piece of uplifting prose or another moral tract or poem. Trimmer's request that More comment upon Trimmer's own work is both a request for editorial guidance and, as well, a hope of publicizing her own work through More's extensive circle. In addition, More clearly has been giving Trimmer advice not simply on the stylistic but on the business side of her work, as More's counsel about how Trimmer should demand the money her publisher owes her illustrates. On this subject, an earlier letter from More to one of her sisters that talks about Trimmer and her problems in getting paid for her work is interesting, as it shows More to be a hard-headed business person when it comes to money for writing. She mentions a long visit from Trimmer, and her satisfaction with Trimmer's "good sense and propriety." She really likes Trimmer's work: "She is the author whom I venture most to recommend. I made one lady take three dozen of her books yesterday." And then More adds, "I presumed to give her a great deal of wholesome advice about booksellers; for would you believe it, popular as I am persuaded she must be, she has got little or nothing by her writings except reputation, and the consciousness of doing good: two things on which though I set due value, yet where there are ten children, money must have the eleventh place in maternal consultation" (II, 52). This observation provides an interesting commentary on More's own reasons for writing, for while she and her correspondents discuss the uplifting, moral, Christian aspects of her work constantly, it seems that there is one reason for writing that is quite as important as these although, unless in a context such as this discussion of Trimmer's problems, it is reflected in the discourse hardly at all. More believes in getting paid for her work; that she seems to have had an exceptionally cordial relationship with Cadell does not mean that she is unaware of the monetary base of the issue. Finally, a brief final comment on Trimmer's letter to More: we should note those twelve happily working little girls at the spinning wheel. We shall see many happily working small children in More's Tracts. But this discussion will be taken up again in later chapters.

More is directly involved in writing to try to influence current events even before she is pulled into the fracas with Tom Paine and the revolutionary movement. In 1788 she tells her sister that she has been writing all the days and half the nights either in prose or verse. She must write quickly, she says, because if her work is to influence events, it must appear before the issue is discussed in Parliament. "I am now busily engaged on a poem, to be called 'Slavery.' I grieve I did not set about it sooner; as it must now be done in such a hurry as no poem should ever be written in, to be properly correct; but good or bad, if it does not come out at the particular moment when the discussion comes on in parliament, it will not be worth a straw. This I shall bring out in an honourable manner, with my name staring in the front" (II, 97). She expects her poem to make a difference; she expects her name to make a difference. She writes to a deadline of real-world events. Thus the pattern is in place for her to use her pen in social causes that have direct political and social implications. For More to use her influence, whether in helping Sarah Trimmer to find an audience of powerful people—or indeed for Trimmer to be paid for her work—or to foreword a social cause in which she believes, Hannah More does not doubt her own power. It does not occur to her, to bring in our own contemporary cliché, to feel marginalized, as, of course, she is not.

One brief detour from our main discussion might be worth making here. I have been alluding repeatedly to the separation between the conservative social circles in which More travels and the radical movement which for her and her friends is so powerfully suspect. The area where the two groups, if unwittingly and perhaps grudgingly, meet is of course in the antislavery arena. The extraordinary battle in England to outlaw slavery is taken up by radical and conservative alike, with Wilberforce at the center of the movement. Edward Royle and James Walvin discuss the components of the antislavery movement in *English Radicals and Reformers: 1760–1848,* and one of the fascinating points they make is that the period from the beginnings of the campaign to the outlawing of the slave trade was "a mere twenty years."[7] Most of the push came from radicals such as Thomas Walker and Thomas Cooper, a former student of James Burgh; Royle and Walvin note that "dissenters were frequently at the front of the initial abolitionist push."[8] Then there was Wilberforce, "who does not fit easily, even amongst this heterogeneous group,"[9] and with him, people like Hannah More and Walpole. So while on most issues of reform the parties and partings are clear, the issue of slavery cuts across just about all the social boundaries we otherwise find so fixed.

One of the aspects of More's social circle that is perhaps difficult for a modern reader to conceptualize is how personal her relationships were with those in the highest reaches of the church and of the secular government. In addition to her friendship with the Bishop of London and his wife, for example, various other church leaders are mentioned as a constant presence in her life. She writes to her sister that "[t]he Bishop and Mrs. Porteus are already gone to take possession of the Palace at Fulham, having left London for good; but they are so near that we shall be no great losers. With the most affectionate kindness they both pressed me to go and spend some time with them, and they would nurse me, and cure my cough. They were so earnest in this request, that I certainly should have accepted it, if I had not been quite well. I have however promised to spend a few days with them before I go to Bristol" (II, 110–11). This is clearly a relationship of friendship, not simply of acquaintanceship. And so we should not be surprised to have Bishop Porteus writing some time later to More (and very late indeed—the note is dated "four in the morning,

1789"!)—in a tone of cordial compliment and fun. "Had I the good fortune to be a papist and a sprite," he tells her, "I would send you in return for an exquisite little poem . . . the prettiest copy of verses in the world; for no one I do affirm writes such delicious poetry as the *Ghost of a popish Bishop*. But as I am unluckily nothing more than a *live protestant Monk*, it is impossible for me . . . to soar so high into the regions of fancy, wit, and taste. . . . I must content myself at present with thanking you very heartily and very humbly in plain, dull, heretical prose, for the very great pleasure you have given us, both in person and by your pen" (II, 172). Another letter from Porteus to More is if possible even more complimentary:

> *Aut Erasmus, aut Diabolus,* was, you know, the laconic and expressive speech of Sir Thomas More, to a certain stranger who had astonished him with a torrent of wit, eloquence, and learning. *Aut Morus, aut Angelus,* exclaimed the Bishop of London, before he had read six pages of a certain delicate *little book* that was sent to him a few days ago. . . .
>
> Indeed, my dear friend, (if you will allow me to call you so,) it is in vain to think of concealing yourself. Your style and manner are so marked, and so confessedly superior to those of any other moral writer of the present age, that you will be detected by every one that pretends to any taste in judging of composition, or any skill in discriminating the characteristic excellences of one author from another. . . . There are but few persons, I will venture to say, in Great Britain, that could write such a book ;— that could convey so much sound, evangelical, morality, and so much genuine Christianity, in such neat and elegant language. It will, if I mistake not, soon find its way into every fine lady's library, and if it does not find its way into her heart and her manners, the fault will be her own. (II, 232–33)

This is the man who asks More to write something to answer Paine's *Rights of Man*.

We have seen More's many references to meetings with Burke. She also speaks often, and with real personal affection, about the royal family. An early allusion comes in her comment on Fanny Burney's position at the court. More writes to Pepys, "I was in the very joy of my heart, on seeing the other day in the papers, that our charming Miss Burney has got an establishment so near the queen. How I love the queen for having so wisely chosen!" (II, 42). Much comment has been made in recent discussions of Burney about the misfortune of her appointment to court, but Burney's own commitment to the queen and the king as well, and her own emotional ties to them, generally are overlooked. It is well to remember that Burney's service in fairly large part was demanding because she herself took it so seriously. During the difficult days of the king's illness Burney writes (November 5, 1788), "How reluctantly did I come away [from the queen]! how hardly to myself leave her! Yet I went to bed, determined to preserve my strength to the utmost of my ability, for the service of my unhappy mistress. I could not, however, sleep. I do not suppose an eye was closed in the house all night." The next day she writes, "It was only therefore at night and morning I could see her; but my heart was with her the livelong day. And how long, good Heaven! how long that day became! Endless I used to think it, for nothing could I do—to wait and to watch—starting at every sound, yet revived by every noise."[10]

Burney's personal affection for the royal family is not unusual among her peers. More's enthusiasm for Burney's appointment at court reflects More's regard both for Burney and for the queen. The king's illness, and the queen's strength, are issues close to More's heart too, and she discusses the royal family frequently in her letters to her sisters much as she discusses any of their other acquaintances. In January 1789 she writes, "Does Pitt not fight like a hero for the poor Queen? but who will fight for *him*, since he has not a hundred a year in the world. . . . The poor King the other night, after Dr. Willis had read prayers to him, prayed aloud for himself. On the 17th he said to the page, Remember that tomorrow is the Queen's birth-day, and I insist upon having a new coat. As for Pitt, he goes on triumphantly.—Excellent accounts of the king to-day; private accounts too, better than have yet been circulated" (II, 140–41). On February 25, 1789, More tells her sister about the marvelous moment when she and her friends found out that the king was recovered; she would have written immediately, she notes, but the post had already gone out for that day, "that blessed Thursday, when the chancellor made the memorable communication of the King's being convalescent. . . . I was out at dinner, and we were talking on what would probably be the event of things, when lo ! a violent rap at the door, and Lord Mount Edgecombe was announced. He came in almost breathless, directly from the House of Lords, and told us that the King was recovered. We were quite transported, and Mrs. Garrick fairly got up, and kissed him before the company. Soon afterwards arrived the Duke of Beaufort, confirming the good news" (II, 143). The personal quality of the thanksgiving is as marked here as in the letters of Burney. This is more than a polite or even interested response; the joy of More and her friends is based in affection, not simply duty or respect.

This affection for the royal family is evident in a letter from More to one of her sisters of March 17, 1789, which recounts a charming anecdote about the very human responses of the king and queen to each other. More tells her sister that "The Queen and Princesses came to see the illumination, and did not get back to Kew till after one o'clock. When the coach stopped, the Queen took notice of a fine gentleman who came to the coach door without a hat. This was the King, who came to hand her out. She scolded him for being up, and out so late; but he gallantly replied, 'he could not possibly go to bed and sleep till he knew she was safe.'" The domestic incident here is charming for More in itself, and it is charming because it is about the king and queen. More's relief at the king's recovery is shared by all in her circle, and, of course, by many of her countrymen. She notes about this public celebration that "There never was so joyous, so innocent, so orderly a mob."

More herself had been invited to a somewhat smaller celebration, and regrets that she could not go "to Lady Cremorne, to see *her* way of celebrating the festivity. She had two hundred Sunday school children, thirty-six of whom she clothed for the occasion; they walked in procession to the church; after service they walked back to her house, where, after singing a Psalm of praise, and God save the King, they had a fine dinner of roast beef and plum-pudding. Then the whole two hundred marched off with baskets under their arms, full of good things for their parents" (II, 145–46). (It is worth stopping for a moment to remark Lady Cremorne's dinner for the children, obviously the poor children, of the neighborhood. This particular sort of gesture is a fairly standard one. Mrs. Montague has an *annual* dinner for the Chimney sweepers each May; not surprisingly, their dinner too is roast beef and plum

pudding [2,155]. More's annual dinners for her Cheddar scholars, then, come within this context.)[11] The king of France too celebrates King George's health: "The king of France has written so
very kindly to the king on his recovery, and behaved so handsomely,
that the queen and princesses are to be at the French Ambassador's
Gala; an honour never before paid to anybody" (II, 154).

The king of France also for More and her friends is seen in
human terms, not simply as a sovereign or a figurehead. This personal level is important because the response of More's circle to
the French Revolution is colored by their affection for their own
monarch and even, as here, a distinctly personal regard for the
French king. Typical is More's rawly emotional letter to Mrs.
Garrick after the events in France have played themselves out.
More writes on February 2, 1793, "If any one king of France deserved the appellation by which they have been distinguished, of
*Most Christian King* it is this innocent victim. His wife is quite a
model of piety, charity, goodness and Sense [*sic*]. We have done
little else but weep for him, talk of him, and read of him."[12] The
people in More's circle are horrified by what happens in France
not merely on an intellectual or political level but out of a genuine dismay at the treatment of the royal family and its attendants.
We will note this personal context repeatedly in More's correspondence with Walpole, and we should remember this layer of response when we analyze More's responses to homegrown unrest.

Most of all, like her friends, More truly believes in the order
that she is upholding. For her, the poor really are different from
the better off, and when she is acting or thinking about the poor
with what she takes to be purest compassion, she cannot imagine
that her conception of them is any but what the poor could desire.
This schism in perception is clear in the Milkmaid episode; a very
short quote from one of More's letters will perhaps underline it.
The passage comes in a letter to her sister in 1789 that talks about
the procession to St. Paul's in honor of the king's recovery. "The
poor soldiers were on guard from three in the morning; I would
willingly relinquish all the sights I may see this twelvemonth, to
have known they had each some cold meat and a pot of porter,"
she writes, and we know that it is kind of her to think of "the poor
soldiers" out on guard for such a long time. She continues, "I was
troubled too about the six thousand charity children, but the
Bishop assures me they had each of them a roll and two apples"

(II, 154). This remark is wonderful, it seems to me, for what it says about More's conception of what poor people need, for one must wonder which of her friends would be happy to march in such a procession with so meager a sustenance. Yet this reassurance that the bishop gives her about the children being properly taken care of does satisfy More, obviously.

The company More keeps at forty is quite the same as the circle she had when she was young. It comprises many of the most important people of her time, intellectuals, artists, politicians, and churchmen. All of the letters reflect a group totally at ease with all of its members. The conversation is always good, but it is never argumentative: perhaps the most serious disagreement More has is with Mrs. Piozzi for recording Johnson's criticisms of Garrick. Within our context, it is the political and social agreement that is so important. We see the congruence of opinion in the discussions about Yearsley, both in the support people give to the project of helping Yearsley and then in their disgust at her response to More's handling of the affair. We shall see the same conformity of viewpoint in the More-Walpole correspondence regarding the aftermath of the French Revolution. That no dissident voices are included at these gatherings partially is a matter of class, but it is also a matter of belief or outlook. People in More's circle see society, and within it, the poor, in the ways that More reflects in all her writings, and especially in the Cheap Repository Tracts because those Tracts are meant to uphold a specific way of life for all classes in terms of the interactions among classes. Townsend, we have seen, represents precisely the same images of order that More and her friends are comfortable with. That nineteenth-century concept of "the two Englands" is over-simple, for before counting the lower classes, even among the relatively well-off there already are two Englands. Certainly the England of More's circle is a very different one from the England described or desired by the radicals against whom More labored so diligently in the Tracts and other writings.

The series of letters between More and Walpole reflect the prevailing discourse in More's circle on the French Revolution and its aftermath. We shall see an increasing sense of horror, an almost hysterical awareness that the bloody events in France could turn into a domestic threat. It is this sense of danger that precipitates More's entry into the pamphlet wars of the 1790s and that calls forth the extraordinary support that results in those "millions" of her Tracts sold. In the Walpole-More correspondence, the first mention of the events in France comes in a letter from Walpole to More dated 10 September 1789. "I congratulate you on the Bastille," Walpole writes. "I always hated to drive by it, knowing the miseries it contained." But, he notes, "the destruction of it was silly, and agreeable to the ideas of the mob, who do not know stones and bars and bolts from a *lettre de cachet*."[13] His sympathy for those inside, then, from the beginning is tinged with a distaste for the "mob" that has set them free—this was not, he implies, the right way to go about the business of change. "If despotism recovers, the bastille will rise from its ashes—recover, I fear, it will. The *États* cannot remain a mob of kings, and will prefer a single one to a larger mob of kings and tyrants. The nobility, the clergy, and people of property will wait, till by address and money they can divide the people. . . . In short, a revolution procured by a national vertigo does not promise a crop of legislators" (324). This first letter is relatively temperate, with some sympathy apparent for the impulse behind the overthrow of the Bastille, though with strong reservations about the manner and the direction of events. When More writes to Walpole on November 2, 1789, she claims with some humor that she is "edified by your strictures on the French distractions" (329). She jokes about the Catholic French king that she would be tempted to forgive him "all the spite I owe him, if he could know that the throne of the *grand monarque* has been overturned by fishwomen!" (329). More seriously, she fears that "These people seem to be tending to the only two deeper evils, than those they are involved in; for I can figure to myself no greater mischiefs than despotism and popery, except anarchy and atheism" (329).

By September 29, 1791, all traces of sympathy or humor on the subject of revolution disappear, replaced by alarm and urgency. Walpole is furious that Mrs. Barbauld does not properly respect the English clergy, and, of course, that she supports the French revolution. "I cannot forgive the heart of [such] a woman," he writes to More. The next sentence of the letter is of particular interest; Lewis' note to it[14] says that "Hannah More altered the sentence to read:'-they all contributed their faggot to the fires,' etc." The sentence, then: "Can I forget the 14th of July, when she contributed her faggot to the fire that her Presbytyrants . . . tried to light in every Smithfield in the island, and which as Price and Priestly [sic] applauded in France, it would be folly to suppose they did not only wish but meant to kindle here" (361). So the fear—shared by Walpole and More—is that the Revolution will come to England, indeed, will be imported by the radicals such as Price and Priestley. Walpole is horrified and furious. "Were they [Price and Priestley] ignorant of the atrocious barbarities, injustice, and violation of oaths committed in France?" He warns More to stay away from Barbauld, whose sympathy even for "the poor blacks" is suspect: "she is a hypocrite" whose supposed compassion is merely "a measure of faction" (361–62).

If Price and Priestley are not bad enough (Walpole's sympathy is all with "the poor man executed at Birmingham, who declared at his death he had been provoked by the infamous handbill"[15] [361]), 1792 also brings Mary Wollstonecraft's *Vindication of the Rights of Woman*. More writes to Walpole on August 18, 1792,

> I have been much pestered to read the *Rights of Women* [sic], but am invincibly resolved not to do it. Of all jargon, I hate metaphysical jargon; besides there is something fantastic and absurd in the very title. How many ways there are of being ridiculous! I am sure I have as much liberty as I can make use of, now I am an old maid, and when I was a young one, I had, I dare say, more than was good for me. If I were still young, perhaps I should not make this confession; but so many women are fond of government, I suppose, because they are not fit for it. To be unstable and capricious, I really think, is but too characteristic of our sex; and there is perhaps no animal so indebted to subordination for its good behaviour, as woman. I have soberly and uniformly maintained this doctrine, ever since I was capable of observation. . . . I really maintained the opinion in sincerity and simplicity, both from what I felt at home and have seen abroad. (370).

The ironies in this denunciation of Wollstonecraft are many, but perhaps foremost is More's comment about women being fond of government just because they are not fit for it—More never doubted her own ability, not to mention her right, to reorganize the lives of the poor in parish upon parish. She also was one of the best-selling authors of her time, her own letters constantly counting off to her correspondents the number of editions her latest work had gone into, and they responding with adoring comments. If it is characteristic of women to be "unstable and capricious" and in need of "subordination," More surely did not arrange her life according to her own prescription.

And yet we cannot accuse her of conscious hypocrisy, for she seems genuinely to have believed what she writes here about the distastefulness of Wollstonecraft's view: as we will see over and over both in the Tracts and in her *Strictures on the Education of Woman*, More's view of woman as the subordinate of man and of woman's role in society is consistent in all of her writings. Wollstonecraft is vilified not just for her view of woman but for her place in the radical circle, and when Walpole answers his "dear Saint Hannah" (371), he responds (August 21, 1792) that he is "glad you have not read the tract of [Wollstonecraft]: I would not look at it, though assured it contains neither metaphysics nor politics; but as she entered the lists in the latter, and borrowed her title from the demon's book, which aimed at spreading the *wrongs* of men, she is excommunicated from the pale of my library." He comments plaintively, "We have had enough of new systems, and the world a great deal too much already. There is still tranquillity [*sic*] and happiness in this country, in spite of the philosophizing serpents we have in our bosom, the Paines, the Tookes, and the Wollstonecrafts" (373).

But the danger cannot be ignored. The earlier part of his letter talks in detail about France, where "a whole nation of monsters is burst forth" (371). He recounts with disgust and pity the treatment of the king and queen and their friends: "Even the Queen's women were butchered in the Thuilleries, and the tigers chopped off the heads from the dead bodies." The king and queen were "shut up in a room without nourishment for twelve hours" (372) with the queen sitting trembling on the floor. Walpole's horror and indignation are obvious; what we want to notice, also, is the serious and lengthy discussion of these political issues in these letters. Here, for example, a letter that takes up the equivalent of three long pages of text devotes two of them to political discussion before "descend[ing] to private life" (373).

On March 23, 1793, Walpole responds to an earlier letter of More in which she had told him about her work in support of the distressed emigrant French clergy. He too has been enlisted in their cause, although it is against his usual practice to allow his name to be put into subscriptions. He goes on to a long discussion of the events in France, intermixing comments about France with furious commentary about Priestley. Note the broken sentences, so unlike Walpole's normal letter style, as if he can barely contain his anger.

> Well! That bloody chaos seems recoiling on themselves! It looks as if civil war was bursting out in many provinces, and will precipitate approaching famine—when till *now* could one make such a reflection without horror at one's self!—but alas! Have not the French brought it to the question whether Europe or France should be laid desolate? Religion, morality, justice, have been stabbed, torn up by the roots: every right has been trampled under foot. Marriage has been profaned and undermined by law—and no wonder that amidst such excesses, the poor arts have shared in the common ruin!—and who have been the perpetrators of, or advocates for such universal devastation? Philosophers, geometricians, astronomers—a Condorcet, a Baillie, a Bishop of Autun and a Doctor *Priestley*—and the latter the worst—the French had seen grievances, crying grievances!—yet not under the good late King—but what calamities or dangers threatened or had fallen on *Priestley,* but want of papal power, like his predecessor Calvin—if you say, Priestley's house was burned—but did he intend the fire should blaze on that side of the street? *Your* charity may believe him innocent—but your understanding does not—well! I am glad to hear he is going to America—I hope he will not bring back scalping—even to that National Assembly of which he was proud of being elected a member! . . .
>
> Some windows of the poor French emigres at Richmond have been broken; but you will say with the Archbishop of Aix, who is there, "I am sorry for the fact, but I like the motive" for the mob declared it was for their having murdered their King.
>
> I wish I had any other topic but France and all that is the consequence. (385)

Note how often Priestley enters this correspondence in the guise virtually of the devil himself. Even the burning of his house calls forth no pity.

Pity, actually, is reserved generally in this correspondence

either for members of one's own class or for those who agree with
one's own views. After years of watching and lamenting the events
in France, Walpole finds that "the sanguinary inhumanity of the
times has almost poisoned one's compassion and makes one abhor so many thousands of our own species and rejoice when they
suffer for their crimes. . . . I will check myself, or I shall wander
into the sad events of the last five years. . . . May we have as much
wisdom and courage to stem our malevolent enemies, as it is plain
to our lasting honour, we have had charity for the French emi-
grants, and have bounty for the poor who are suffering in this
dreadful season!" He takes leave of More, however, not in a spirit
of compassion but of intense rancor, with a parting shot at one of
their favorite villains: "Adieu! Thou excellent woman! Thou reverse of that hyena in petticoats, Mrs. Wollstonecraft, who to this
day discharges her ink and gall on Marie Antoinette, whose unparalleled sufferings have not yet staunched that Alecto's blazing
ferocity. Adieu! Adieu! Yours from my heart. . . . PS. I have subscribed five guineas at Mr White's to your plan" (397).

And what plan is that? More has sent him a prospectus for
the Cheap Repository Tracts. "Thank you a thousand times for
your most ingenious plan," Walpole writes on January 24, 1795.
Walpole is quite carried away with enthusiasm. "I sent one instantly to the Duchess of Gloucester, whose piety and zeal imitate
yours at a distance, but she says she cannot afford to subscribe
just at this severe moment, when the poor so much want her assistance—but she will on the thaw, and should have been flattred
by receiving a plan from yourself. I sent another to Lord Harcourt,
who I trust will show it to a much greater lady; and I repeated
some of the facts you told me of the foul fiends, and their anti-
More activity. I sent to Mr White for half a dozen more of your
plans, and will distribute them wherever I have hopes of their
taking root and blossoming—tomorrow I will send him my subscription, and I flatter myself you will not think it a breach of
Sunday," he tells her, ending, "how calm and comfortable must
your slumbers be on the pillow of every day's good deeds" (395–
96)! Good deeds, like beauty, are in the eye of the beholder. More's
attentions to the poor are not always received by the objects of
her benevolence in quite the way she wishes or expects, but the
support of More's friends, Walpole among them, is unwavering.
The extraordinary success of the Tracts is due in large part to the

distribution networks set up by More's peers, and we have seen earlier the response of her circle to the Ann Yearsley episode. Implicit in all the More-Walpole correspondence on issues having to do with the poor is a stance that delimits compassion by obedience; Ann Yearsley finds universal disapproval among More's friends because she does not conform to what they see as an appropriate model of deference.

Walpole's letters in this context too are typical. When More sends Walpole some of Ann Yearsley's poems, he devotes most of a very long letter (November 13, 1784) to them. He is at once surprised at Yearsley's talent and suspicious of the effect public recognition will have on this woman who seems to him essentially to be a freak of nature. He is "surprised," he says, "at the *kind* of genius of this unhappy female: I mean at the dignity of her thoughts and the chastity of her style. Her ear . . . is perfect—but *that* being a gift of nature, amazes me less" (219). He goes on to analyze seriously and with technical discussion aspects of her poetry: she should not, for example, write in blank verse because, not being learned, she cannot sufficiently "enrich [her] language" (220).

But he spends more time discussing Yearsley's social situation: "Were I not persuaded by the samples you have sent me, Madam, that this good thing has real talents, I should not advise her encouraging her propensity lest it should divert her from the care of her family, and after the novelty is over, leave her worse than she was" (220). Walpole's expression for Yearsley, "good thing," is eloquent of his sense of distance from her. The feeling is that this poet of a milkmaid is somehow unnatural, a "novelty" like a performing monkey. She should be doing normal things—caring for her family—instead of making poems. And her performance is dangerous, for her and for others. There is, he reminds More, the sad example of Stephen Duck: "When the late Queen patronized Stephen Duck, who was only a wonder at first, and had not genius enough to support the character he had promised, twenty artisans and labourers turned poets and starved" *Walpole*, 220). More carefully should monitor Yearsley, making sure that Yearsley always realizes "that she is a Lactilla, not a Pastora, and is to tend real cows, not Arcadian sheep" (221). The distaste Walpole evinces for a milkmaid who thinks of herself, even acts as if she is, a poet is precisely that of More's other friends.

More knows she is assured of a sympathetic audience when she writes to Walpole in October 1785 that, "as a contrast" to decent, kind people,

> I must produce my old friend the milkwoman. She has just brought out another new book, which you may possess for five shillings, and which she has advertised to be quite free from *my* corruptions. What is curious, she has prefixed to it my original preface to her first book, and twenty pages of the scurrility published against me in her second. To all this she has added the deed which I got drawn by an eminent lawyer, to secure her money in the funds, and which, she asserts, I made Mrs Montagu sign without reading.
>
> Do, dear Sir, join me in sincere compassion, without one atom of resentment (for that I solemnly protest is the state of my mind towards her) for a human heart of such unaccountable depravity, as to harbour such deep malice for two years, though she has gained her point, and the money is settled to her wish. (253)

More's language hardly could be stronger: "a human heart of such unaccountable depravity" implies monstrous malfeasance. Almost another year later, Ann Yearsley is still a bitter topic. Walpole suggests to More that Yearsley's behavior perhaps is to be laid at More's door, for More simply made it possible for Yearsley to have too much. "Could the milkwoman have been so bad, if you had merely kept her from starving, instead of giving her opulence? The soil, I doubt, was bad; but it could not have produced the rank weed of ingratitude, if you had not dunged it with gold, which rises from rock, and seems to meet with a congenial bed when it falls on the human heart" (283).

Walpole, like More, sees himself as a benevolent person with a committed interest in the good of humanity. The context for this comment on Yearsley is a discussion that begins with the education of princes. "[R]oyal brats" should be taught about human suffering rather than "corrupted early" by wealth and flattery: "To be educated properly, they should be led through hovels, and hospitals, and prisons. Instead of being reprimanded (and perhaps immediately after, *sugar-plummed*) for not learning their Latin or French grammar, they now and then should be kept fasting, and if they cut their finger, should have no plaster till it festered."

Human beings are "corrupted and perverted by greatness, rank, power, and wealth." All well and good: Walpole casts a critical eye on his own class and those above. Not exactly, for his sentence continues, à la Soame Jenyns, "I am inclined to think that virtue is the compensation to the poor for the want of riches" (Walpole, 282–83). There is a peculiar twist here in the rhetoric that is very typical of those in More's circle. The well-off do not need to feel sorry for the poor—the poor are in some ways better off than the rich—because poverty keeps the poor virtuous, even makes them virtuous, and virtue is to be desired over comfort. We meet these ideas in other late-century contexts, in Jenyns, of course, but also, most oddly, at the end of Elizabeth Inchbald's radical (!) novel *Nature and Art*. It is good to be poor, Walpole says, for the poor labor naturally. Probably "the first footpad or highwayman had been a man of quality, or a prince, who could not bear having wasted his fortune, and was too lazy to work; for a beggar-born would think labour a more natural way of getting a livelihood than venturing his life" (283). And so Yearsley probably would not have turned bad if she had not had the occasion to escape her poverty.

To modern ears these arguments sound self-serving if not ridiculous, but to Walpole, More, and their friends these ways of looking at social issues mark them as understanding, concerned, and benevolent. When Mr. Fenton in "The Shepherd of Salisbury Plain" insists to the poor shepherd that he would not take the shepherd from his poverty if he could, this stance represents the epitome of concerned, responsible behavior. Mr. Fenton could be characterized in the same words that Walpole uses to describe More: "You are not only the most beneficent, but the most benevolent of human beings—not content with being a perfect saint yourself, which (forgive me for saying) does not always imply prodigious charity for others, not satisfied with being the most disinterested, nay the reverse of all patriots, for you sacrifice your very slender fortune, not to improve it, but to keep the poor honest instead of corrupting them" (401). I think it is difficult for a modern reader to understand how important it was for those in More's circle "to keep the poor honest instead of corrupting them."[16]

This desire, after all, is a large part of the motivation for the labors of Hannah and her sisters at Cheddar and the subsequent schools for the poor. As Roberts puts it in the *Memoirs*, "finding in

rural life and the peasant's cottage the same crimes, in other forms
[that she had seen in the higher classes], disfiguring the moral
scene, and intercepting the prosperity of the rising generation,
she could not . . . withhold herself from taking an active part in
the instruction of the poor population around her. . . . In the course
of [the sisters' excursions to Cheddar and the other villages], finding the poor in their neighborhood immersed in deplorable ignorance and depravity, they resolved to supply their spiritual wants"
(II, 205–6). The "wants" of the poor, spiritual or otherwise, however, as with Ann Yearsley, are defined very narrowly within the
terms of what More sees fit for them. Literacy, for example, clearly
only is to be encouraged to the point of an ability to read the basic
religious documents, and only for this purpose. More comments
to Mrs. Kennicott, for example, that she has had good success at
Cheddar: "we have a great number there who could only tell their
letters when we began, and can already read the Testament, and
not only say the Catechism, but give pertinent answers to any
questions which involve the first principles of Christianity." This
progress is indeed wonderful, for More has found the poor in these
neighborhoods to be "more vicious and ignorant than I could have
conceived possible in a country which calls itself Christian" (II,
210–11).

She writes in a similar vein to Wilberforce: "What a comfort
I feel, in looking round on these starving and half-naked multitudes, to think that by your liberality many of them may be fed
and clothed," but the truly important thing is that their souls be
saved, and toward *that* end, much of the letter explores sources of
proper religious printed matter to stock her schools. "Mr. H. T—
—I think belongs, to the Society of Sunday Schools in London, for
assisting necessitous villages with books, &c. There cannot be a
fairer claim on them than the present. If you and he approve it,
perhaps we may apply for a quantity of New Testaments, Prayer
Books, and little Sunday School books, with a few Bibles. The
sooner we get them the better, otherwise you or he will be so good
as to order a supply from the Society for Promoting Christian
Knowledge" (II, 217). Later (in 1790), she decides that it would be
a fine idea if the parents of the children are allowed to get instruction too, although the instruction is to be limited only to an hour
in the evening, and its subject matter, not surprisingly, is solely to
be religious instruction: "They are so ignorant that they need to

be taught the very elements of Christianity" (II, 224). Ignorance in any other area she does not even mention. The previous year, within the same context, she had written to Mrs. Kennicott, "It is grievous to reflect, that while we are sending missionaries to our distant colonies, our own villages are perishing for lack of instruction." But the instruction, whatever the extent of the ignorance, shall only be religious. "As the land is almost pagan," she writes, "we bring down persons of great reputation for piety from other places, and the improvements are great for the time." Not that things are easy for her and her instructors: "But how we shall be able to keep up these things with so much opposition, vice, poverty, and ignorance, as we have to deal with, I cannot guess" (II, 213).

More will shoulder a significant burden of the education of these misguided poor people, not only in setting up the schools but in herself writing for them material that is fitting. For "it is the profligate multitude that want to be drawn off from that pernicious trash, the corruption of which is incalculable. I have, therefore [she writes to the Reverend J. Newton in 1794], thought it lawful to write a few moral stories, the main circumstances of which have occurred within my own knowledge, but altered and improved as I thought would best advance my plan, carefully observing to found all goodness in religious principles." These, of course, are the Tracts. Some people, she notes, will say that "invention should have been entirely excluded," but "alas! I know with whom I have to deal, and I hope I may thus allure these thoughtless creatures on to higher things" (II, 429). Many critics have commented on More's respect for the poor people she wants to "help"; it seems clear, however, that More's view of the poor, of the "thoughtless creatures" for whom she writes the Tracts, is that they are at best pitiable, if not downright dangerous, but certainly not worthy of the same sort of respect that she unerringly expresses for her own peers. Rather, like not very bright children, they can be led to better things through the right kind of exposure to ideas that have been tailored, and sugar-coated, for them. Indeed, More glories in her own intransigence in the view that she is promulgating. "I forgot to tell you one thing which diverted me vastly," she writes to her sister. When the "Duke of ——" said that he would not subscribe to the Tracts because "he took it for granted, knowing the character of [More], that all the doctrines would be on one side[,] I desired my friend to tell his grace that they certainly would" (II, 430). The duke's hesitation notwithstanding, the warm support of her friends for her project comes up over and over again.

She notes that she is "afraid we shall be ruined by the very success of our Tracts. Cadell says, he would not stand in my shoes at the end of the year, for five hundred pounds over and above the subscription; nay according to another calculation, a *thousand* pounds would not do it at any rate." Her friend the Bishop of London has "his table full of our penny literature. Above a thousand, I suppose; some of which he gives to every hawker that passes; and he kindly says that by letting them stand always on his library table, he cannot forget to make them the subject of conversation with all comers" (II, 431). The Tracts are distributed by organizations formed for this purpose: "Two highly respectable Committees are formed, one in the city, and the other in Westminster, members of parliament, &c. for the regular circulation of our Repository Tracts." And "the Bishop of Dromore has been with me, to put me on a good plan about hawkers. The Bishop of London received the enclosed note to-day from the Archbishop of Canterbury; . . . how much the heads of the church condescend to deal in our small wares." News comes from India that the Tracts are being read there: "The Rajah preferred [the Tracts] to the Rambler, which somebody had given him, and declared he liked Mrs. More's works better than any of the English books he had ever read" (II, 434).

Bishop Porteus is delighted with the beginnings of the project. "Pray send me a few more copies of your 'Market-woman,' and any thing else you may have ready, that I may send some with the proposals to my country friends, for the nature of these compositions will be a better recommendation of the plan, than any thing you or I can say in favour of it." He goes on that "both the Bishop of Durham and myself (and I hope many others of our brethren) will be in the number of your subscribers." And then there is a telling comment, in the form of a wry joke. Porteus refers to the fact that because the Tracts are being distributed in such numbers, but producing them costs more than they are being sold for, More needs money to subsidize their production lest she herself wind up seriously in debt. Porteus notes that "though the times are bad for raising new levies of money at present, yet if we can but keep the French out of England, and all things quiet at home, I hope there will be still both money and piety enough left in the country to keep you out of the King's Bench. It would, to be sure, be very pleasant to have you for so near a neighbour; but as they would only let you out on Sundays . . . I do not much relish the idea of your withdrawing . . . to that reputable and elegant retreat" (II, 453).

More's "magnificent and ambitious project" is a huge success, Porteus tells her. Commenting on his recent trip of eight hundred miles, he tells her that "wherever I went, I heard of you and your *good works.* Some of them I saw in a shop window at York, and stopped to talk with the mistress of it, a fine fat, round-faced, well-looking quaker, who said she sold a great number of them, and gave many away to the poor people, who were very fond of them" (II, 454–55). This is one of the very few citations that actually talk about the poor and their response to the Tracts. As G. H. Spinney suggests, poor people probably in fact were not terribly enthusiastic about them. He notes that the methods of distribution used for the Tracts "made the scheme look far more successful than it really was. It is hard to say what proportion was bought directly from hawkers by the poorer people, but it was probably not very high."[17] Among her own class, on the other hand, the Tracts are highly approved. "The sublime and immortal publication of the 'Cheap Repository,'" her friend Bishop Porteus tells her, "I hear of from every quarter of the globe. To the West Indies I have sent shiploads of them. They are read with avidity at Sierra Leone, and I hope our pious Scotch Missionaries will introduce them into Asia" (III, 5). In another context Porteus asks her for "Part of 'Will Chip' or a similar pamphlet under a different name" to help to spread a subscription; "I am confident . . . that your pen might work wonders, and perhaps contribute, under providence, to save your country" (III, 35).

And this is precisely the context in which More herself sees her labors: "we labour strenuously to attach our people to the state as well as to the church" (III, 52), she writes to Mrs. Kennicott. For the poor really are frightening, as we know, and so they must be shaped by those above them who know better than they not only about moral but about political values. Even in religion, they are "more liable to enthusiasm than the better-informed" (III, 137). This is why, even when the poor are educated, they must be provided with safe materials and educated only to the point of being able to deal with these defined readings but no more. Thus "my plan of instruction is extremely simple and limited. They learn, on week-days, such coarse works as may fit them for servants. I allow of no writing for the poor. My object is not to make fanatics, but to train up the lower classes in habits of industry and piety" (II, 133). The Cheap Repository Tracts were created with just these goals in mind: "To teach the poor to read without providing them with *safe* books, has always appeared to me an improper measure, and this consideration induced me to enter upon the laborious undertaking of the Cheap Repository Tracts" (III, 135), More writes years later (1801). In fact, looking back, she sees what she has always been doing as "devoting my time and humble talents to the promotion of loyalty, good morals, and attachment to church and state among the poorer people" (III, 124). Notice that even in her own retelling, her efforts were not simply toward the moral improvement of the poor but to the cultivation among the poor of political allegiance to the state.

It seems fitting as a coda to this chapter to point out that nearly twenty years after the beginning of the Cheap Repository project More still was being asked to put out political fires with her pen. "Towards the close of [1817]," Roberts notes, "the universal stagnation of trade, and depression of landed property, afforded too plausible an occasion to ill-intentioned men, for perverting the minds of the working people, irritated by the disappointment of their ill-founded expectations, that plenty would be the immediate attendant upon peace, and by the severe distress consequent upon the general scarcity of employment. *The services Mrs. More had already rendered to the cause of loyalty and subordination,* by her skill and success in accommodating sober sense and sound reasoning to plain and plebeian understandings, in the form of narrative and dialogue, and in a playful and popular style, occasioned *fresh applications to be made for her powerful assistance at this alarming juncture.* Without a moment's hesitation, she set to work and with her usual celerity produced several appropriate and admirable Tracts and ballads, which she continued to supply while the pressure of the danger existed, and which were circulated in great numbers throughout every part of the country, with very visible effect. *Those who called upon her for this fresh public effort* [all italics mine], were surprised at the sudden success of their application, and beheld with astonishment the rapid succession of these little pieces that flowed from the pen of this ready writer, and the zeal and animation she displayed in the cause" (III, 466–67).

Loyalty and subordination are paired here, as they always have been in all of More's work with the poor. There is no sense that the poor could be loyal and not be subordinate, for in the nature of the political and social state a function of their loyalty is in fact their acceptance of their own subordination to those above them. Put another way, not willingly to accept subordination itself constitutes disloyalty to their country. This is the argument in *Village Politics,* it is the argument in the Cheap Repository Tracts, and, as we will see in the next chapter, it is the argument put forward whenever the poor threaten, even implicitly, to attempt to choose for themselves their place in society.

More's special skill is to accommodate "sober sense . . . to plebeian understandings," with the assumption being that these understandings are not very good at all and can be shaped effectively by the kind of simplistic prose and verse that More produces to this purpose. As with the Cheap Repository Tracts, special systems of dissemination are set up to circulate her work to the dangerous poor. Roberts notes that in 1817 "A committee was formed, as on a former occasion in London [the publication of the Tracts], to accelerate the circulation of these seasonable publications; with the leading members of which, she maintained a correspondence, which drew from her many communications of practical and experimental wisdom."

Perhaps not surprisingly, some of the old artillery is brought out: "Her admirable little dialogue of Village Politics, was now reprinted" (III, 467). The new version of the pamphlet, *Village Disputants,* is distributed in dangerous areas: More writes to some friends that "Lord K—— has sent 600 Village Disputants to six gentlemen at Manchester for distribution, in their separate districts" (III, 469). To Sir W. W. Pepys she writes on January 24, 1817, that she has accepted the duty of working to calm the spirit of revolution fomenting in the manufacturing towns; she has been asked to do so by those in the very highest quarters. "And now shall I confess how low I have been sinking in the ranks of literature? I did not think to turn ballad-monger in my old age. But the strong and urgent representations I have had from the highest quarters of the very alarming temper of the times, and the spirit of revolution which shews itself more or less in all manufacturing towns, has led me to undertake as a duty a task I should gladly have avoided. I have written many songs, papers, &c. by way of antidote to this fatal poison." She has had this literature produced anonymously, because, she says, she was afraid to have the pieces attributed to her: "Thousands and tens of thousands have been circulated without its being known from what source they proceeded. As to some of them, my quiet, perhaps my safety, requires silence, where obnoxious names are mentioned" (III, 473–74). She plans to have these dangerous allusions expunged in future editions, she says.

*Village Disputants*, she notes, she has "accommodated . . . to the present times" (III, 474). In March, she writes to Pepys that she is sending some of her "very *profound* and *learned* halfpenny and penny lucubrations, as a present to your servant's hall," although she hopes that he will take a look at them too. She jokes, rather wryly, that one of her most "elegant" occupations is "that of furnishing the baskets of hawkers," but her purpose is absolutely serious: her hope is to "counteract . . . the blasphemous and seditious Tracts which they carry with too much success" (III, 479). Finally, toward the end of April, in a letter that talks about the imminent death of one sister and the very serious illness of another—in the very same paragraph that recounts these personal tragedies and asks God for the grace to bear and suffer "his whole will"—she continues, "The spirit of insurrection which has shewn itself in so alarming a way,—the blasphemous and seditious Tracts which have deluged our whole country, called upon every lover of religion and social order to furnish some counteraction. I, for one, have set to work, and I think, in six or eight weeks I produced above a dozen of these halfpenny and penny compositions; I fear the antidotes are not powerful enough to expel the deeply-rooted venom, yet as they had a very wide circulation, my friends think they have been useful. I did not think to turn ballad-monger in my old age, but I thought it was my duty" (III, 481).

The introduction to the "Tracts written during the Riots in the Year 1817" in the eleven-volume collected edition of More's works published by Cadell only three years before her death emphasizes the political motivation of these works; the Cheap Repository Tracts in this edition are preceded by a parallel statement making clear their political motives. More's Tracts of 1817, we are reminded, were necessary because

"in the year 1817 very dangerous alarms were excited in this country by the mischievous activity of a number of disaffected persons. The temporary decay of trade, and the scarcity arising from inclement seasons,—calamities over which no human power had any control, instead of being considered as the visitations of Providence, were attributed to Government, and seized on as a pretence for promoting anarchy, riot, and treason. With a wish to raise an insurrection, a multitude of seditious and blasphemous pamphlets were circulated with incredible industry, and read with avidity. In consequence of which the writer of the Cheap Repository Tracts at the beginning of the French Revolution was again earnestly called upon to contribute her feeble aid towards furnishing antidotes to this spreading poison. The following little pieces [the 1817 Tracts] were written with this view."[18]

Note the explicit connection made here between the French Revolution and the project of the Cheap Repository. More's writing directed to the poor has been discussed by generations of commentators as her religiously motivated attempt to provide moral guidance for them. There is undoubtedly that element to her productions, but in her writing to the poor, as I have been suggesting throughout this study, the moral always has a strong political base. From the early *Village Politics* through all the Tracts of the Repository and afterward in these Tracts written in her seventies, More is, so to speak, a hired polemicist for the upper classes.

Five

# Two Sides of a Question

## Hannah More's *Village Politics* and Josiah Wedgwood's *Address to the Young Inhabitants of the Pottery*

WILLIAM ROBERTS dramatically tells the story of that terrible year, 1792, when "affairs began to wear a very gloomy and threatening aspect in this country. French revolutionary principles seemed to be spreading wide their mischievous influence. Indefatigable pains were taken, not only to agitate and mislead, but to corrupt and poison the minds of the populace, by every artifice that malice could suggest; and such had been the success of these efforts, and of the inflammatory publications by which they were prosecuted, that the perverted feelings and imaginations of men appeared to be propelling them fast into the same abyss into which the French had already fallen."[1] At this awful moment, if we are to take him quite at his word, More was besieged by letters "from persons of eminence" begging her to produce "some little popular tract" to counteract "those pernicious writings. The sound part of the community [!] cast their eyes upon her as one who had shown an intimate knowledge of human nature . . . from the highest to the lowest classes" and who, it was hoped, could "stem so mighty a torrent" (*Memoirs*, II, 345–46).

Whether letters really "poured in upon Hannah More, by every post" (II, 345) at this juncture, as Roberts says, we don't know; it is clear, however, fhat Bishop Porteus asked More to respond to the moment's horrors. More writes to Mrs. Garrick a bit after the fact, on January 8, 1793, that "He [the Bishop of London] importuned me in the most earnest manner to write some little vulgar two penny thing to try to open the eyes of the common people on the . . . rage for liberty and equality. So sick as I was, I spent one day writing a little book mean enough for the capacities of such readers as Mr. Pepperdey, and Mr. Peter Alexander. It is called *Village Politics by Will Chip a Country Carpenter.*" More explains that she did not want her name attached to the pamphlet, and so she went through a number of moves to try to keep people from making the connection: "I changed my Bookseller the better to avoid Suspicion, and I did not send it to any of my friends, as I have usually been found out by that. You may get it for two-pence, for I would not send it you [sic] for the reason above-mentioned. I tile [sic] you fairly you wont like [sic], and I shall not be affronted if you tile me so, for it is not written for the polished but the ignorant." The letter ends, "Poor Louis Capet!"[2] As for secrecy, then as now it was not so easy to keep things quiet; having confessed her authorship of *Village Politics* to Mrs. Boscawen, More is promised that the secret shall not be spoiled by her, but is told that More herself may have let it out unwittingly—More's letter to Mrs. Boscawen had no seal, and thus could have been read by anyone along the way! At any rate, it does not take long for More's authorship to be widely known and for endless thanks to roll in.[3] We shall get to some of these letters later, for in their extravagant praise the letters themselves provide significant commentary on More's political work here. But first we should look at the tract itself.

Poor Louis Capet, indeed. The horrors of the revolution in France and its aftermath, as we have seen in the last chapter, are constantly on the minds of those in More's circle, as is an intense fear that events in England could take something like the same direction. More sets out to counteract the pernicious influences of Paine and his ilk with an attack directed at the same audience that seemed to be so malleable in his hands. *Village Politics* is written in language so simple that a child would understand it; clearly, More's idea of the intelligence of her lower-class audience, notwithstanding her experience with Ann Yearsley, is that to be lower class is to be of low mental ability. Neither she nor her friends seem to hear the contemptuous quality of an argument that is couched in diction and supported by logic that might be appropriate for a five year old. Indeed, More will be praised repeatedly for bringing the arguments of *Village Politics* to the level appropriate for her intended audience. There is a good deal of humor here, but it too is always sophomoric, although More's own friends seem to find some passages of *Village Politics* so funny that their own readings are interrupted. All of the arguments are as basic as they can be, as are the actions and situations described. The names, going back to medieval morality plays (which used the device for the same effect), identify the speaker not simply as an individual but in terms of his group, trade, or moral position.

The "author," Will Chip, is "a Country Carpenter." He is, then, a good ole country boy, as our own country-western songs would say, and his identification as someone not of the city, and someone with a down-to-earth trade, places him as a coequal with his audience of good and uncorrupted working Englishmen. Jack Anvil, the blacksmith, similarly is part of the same set; Tom Hod, the mason, while at first he seems to fall for the pernicious arguments of Liberty, Equality, and so forth, can be relied on, with proper guidance, to see through the ruses of Tom Paine and company and to come back to the values of a true-born Englishman. The brilliant beginning of the dialogue, with Tom looking "like a hang dog" because he is so miserable and Jack's ferreting out the trouble—Tom's book—sets the tone and level of the entire work.

It's not that the "old mare" is dead, or that he's out of work, that makes Tom unhappy—in fact, he never knew that he *was* unhappy until he came across this book. The clear implication, that if someone needs a book to tell him he's unhappy things can't be very bad, More makes explicit: "A good sign, though, that you can't find out you're unhappy without looking into a book for it,"[4] Jack tells Tom. The problem is that Tom wants liberty; Jack, feigning misunderstanding, asks Tom if he's the subject of a warrant and promises to vouch for him. Law-abiding Englishmen have liberty enough, Jack says; the only threat to their own liberty would come, rightfully enough, if they disobey the law. But no, Tom insists, his problem is that he needs "a new Constitution." Jack offers to send for the doctor,[5] and Tom, exasperated, finally makes himself absolutely clear: "I'm not sick; I want Liberty and Equality, and the Rights of Man." The vile formulation out in the open, Jack sees Tom for what he is. "O, now I understand thee," he says; you're a "leveller and a republican." Tom cannot see that his ideas are wrong; he just knows that he wants reform. Clearly, he has not thought through what he means by "reform," for when Jack tells him to change himself, Tom insists that he wants "a *general reform.*" Finally, the truth comes out; Tom has been brainwashed by current propaganda. What he thinks he wants is what he understands the French—the French!—to have: "I want freedom and happiness, the same as they have got in France."

Jack has an easy answer, one More is sure easily will win the argument. She calls up hundreds of years of rivalry between England and France. Jack exclaims, "What, Tom, we imitate *them!* We follow the French!" The English have what the French have turned their world upside down to get. He would not, he tells Tom, look to the French for "freedom and happiness." And, turning around Tom's suggestion that the French have freedom, Jack insists that the only freedom they have is the freedom to be victimized by crime and by anarchy because they have "no king to take them up and hang them" if they misbehave. Jack admits that the French system had imperfections, but which system does not? And yes, they are Catholics, but "bad [religion] is better than none, Tom." Discussion of French jails leads to complaints about English ones; Tom is for tearing them all down: "all men should be free." This is an argument that will appear in a number of the tales of the Cheap Repository Tracts, and More's answer here is the same one she will make later: "a few rogues in prison keep the rest in order, and then honest men go about their business in safety, afraid of nobody; that's the way to be free."

Jack gives Tom a lesson in English civics. You and I, he says, are tried by our own peers just as much as a lord is. Even the king can't send a man to prison if he has done no wrong, and if he has, well then he deserves punishment. An ordinary man can "go to law" with anyone, with "Sir John at the great castle yonder," and the law treats them as equals. A lord will be hanged for the same crime as anyone else would be. William Godwin's *Caleb Williams,* published just the following year, suggests some of the most obvious points for rebutting Jack. Godwin's novel largely is a chronicle of the inequality before the law of different classes of men. The wealthy land owner Tyrrel uses the law to hound to death his impecunious ward Emily when she dares to disobey him, just as he uses it to destroy his tenant farmers, the Hawkinses; Falkland in the same novel uses the law to attempt to destroy Caleb, and he very nearly succeeds as Tyrrel had done in his vindictive pursuits. In *Caleb Williams,* as in Mary Wollstonecraft's *Maria,* the law never is available equally to those under its jurisdiction. An ordinary man may go to law with whomever he chooses, but his resources will never hold out against the richer man, and this is only one of the many ways in which the law favors the powerful.[6] But of course More gives Tom none of these responses: all he can say to Jack's rosy picture is "Well, that is some comfort."

Tom switches to another topic. "But have you read the Rights of Man?" Tom asks, and Jack responds that he would not waste the little time he has for reading on such a book; he would "only read a bit of the best." Again, Tom does not respond to what Jack says but answers instead with an unrelated complaint. Repeatedly, More shows that while Jack's arguments are logical, Tom jumps from point to point, incapable of putting together a rational discussion of his own because his own protests are not, after all, supportable. And so Tom demands to know why he cannot have those "same fine things they have got in France?" But he does not even understand what he is asking for. It is clear that the big words that he uses—"I'm for a *Constitution,* and *Organization,* and *Equalisation*"—are not concepts he comprehends. Jack loses his patience a bit, as More intends her reader to do, with Tom's silliness. "Do be quiet," he snaps. "Now, Tom, only suppose this nonsensical equality was to take place," it couldn't last long. Let's say everyone was given half an acre of ground. Each man could raise potatoes for his family—but if each were doing the same thing, no one would be around to do all the other things people need in order to survive and prosper. A broken spade could not be mended, for there would be nobody to mend it. "Neighbour Snip" would not be mending clothes, nor clothiers making cloth, "And as to boots and shoes, the want of some one to make them for us, would be a still greater grievance than the tax on leather." This last is really a brilliant stroke, for we remember that one of Paine's main arguments is that the taxes on commodities are driving the laboring classes into poverty. More's argument, that any taxes are better than not having the commodities themselves, surely sounds convincing, especially when she continues with the list of things that would not be available under equality, such as a doctor's care (he too would be out digging).

The argument here, that everyone works together in society for the good of all, and that each man in his place supports the rest, is basic to much eighteenth-century thought on society and, of course, religion. For it all really is God-ordained, and for the individual to question the hierarchies of society is to question God's order. Pope's *Essay on Man* was enunciating this view early in the century, and More, at its end, uses this basic principle as the foundation of all her writing to the poor. So when Tom says that even if he did not have all these services that Jack warns would disappear when all men were equal, "still I should have no one over my head," he does not realize that that never could be true, because by nature some men are smarter, some stronger than others. It is the law—not these new-fangled laws that Tom wants but the good old constitution of England—that prevents such as Tom from being at a disadvantage to or in danger from those better endowed than he. Jack says, "we have a fine constitution already, and our forefathers thought so." But Tom is contemptuous: "They were a pack of fools, and had never read the Rights of Man."

Up to this point *Village Politics* has been more or less a dialogue, that is, a fairly equal give and take between Tom and Jack. Jack's answers to Tom's objections generally have been longer than Tom's comments, but the disparity in length was not very obvious. From this point, however, until near the end of the story, Tom's comments for the most part are one-liners, essentially prompts for tales and vignettes designed to teach specific lessons of common sense, morality, and, of course, good citizenship. Tom's statements, as in this last one about *Rights of Man*, are thoughtless and unformed, and they almost always show disrespect for those wise men who have crafted the near-perfect England that Jack finally will make Tom see. If "our forefathers" were a pack of fools because they had not read *Rights of Man*, as Tom says, then it must be Tom who is wrong in his perspective because a blanket attack on those who have come before cannot be valid. Underlining his unreasonableness, Tom demands that which is not possible: how *could* they have read something that had not yet been written? Tom's thinking is sloppy; Jack patiently makes a careful case against Tom's harebrained demands.

But Jack must couch his rebuttals and explanations in terms that Tom will understand. And so he gives Tom a metaphor for good old England, a "fine old castle" over there that belongs to Sir John. Sir John's wife, who "likes to do every thing like the French," wanted to pull down the castle and "build it up in her frippery way." Of course, Sir John would not let her do any such thing: "shall I pull down this noble building, raised by the wisdom of my brave ancestors; . . . a castle which all my neighbours come to take a pattern by?" And so, rather than destroying the old and valuable, they mend the building as it requires fixing. English law and custom, even Tom should be able to understand, are noble; others use the English as models. Naturally from time to time some small changes need to be made, but certainly not major, revolutionary ones. The French destroy what is valuable to replace value with frippery; good Englishmen should not follow *that* example. We notice that, as happens without exception in More's work, when in a couple there is one who is mindless or stupid or thoughtless, it of course is the woman who is so portrayed. Good old Sir John has his feet planted firmly on the earth; it is "my Lady" who has these stupid and destructive French ideas.

Tom misses the point entirely. This obtuseness on his part discredits his arguments, for if he isn't capable of following Jack's story—which More's reader has had no problem with—why should the reader find Tom's arguments important? So Tom interrupts Jack's nice story about Sir John and his ditzy wife to demand "a perfect government," having just been shown that s ch a thing cannot be created: Jack tells him he "might as well cry for the moon. There's nothing perfect in this world."

Simply jumping to another subject, Tom complains "I don't see why we are to work like slaves, while others roll about in their coaches, feed on the fat of the land, and do nothing." Jack tries to make Tom understand once again that in society everything and everybody is connected. Jack's little girl brought home a story from her charity school the other day that might help Tom understand (note the commercial here for educating little girls and for charity schools!): it seems the limbs decide one day that they will not feed that lazy stomach, who just sits there and doesn't work. The feet won't carry him around and the hands won't work "to feed this lazy belly, who sits in state like a lord, and does nothing. . . . [S]o said all the members; just as your levellers and republicans do now." The tummy of course is "pinched," but the limbs find themselves in dire condition "and would have died, if they had not come to their senses just in time to save their lives, as I hope all you will do."

Next Tom brings up the subject of taxes and in return gets a lecture on civic responsibility and economics. Jack admits that

"Things are dear," but he warns that "riot and murder" don't make them cheaper, and that, in fact, civil disorder brings ever higher costs: "the more we riot, the more we shall have to pay." The tax burden is equitable here in England, with each paying a share, unlike France, where "the poor paid all the taxes . . . and the quality paid nothing"—precisely the opposite of the argument Paine makes that in France the tax burden is far less than in England, and that in England the rich get by without paying their share of taxes because it is the rich who make the laws. Jack admits that taxes are high, but he contends that much of the tax burden goes to paying off old debts, and the current government is not responsible for those. Besides, things are getting better for the poor, and "if the honest gentleman who has the management of things is not disturb'd by you levellers, things will mend every day." Jack eventually brings to mind Candide, but there is one very important difference: More wants her audience to take Jack at his word.

For Jack, this England is the best of all possible worlds, if those naughty levelers would just stop shaking the foundation. And the foundation of this world is the order imposed by hierarchy. But that is the problem, for "Levellers" by definition want to do away with hierarchy. And so Tom asserts, "I know what's what, as well as another; and I am as fit to govern." Again Jack answers him patiently. To be as good as any man does not mean to be the same. You are as good as any one, he tells Tom; you can work and you have a soul. But different men have different talents, and these must be respected. Jack is a "better judge of a horse-shoe than Sir John," but Jack is not so fit to govern. Indeed, each needs the other. And most of the poor can vote, "and so you see the poor have as much share in the government as they well know how to manage."

As for equality, and one man being above another, that question Tom must take up "with Providence, and not with government. For the woman is below her husband, and the children are below their mother, and the servant is below his master." In two sentences, More here sums up her entire moral and social philosophy; this belief in hierarchy is at the heart of her life view. Tom Paine, the French revolt, Mary Wollstonecraft, anything that challenges the order of the world as More and her friends perceive it, is execrable precisely because it challenges an order that Providence itself has decreed. All of More's written works and public projects are in support of the status quo. The poor are not to be taught to write, only to read enough to deal with properly moral and religious texts, because to be able to write would present the potential for altering their state in life; such change would go against the divine plan. Inherent in the social order is the concept of the royal family at its head. We remember Tom Paine's argument that kings are men like any other, just more greedy and less useful. He takes away the "God-ordained" rationale and finds a fraud; More sees even the questioning of a divinely ordered structure as threatening the whole of moral order. So when Tom answers Jack's accounting of the social hierarchy by arguing that "the subject is not below the king: all kings are 'crowned ruffians;' and all governments are wicked," Jack resorts to the Christian rules. This is nonsense, he tells Tom; if you went to Church more often, you would remember the injunction to "'Render unto Caesar the things that are Caesar's; and also, 'Fear God; honour the king.'" Tom's book, that evil thing of Paine's, is contrasted with Jack's book, the Bible.

Tom's book tells him that we need to obey "no government but that of the people; and that we may fashion and alter the government according to our whimsies," but the Bible says that everyone is "'subject to the higher powers, for all power is of God; the powers that be are ordained of God; whosoever therefore resisteth the power, resisteth the ordinance of God.'" More brings the full weight of religion to bear on the question of civil disobedience. To rebel against the king is to challenge God himself; to refuse to pay civil taxes goes against religion, in a quite literal sense. "Dost thou know who it was that worked a miracle, that he might have money to pay tribute with, rather than set you and me an example of disobedience to government?" Jack asks Tom. If this is heavy-handed, it is also direct. Paying taxes is a religious duty; to challenge the right of the government to demand taxes is to challenge the authority of God.

Tom, in his usual way, stubbornly ignores Jack's lecture, insisting that he will never be happy until "we do as the French have done." We need "a new *constitution*—that's all." Like a mantra, to whatever argument Jack makes, Tom keeps repeating, "I should like to do as they do in France." The more Tom disregards Jack's answers, the more the reader sees Tom as unreasonable and the more France comes to embody everything that is terrible. Jack ticks off what life in merry old England would be like if the English were to change over to things as they are done in France. This is, all in all, the heart of More's argument: "What, shouldst like to be murdered with as little ceremony as Hackabout, the butcher, knocks down a calf? or shouldst like to get rid of thy wife for every little bit of a tiff? And as to liberty of *conscience,* which they brag so much about, why they have driven away their parsons, ay, and murdered many of 'em, because they would not swear as they would have them. And then they talk of liberty of the press; why, Tom, only t'other day they hanged a man for printing a book against this pretty government of theirs." France is really frightening. A man can get killed, he can lose his wife, there's no religion—clearly things are better in England. And if some things really did need changing in France, that's no reason why perfectly sound English institutions should be destroyed.

Even if the English upper class is in need of some reform, that's between them and their God. Any sins of theirs will be answered for "in another place." Jack admits to Tom that "as to our great folks, . . . I don't pretend to say they are a bit better than they should be," but he insists "that's no affair of mine" for "*hoarding's* not the sin of the age." The money of the rich circulates through the economy, "and every body's the better for it." It is true that the rich spend too much on frippery and feasts, but, as for himself, "a poor tradesman, why 'tis but bringing more grist to my mill. It all comes among the people."

Jack discourses at length about the economic benefits to the poor of upper-class spending; this is a favorite theme for More. Many of the stories in the Cheap Repository Tracts will show the economic benefits for the lower classes of upper-class spending. More also discusses this issue in many of her other writings. Always, her argument is the same: the more time His Lordship spends in the countryside with "his" people, the better off the local economy will be.

> Their coaches and their furniture, and their buildings and their planting, employ a power of tradesmen and labourers. Now in this village, what should we do without the castle? Though my Lady . . . flies about all summer to hot water and cold water, and fresh water and salt water, when she ought to stay at home with Sir John; yet when she does come down, she brings such a deal

of gentry, that I have more horses than I can shoe, and my wife more linen than she can wash. Then all our grown children are servants in the family, and rare wages they have got. Our little boys get something every day by weeding their gardens; and the girls learn to sew and knit at Sir John's expense; who sends them all to school of a Sunday, besides.

Although the context for these remarks is the behavior of the poor man, More's emphasis on the place of the Great House in the local economy reminds us also of the duty of the rich to provide work for the poor. If each does his part, the one by providing work, the other by working, all will live happily, in harmony and prosperity. Note too the implication that the poor never should envy the rich but should consider themselves fortunate to have the work that the rich provide. As long as he has horses to shoe and his wife linen to wash, the poor man should be content. All of his children should work, and he is blessed if work is available not only for the older ones but for the youngest as well—each child supplied with a work that fits his capabilities. This lesson will show up in the majority of the Cheap Repository Tracts, and in fact the willingness of a child to work and of his parents to encourage him to work is one of the major characteristics that differentiates the deserving poor from their lazy and irresponsible kin. We should remark too on what it is that these fortunate children learn at the school that the good Sir John so munificently underwrites: sewing and knitting.

Tom is convinced by this last argument of Jack, but, alas, Tom laments that "there's not Sir Johns in every village." Yes, "[b]ut there's other help." The system of parish support and poor relief, Jack reminds Tom, is his whenever he is in need; go find *that* in France, he challenges. You were nine weeks in the Bristol infirmary last year, Jack says, "where you was taken as much care of as a lord, and your family was maintained all the while by the parish." Well, maybe that standard wasn't quite up to what a lord might have, but the sum of "four millions and a half for the poor every year" is impressive. When you get your "levelling . . . there will be no infirmaries, no hospitals, no charity-schools, no Sunday-schools, where so many hundred thousand poor souls learn to read the word of God for nothing. For who is to pay for them? *Equality* can't afford it; and those that may be willing won't be able." This threat, that if the social system is changed all the support for the poor man in times of trouble will disappear, seems ready at hand whenever a perceived need to keep the working man in line arises. When we turn to Josiah Wedgwood's *Address to the Workmen in the Pottery*, we will find precisely this theme of dire consequences for going against the status quo. Here in *Village Politics*, the threat also has been implicit from the beginning of the dialogue: the poor man who wants to change the English system simply cannot imagine the horrible consequences to his and his family's safety should he manage to get that which he thinks he wants.

But if naïve Tom cannot see where his ideas would lead, Jack can. We'll still have to work, Jack says, but no one will be able to pay us. And then Jack alludes directly to Paine's *Rights of Man* in a way that seems considerably more sophisticated than one would think More's intended audience could follow since it requires her reader to compare her definitions with Paine's. "I have got the use of my limbs, of my liberty, of the laws, and of my Bible," Jack tells Tom. "The two first I take to be my *natural* rights; the two last my *civil* and *religious* rights: these, I take it, are the *true Rights of Man*, and all the rest is nothing but nonsense, and madness, and wickedness." Jack's list, taking in the simple things available to all able-bodied working men in England, suggests that the elaborate distinctions Paine makes are nothing but demagoguery. Jack insists that he has "peace and thankfulness" in his cottage and the security of not living in fear. To desire equality, he says, is simply to be envious of those who are richer "in this world"; we know where that idea will lead in More's work: the good man does not desire more than he has because his place in the hierarchy is divinely ordered. Jack is a good man; "[i]nstead of indulging discontent, . . . I read my Bible, go to church, and look forward to a treasure in heaven." Poor silly Tom thinks "the French have got it in *this* world," but Jack disabuses him of this false notion. Sir John has received letters proving that in France "'Tis all murder, and nakedness, and hunger." And not only that, but ever since this Levelling came in, the French, who "used to be the merriest dogs in the world," have become positively morose!

By this point More clearly feels that she has gotten her message across. We have reached page twenty of twenty-four, and from here on she will sum up and then turn the argument around so that Tom, who has been presented not as bad but merely as mistaken in his views, will see the light and join Jack on the side of roast beef and ale. The first step in the summing up is a kind of catechism: What is French liberty? "To murder more men in one night than ever their poor king did in his whole life." What is a democrat? "One who likes to be governed by a thousand tyrants, and yet can't bear a king." Equality? "For every man to pull down every one that is above him; while, instead of raising those below him to his own level, he only makes use of them as steps to raise himself to the place of those he has tumbled down." And, Tom asks, "What is *the new Rights of Man?*" Jack's answer is "Battle, murder, and sudden death." He points out that the French have even renounced the sabbath, with their Parliament meeting on Sunday as naturally as good Englishmen go to church. And "they don't even date in the year of our Lord." This is too much for Tom, who turns pale—presumably with horror at the idea that his "Rights of Man will lead to all this wickedness." Naturally, he "begin[s] to think we're better off as we are." Even further, "I begin to think I'm not so very unhappy as I had got to fancy," he confesses to Jack.

Clearly making reference to Paine's discussion of commodity taxes and their unfair burden on the poor (specifically Paine's observation that since the rich generally brew their own beer, they essentially are untouched by taxes that are a significant charge on the poor), Jack sanctimoniously tells Tom that though he himself does not drink, he'll put the case in terms Tom can understand: "when there's all equality there will be no *superfluity!* when there's no wages there'll be no drink; and levelling will rob thee of thy ale more than the malt-tax does." This is really a quite marvelous argument on More's part in a number of ways. We should note here how carefully she is refuting the precise points that Paine makes in *Rights of Man.* One would like to know, although I have not been able to find any evidence one way or the other, whether her refutation of specific arguments, such as Paine's comments on the malt tax, comes from her own study of his pamphlet, from popular attention paid to certain of the arguments, or both. Absent a definitive statement from More or someone close to her, I think we must assume that the points she picks up are those that had been the subject of the most comment in contemporary popular discourse, as was the case with the malt tax.

Tom is convinced. Now it is his turn to sum up. This is a brilliant device, for to have the "evidence" summed up by the formerly rebellious Tom shows both that he fully understands the fallacy of his original position and that to have erred and believed the "nonsense" of Paine and his friends does not mean that the good man cannot afterward awaken to the truth. And thus Tom volunteers to "sum up the evidence, as they say at 'sizes—Hem! To cut every man's throat who does not think as I do, or hang him up at a lamp-post!—Pretend liberty of conscience, and then banish the parsons only for being conscientious!—Cry out liberty of the press, and hang up the first man who writes his mind!—Lose our poor laws!—Lose one's wife, perhaps, upon every little tiff! [This is my personal favorite.]— . . . No sabbath nor day of rest!" Tom has scared himself with this recitation, and Jack must reassure him that, fortunately, things are still fine in England. "We have a king, so loving that he would not hurt the people if he could; and so kept in that he could not hurt the people if he would. We have as much liberty as can make us happy, and more trade and riches than allow us to be good. We have the best laws in the world . . . and the best religion in the world." Tom is so moved by Jack's rousing patriotic summation—"While Old England is safe, I'll glory in her, . . . and when she is in danger, I'll fight for her, and die for her"—that he breaks into song: "O the Roast Beef of Old England."[7] And now, for More, there is only one more item on the agenda.

For if Tom has been saved and no longer poses a threat to Old England, there are still others who do. More must show a delicate balance here. Her readers must be pumped full of patriotic fervor so that they will be impervious to the dangerous arguments of the those who would have them follow the French ways, but she does not want to encourage violence and civil unrest in the course of the correction. Tom has a tendency—as More and her friends undoubtedly fear too many of the laboring and poor have—to swing too far in any direction. And so Tom's response to his new understanding is to go along to the tavern and "put an end to" the work of those who would incite to revolution. All well and good. But first he wants to "burn my book, and then I'll go and make a bonfire and—." Jack, ever level-headed, puts a stop to these enthusiasms. No, he says, let's be moderate and reasonable; not to be so, is to be not a friend but an enemy to your country: "There is but one thing worse than a bitter enemy—and that is an imprudent friend. If thou wouldst show thy love to thy king and country, let's have no drinking, no riot, no bonfires; but . . . 'Study to be quiet, work with your own hands, and mind your own business.'" And Tom, who has become the model More wishes all those troublemakers would turn into, meekly says, "And so I will, Jack." And off they go to the tavern to tamp down the fires of ill-considered revolt.

We don't have much firsthand evidence of how the intended audience for *Village Politics* received More's little work, but her friends are delighted with it. More's circle, as we have seen, was horrified by the events in France, and at times More's own letters strike precisely the tone of shocked disbelief at the displacement of common sense and supposedly commonly held values that Jack shows in *Village Politics*. On March 20, 1790, More writes to one of her sisters, "Things are getting worse and worse in France. A lady of quality the other day in Paris, rung her bell, and desired the footman to send up her maid Jeannotte. In vain she rung and rung; the man told her, Jeannotte refused to come; or be any longer under any body. At last Jeannotte walked into the room with a pamphlet open in her hand, and sat down. The lady astonished, asked her what she meant. '*C'est que je lise,*' said Jeannotte, without taking her eyes off the book. The lady insisted on an explanation of this impertinence. The maid replied with great sang froid, '*Madame, c'est que nous allons tous devenir egaux, et je me prepare pour l'egalité.*' I have conceived an utter aversion to liberty according to the present idea of it in France" (II, 225), More ends. I have noted repeatedly the fear that More evinces of the power of the wrong written words in the hands of those too easily swayed by them. My last chapter will explore in some detail the belief of More and her contemporaries that written words could work extraordinary changes both in individuals and in society. As I show in that discussion, and as has been evident in my analysis of *Rights of Man* and *Village Politics*, this perception of the potency of words is the same on both sides of the political divide.

Perhaps the most clever response to *Village Politics* comes from the bishop of London. Addressed to "My Dear Mrs. Chip," he tells More, "I have this moment received your husband's Dialogue, and it is supremely excellent. I look upon Mr. Chip to be one of the finest writers of the age; this work alone will immortalize him; and what is better still, I trust it will help to immortalize the constitution. If the sale is as rapid as the book is good, Mr. Chip will get an immense income, and completely destroy all equality at once. How Jack Anvil and Tom Hod will *bear* this, I know not, but I shall rejoice at Mr. Chip's elevation, and should be extremely glad at this moment to shake him by the hand, and ask him to take a family dinner with me. . . . I have kept your secret religiously" (II, 348). Roberts notes that a few days later Porteus sends another note: "'Village Politics' is universally extolled, it has been read and greatly admired at Windsor, and its fame is spreading rapidly over all parts of the kingdom. I gave one to the Attorney General, who has recommended it to the Association at the Crown-and-Anchor, which will disperse it through the country. Mr. Cambridge says that Swift could not have done it better. I am perfectly of that opinion. It is a masterpiece of its kind. I congratulate myself on having drawn forth a new talent in you, and on having thereby done much service to my country" (II, 348).

If there was any doubt that More's work is part of a concerted effort to try to control the potential unrest of the laboring classes, we have here Porteus' documentation of the paths of More's pamphlet. It has gone to Windsor, where it has met with unqualified approval; it has gone to the attorney general, who will see to it that it reaches channels of dispursement throughout the country. It is no accident that the pamphlet quickly finds its way around the nation, for formal channels are in place to see that it is disseminated swiftly and widely. Porteus feels that he has done "much service to my country" in getting More to pen this work, and his enthusiasm is shared by all of More's circle.

Elizabeth Montagu writes that "you can hardly doubt that your 'Village Politics' is allowed to have been the most generally approved and universally useful of any thing that has been published on the present exigency of the times." We should stop to note a number of things about this remark. First, it is totally political. Montagu is very concerned about the political situation, and, like Porteus, she is deeply appreciative of More's contribution. Second, Montagu clearly has been in touch with many people regarding More's pamphlet, which means that the "present exigency of the times" is a topic of immediate interest and wide discussion among her acquaintances. She goes on, "I sent many copies to all the counties where I had any correspondence, and had the satisfaction to hear of their most happy effect; particularly in Northumberland, where the worthy parson of my parish found them so useful, that he intended to get a thousand copies printed" (II, 348–49). To the official, governmental or quasi-governmental routes are added the private efforts, literally, to get the word out. Mrs. Montagu has sent copies to everyone she knows, and some, like the parson, will themselves make more copies to send the good texts on. The question of royalties does not enter into this discussion; Mrs. Montagu and the parson of her parish in Northumberland certainly do not fear that they are depriving More of her financial share in the pamphlets by having them privately reprinted for further distribution. Finally, here, it is interesting that the parson, like Bishop Porteus, is directly involved in distributing the pamphlet. The men of God recognize in themselves a duty to preserve the status quo. Mrs. Montagu devotes all but a short concluding paragraph to these accounts of politics and economics ("Speculation in politics has brought a bankruptcy on the French constitution, and speculations in trade on our bankers"). Although she is not herself writing in the pamphlet wars, Mrs. Montagu is as involved in these political debates as More.

And then there's Mrs. Boscawen, who begins *her* letter to More with an account of her own large-scale efforts to get the word out. "It must have been *instinct* then that has made me send for a quarter of a hundred more of 'Will Chip,' and still for more and more; the last bale came in yesterday, and I see they will not last the week out; I had better have had a hundred at once. Last week I sent a packet to Badminton, and my Duchess answers me thus, 'We have all read, and delight in your "Village Politics." I have not had a gross, to be sure, like this Gloucestershire gentleman, but I have had them past counting.'" She goes on to tell More about the first time she came into contact with Tom Hod and his neighbor Jack Anvil; it "was one night at Lady Cremorne's, where the Bishop of London pulled them out of his pocket, and read the delectable dialogue to us . . . and when he came to 'my lady' and sent her 'to cold water, and hot water, and salt water, and fresh water,' he could not get on at all, we laughed so immoderately." More's friends find the pamphlet delightful and amusing, and they also find it most seriously socially useful. They can appreciate More's satire on the silliness of her ladyship, but they also intensely support the message that they intend *Village Politics* to convey to those frightening masses on the verge of revolt.

The moment that Mrs. Boscawen arrived home, she says, "I wrote upon a bit of paper that minute 'A quarter of a hundred of Will Chip; or Village Politics, to be had at Rivingtons,' and this I gave to citizen Brown, and bid him carry it . . . [to her bookseller], but did not hold me (as I said) three days. I have had many re- cruits since, and must have more." She compares More's pam- phlet with *Reasons for Contentment* by Archdeacon Paley, "addressed to the labouring part of the British public," but finds More's effort much the best and so sends *Village Politics* to the person who had given her *Reasons*. More, she says, "understood the language much better; and accordingly I despatched a little packet of Will Chip, before I sat down at home." She has suppled Richmond, she says. "Our minister and our apothecary are sup- plied. . . . Mr. Rivington still dispenses them by thousands, (I hope some will go to France) and though he cannot get anything by them, nor the pleasant author, yet both will allow that this is suc- cess." This is a rather extraordinary letter, perhaps not least so in the context of recent scholarly debate about the role of women— their empowerment, if you will—in the eighteenth century. It is quite clear here that Mrs. Boscawen actively is helping to negoti- ate the dispursement of More's tract. She is sending them, in "lots," to all the influential people she knows, intending each of these people in his turn to send them on. She is aware of the nature of the work More has produced; obviously, More's was not the only pamphlet sent into the war, but it was the best tuned to the lan- guage of those it was meant to tame. Mrs. Boscawen, like Bishop Porteus, promises More her secrecy, but, as we have seen, she warns that More's kind letter acknowledging authorship came without a seal. No matter, she insists, if all those "on the road know, to whom they are indebted for this incomparable and per- fect code of Village Politics" (II, 350–52).

E. P. Thompson says that the reason revolution did not hap- pen in England in the 1790s ⋅ as that the "'natural' alliance be- tween an impatient radically ᵣinded industrial bourgeoisie and a formative proletariat was ᵦᵣoken as soon as it was formed. The ferment among the industrialists and the wealthy Dissenting tradesmen of Birmingham and the northern industrial towns be- longs in the main to 1791 and 1792; the peak of 'disaffection' among artisans and wage-earners . . . —whether caused by Jacobin agitation or by starvation—belongs to 1795. Only for a few months in 1792 do the two coincide; and after the September massacres all but a small minority of the manufacturers had been frightened by the cause of reform." And then he says something that is remarkably interesting, although I will suggest in a moment that his explanation is not quite correct. Thompson ascribes the lack of a successful revolution in England to the fear these industrialists had of their own natural allies: "If there was no revolution in England in the 1790s it was . . . because the only alliance strong enough to effect it fell apart; after 1792 there were no Girondins to open the doors through which the Jacobins might come. *If men like Wedgwood, Boulton and Wilkinson had acted together with men like Hardy, Place and Binns . . . then Pitt (or Fox) would have been forced to grant a large instalment of reform* [italics mine]. But the French Revolution *consolidated* Old Corruption by uniting landowners and manufacturers in a common panic."[8]

Thompson's assumption that the industrialists shared the fears of the landowners is surely correct, but I think that the industrialists' suspicion of the workers goes back earlier than Thomson dates it here. Isaac Kramnick makes something of the same misassessment, specifically when he discusses Josiah Wedgwood's *Address to the Young Inhabitants of the Pottery,* which Kramnick sees as a quite collegial lecture on the wondrous transformation wrought by factory masters such as Wedgwood himself. "In his lecture the great potter captured vividly the world view of Priestley's circle as they effected their revolutions in the west of England. He suggested that the workers ask their parents to compare the countryside as it now stood with what they once knew."[9] Naturally, poverty has been replaced with the affluence of wages, huts had become homes, poorly cultivated land "replaced by 'pleasing and rapid improvements.' Convinced that his young employees would agree with him that their lot was much better than that of their parents, a generation earlier," Wedgwood ascribes this progress to "industry." Kramnick goes on, "The foundation of a new England [for Wedgwood] was being laid by people who saw hard work as a commandment of God. Wedgwood, in fact, expanded the decalogue, heaping praise on workers "very good in keeping my eleventh commandment—*Thou shalt not be idle.'"

But this of course sounds very like Hannah More. All those

happy workers, working all the time, working because God (and now their industrialist boss) approves of ceaseless labor, could fit seamlessly into any of More's Tracts. Kramnick is certainly correct that this view of the worker is part of the new industrial philosophy of leaders like Wedgwood, but that philosophy itself is part of the larger sense in England that we have seen in so many contexts as defining the role of the worker and the self-image that the upper classes want to shape in him. Kramnick presents the industrialists' connection to their workers as a new way of dealing with production, labor, and the role of the laboring man in the process of reshaping not only England's economy but also her Zeitgeist, just as Thompson sees a seemingly natural affinity between the industrialists like Wedgwood, Boulton, and Wilkinson and the political dissidents that might have led to revolution if the industrialists had not been scared off by the events of the mid 1790s. But men like Wedgwood did not see the laboring class with quite so radical eyes as such discussions imply; in fact, I would argue, in many important ways these men, like the more traditional upper classes, had a distinct stake in keeping the poor working, and working on their terms. And the industrialists' "panic," to use Thompson's word, clearly would come from the same source—the fear of losing their property—that motivates More and her friends in the face of the Painite campaigns.

Thus when Kramnick quotes Wedgwood on the sanctity of property, in the context of our discussion of More we may put a different spin on Wedgwood's address than might seem obvious if we look at Wedgwood, as Kramnick does, only within the context of the new, radical industrialism. Kramnick notes that the "rest of [Wedgwood's *Address to the Young Inhabitants*] outlined what was necessary to ensure that this seemingly boundless improvement would continue. First, of course, the workers must respect the property that rightfully belonged to the masters; they must not, that is, destroy the machines. The industrialist Wedgwood articulated the liberal theory of the state as he digressed into political theory. 'If property is not secure there would be an end to all government, an end to the state. No man could be secure in the enjoyment of the fruits of his labor for a single day, no man, therefore, would labor . . . without the hopes of reaping for himself and being protected in his property.'" If this does not sound enough like More in *Village Politics* and later in the Cheap

Repository Tracts, we continue with what Kramnick says is Wedgwood's "final requirement for continued progress . . . the proper ordering of [the workers'] own lives. . . . And so Wedgwood turned to middle-class ethical theory. 'If a married man can maintain a wife and four or five children with no more than you do . . . who have only themselves to provide for, surely some small weekly saving may be made, which, I can promise you, you will afterwards find the comfort of, when you marry, and have a house to furnish, and other things to provide for a wife and growing family. Most of you visit public houses, wakes, and other places where TIME AND MONEY IS WASTED and where you acquire habits in your youth which entail poverty and distress on those who depend on you later.'"

As we will see when we turn to the Tracts of the Repository, these are precisely the tenets that More will set out for her poor people and laborers. These precepts cross class and political boundaries; the late eighteenth-century Englishman's view of the poor is much more dependent on his finances than his class or political affiliations. And thus I think it is worth spending some time with Wedgwood's less-often studied lecture, *An Address to the Workmen in the Pottery, on the Subject of Entering into the Service of Foreign Manufacturers*, published the same year as the *Address to the Young Inhabitants*, 1783.[10] For in the *Address to the Workmen* the tone of threat is remarkably similar to that More will use nine years later in *Village Politics*. One wrong step, Wedgwood warns, and the misguided workman will regret his blunder all his life— may even lose his life because he had acted wrongly.

The mistake, Wedgwood cautions, would be to run away to some other country, America or France, for example, in the pursuit of higher wages. We understand why Wedgwood would not want this sort of exodus: not only does he need his labor force, he also needs to safeguard his industrial process. But these are not the arguments he makes to the workers, of course. For them he first draws the picture of the promised land of an England they already enjoy, and then he shows them the horrors of "abroad." The arguments are very much the same as those More will make in *Village Politics*, as is the level of the logic used. Addressing his "countrymen and friends," Wedgwood notes that recently there have been attempts to "seduce" them into "the service of foreign manufacturers." He is "fully persuaded it would be contrary to your own interest, as well as that of your country, to accept such offers." Wedgwood's England, like More's, is a virtual paradise for the laborer. Potters especially get high wages, and all men when sick or past labor are better treated here in England than anywhere else. Wedgwood sounds just like More's Jack: "It may with great truth be asserted, that higher wages are given to manufacturers, particularly to potters, and that greater care is taken of the poor when sick or past labour, in England, than in any other part of the world." Notwithstanding this truth, many men have succumbed to the lures of foreign service, "the flattering promises held forth to them having got the better of their discretion." These are not the sort of people you want to be, Wedgwood cautions his listeners. "These people have indeed, generally, been of the looser kind, such as no advantages could satisfy at home," and they have gotten their just desserts. In the end, they've been "miserably deceived" by the promises they have believed. Their sufferings, in fact, are so severe that they are more like story than reality: "If I was able to give you an account of all these emigrations of our workmen into foreign parts, with the severe distresses they have fallen into, it would look more like romance than real history." He will content himself just with two or three real-life cases of men who chose to go to America.

There was, for example, a Mr. Bartlem, a master potter, who seventeen years ago, having been unsuccessful here, "went to South Carolina, and by offers made from thence, very advantageous in appearance, prevailed upon some of our workmen to leave their country and come to him." They were "puffed up with expectations of becoming gentlemen soon." Note the disapproval implicit here in the very idea that these workmen thought it possible that they might soon become gentlemen. The fact that they think in such terms is itself a hint that they will come to no good, and sure enough, not only do they suffer, they also entice their friends and family to ruin. They write to their friends to come over too, and so others follow these first miscreants. "But change of climate and manner of living, accompanied perhaps with a certain disorder of mind to be mentioned hereafter, (which have always made great havock among the people who have left this country to settle in remote parts) carried them off so fast, that recruits could not be raised from England sufficient to supply the places of the dead men. In Mr. Godwin's own words to me, whose son was one of them, *they fell sick as they came, and all died quickly*, his son amongst the rest."

And then there's the sad case of Mr. Lymer's family. Lymer, "at the solicitation of his brother-in-law [Mr. Bartlem]," goes over with his wife and children and all their effects. They are besieged by stormy weather and shipwrecked. Most of the sailors drown, but the family miraculously survives. However, although they have their lives, they find themselves "destitute of every necessary but the clothes that covered them." Mr. Lymer, his wife, and the two children they took with them, all fall sick and follow the rest of their countrymen into an untimely grave. Mr. Bartlem goes back to England to gather a new crop of recruits, "but the event of this expedition was only more labour and lives lost."

While this is going on in Carolina, an "equally fatal" mission is underway in Pennsylvania. "Here a sort of China ware was aimed at, and eight men went over at first." The outcome is basically the same: when the "proprietors" realize they have no chance of making the project successful, they silence their protesting workmen by having one of them jailed. "[T]he rest who had never received half the wages agreed for, were left entirely to shift for themselves. Thus abandoned, at the distance of some thousands of miles from home, and without a penny in their pockets, they were reduced to the hard necessity of begging in the public streets for a morsel of bread." The workmen, abandoned by their employer, have no recourse but to beg. The possibility that they might have looked for another job does not seem to occur to Wedgwood, or at least he does not want it to occur to his listeners. Rather, of course, Wedgwood's workers should realize just how fortunate they are to have him, and the whole parish system behind him, to support them. The men who were foolish enough to leave England for the promises of higher wages in Pennsylvania die for their foolishness. "Some died immediately, of sickness occasioned by this great change in their prospects and manner of living, being dashed at once from the highest expectations to the lowest and most abject misery." (Even to die of a reversal in love would seem exaggerated; to die of a reversal in employment seems, well, like a threat that Hannah More might make.) Attempts are made to help the survivors of this first wave of deaths by getting up a subscription to supply them "with daily bread." But it is not food alone that they require: "like plants removed into a soil unnatural to them, they dwindled away and died, and not one was left alive, to return and give us any farther particulars of this affecting tale."

These are very frightening stories. Wedgwood won't comment on them further, he says, except "I might here call upon you to reflect on the fate of those, who could not content themselves with the good things of their own land, a land truly *flowing with milk and honey*." Pay heed, he says, if you wish "to escape the like fatal consequences." Having appealed to his workers' fears and emotions, for a moment (a relatively brief moment in this speech), Wedgwood appeals to their reason. The masters abroad must be in their business to make money; this would be difficult to do as long as the English send to them a cheaper and better commodity, and since the foreigners offer double the English wages, the English commodities must be cheaper than theirs. In fact, it seems the wages offered are six times what native workers are paid—"the improbability of such offer being made good will appear . . . manifest."

If you were "unfortunate enough" to be engaged and "carried away" to work abroad, "what may we reasonably expect the consequences would be?" The masters undoubtedly would train up local apprentices; after this was done, why would they pay foreigners six times the local wage? In fact, the likelihood is that, as people generally favor their own, local wages would soon be higher than those paid to foreigners. From here it's a slippery slope downward. "And such low wages would afford but miserable subsistence to Englishmen, brought up, from their infancy, to better and more substantial fare than frogs, hedge-hogs, and the wild herbs of the field!" Wedgwood descends to simple, though rousing, demagoguery. You get angry at the idea "of such wages and such fare," and you say, "*No! At the worst we can but leave them, and their country, when they attempt to reduce our wages.*" But "under arbitrary governments abroad" the masters have ways to keep "those whom they do not chuse to part with; such as inducing them to run in debt, and arresting them for the same; which is a trap that would too easily be fallen into by those who are not content with the wages they get amongst us." Something terrible will happen to you, both Wedgwood and More tell working people, if you are not content with what you have and if you act on that discontent. Wedgwood carries the threat yet further, warning that even if the worker manages to evade this trap of debt, the riled masters simply can call forth the government's power to jail the miscreant worker, even to jail him for life, for industrial espionage: having learned the local manufacturing secrets, the worker would not be allowed to carry those secrets from the country.

It is really, really frightening out there, Wedgwood insists. In France, armed with "a sort of warrant called a *Lettre de cachet*," an officer can rouse even "the first Lord of the land" from his bed, take him from his family, at midnight, to take him to prison. What, then, could happen to a poor workman! And even if you aren't arrested, you won't be able to leave the country anyway. Your description will be at every border-crossing point, your accent and your visage will gave you away. There will be no escape. Wedgwood's arguments build to a peak of terror. Trapped in the loathsome foreign place, "outcasts in a strange land," not least among the horrors will be the inability to communicate in a language not your own: "To whom . . . you cannot unbosom yourselves, nor tell your complaints; nor, if you could, would they care for them." The natives of this foreign land would look on the newcomers with disdain since they are by definition not good citizens, having deserted their own nation, *"endeavoured to ruin its manufactures, and to bring the greatest evil in your power upon the state and neighborhood where you first drew your breath."* All this evil would result, Wedgwood tells his by now presumably terrified audience, because they had *"disregarded the interests of [the] neighbours and friends whom you left behind, and, like Esau, sold your birthright for a mess of pottage. . . .* In this foreign land then, suspected, watched, despised, and insulted, you must continue to the end of your wretched days." Surely, every man listening by now must have begun to cry for his mother's comforting touch. And, indeed, the contrast with what these workers actually have, against what they will get if they venture to stir, is explicit, for "in old England, in Staffordshire, you were happily placed amidst populous and thriving towns and manufactures; —amongst people of the same religion, speaking the same language, and brought up in the same habits of life, as yourselves;—amongst neighbours . . . [and] relations and dearest friends, daily interchanging mutual good offices of love and affection."

One would think that Wedgwood is satisfied by now that he has made his point, but actually he is not quite through. For, he reminds his audience, until now he has been talking about men in

the prime of life, "whilst in full health and vigour." What about
when you are sick; what about when you are old? Like More,
Wedgwood too uses the argument that the parish relief system
gives extraordinary security to the worker, to the poor or down at
luck; and if the parish officers refuse you the aid you have coming, "a magistrate will oblige them to grant it to you." The clincher,
of course, is that "abroad, you will meet with no such institutions
as ours." And even more horribly, not only does "abroad" leave a
man without living wages when healthy and without support
when he is sick or old, it also leaves him heart-sick, for "besides
bodily sickness, there is a disease of the mind, peculiar to people
in a strange land; a kind of heart-sickness and despair, with an
unspeakable longing after their native country; not to be described,
and of which no one can have a just idea but those who have been
under its influence." This horrid mind-sickness attacks even the
casual traveler, but for he who is condemned to live out his days
away from his native land, the disease can be deadly: "Most travellers have felt it, in a greater or lesser degree; many have died of
it; and those who have recovered declare it to be worse than death
itself."

   After this long emotional argument, it comes out that these
have not been theoretical bogeymen Wedgwood has been con-
structing, for apparently there have been actual attempts to steal
away workers by one Mr. Shaw who comes again and again on
such errands from his foreign masters. Wedgwood portrays Shaw
as a deserter from the army who, as such, has "forfeited [his life]
to his country" and thus has no choice but to attempt to curry
favor with his new masters since he has no home to which he can
return. Even so, Shaw is not so hard-hearted a wretch that he does
not shed tears himself at the thought of leaving home once more;
these tears, Wedgwood concludes, give a "sure pledge of that distress which by following his example you will unavoidably be
led into." Wedgwood has threatened his men with the direst horror, even death itself, if they leave their employment in England
to search for higher wages abroad. He has put before them the spectre of evil even worse than death, of emotional privation so intense
that it would make death by comparison seem a lesser fate.

   All of these arguments have dealt with the harm that the
individual would bring on himself if he should go off to America
or France. But Wedgwood has not yet appealed to the men's bet-

ter instincts, to their patriotism, their sense of responsibility to their native land and to their fellows. This appeal he saves for last. You must be fully convinced that it would be folly to leave, he says; but what if, indeed, for some one of you personally it would be in your interest to accept one of these offers? "Would it have no weight with you to think, that you were ruining a trade, which had taken the united efforts of some thousands of people, for more than an age, to bring to the perfection it has now attained?" This attainment—the envy of all Europe—can only be destroyed, as it was created, by Englishmen. The enemy can conquer only by finding traitors from within our ranks, in industry as in military trials. Who among you could, for a "paltry addition to his own wages for a few years," betray his country and his fellow workmen? The question is meant to be rhetorical, for the answer clearly in this context is that no real Englishman possibly could be so base.

Having held out a stick to keep his workmen doing what he wants them to do, he also holds out the carrot of upholding the sanctity of England and the good character of her men. Wedgwood thus appeals to a combination of self-interest and patriotism. Pretending to present a rational argument against entering into foreign service, he instead has put forth scenarios and supposed facts intended simply to frighten his laborers out of thought. He ends his address with an appeal to them as loyal Englishmen—and with a reference to the fact that the laws of the country support everything he has been saying. The text of the laws he simply appends to the address itself. These laws, six pages of them (to eighteen pages of the address), lay out specific punishments for foreign labor, ranging from a fine not exceeding one hundred pounds for a first offense, and three months imprisonment should the fine not be paid, to twelve months for a second offense. Manufacturers who leave the dominion to exercise their trades, or "to teach any of the said trades or manufactories to foreigners," may not return home for six months after they have first been warned to desist; should they after this time continue to practice their trades abroad, they will forever be incapable either of bequeathing or of taking any legacy within the kingdom and also will forfeit all property they may have had within the kingdom. The descriptions of various permutations of this industrial misbehavior along with their punishments go on for several pages.

A final comment on Wedgwood's *Address* is that it is worth noting his assumption that the workmen could, or would, puzzle out the legal language of these appended pages. As I discussed in my chapter on Paine, the level of language relatively simple men seem to have been expected to deal with seems quite impressive. If Wedgwood's own address brings matters down to broad strokes and bold simplifications, his supporting material would demand a good deal of a reader. But even if he did not seriously intend that these legal pages be read, they surely would have served the purpose for which they were intended, that is, to intimidate. As we will see in the following chapters on the Tracts of the Cheap Repository, threats very similar to Wedgwood's appear frequently in More's stories as she, from her side of the political divide, works hard to keep the poor from revolt.

# Six

# Social and Political Circumstances

## More's Cheap Repository Tracts

> To be enabled to acquire, the people, without being servile, must be tractable and obedient. . . . They must respect that property of which they cannot partake. They must labour to obtain what by labour can be obtained; and when they find, as they commonly do, the success disproportioned to the endeavour, they must be taught their consolation in the final proportions of eternal justice.
>
> —Edmund Burke,
> *Reflections on the Revolution in France*

THE 1793 *VILLAGE POLITICS* is soon followed by the Tracts of the Cheap Repository beginning in March 1795. Jonathan Wordsworth sees the Tracts as a response to Paine's *Age of Reason*,[1] but they clearly deal with many of the issues raised in *Rights of Man*, as the "Preface" to *Village Politics: Addressed to All the Mechanics, Journeymen, and Labourers, in Great Britain* in the collected edition of 1830 makes clear: "Those who remember the beginning of the French Revolution need not be reminded how much the lower classes of this country were in danger of being infected with the principles which occasioned it. The effects of those principles began to be actually and seriously felt at home. The alarm was aggravated by the eager circulation of numerous Tracts subversive of all government, social order, and religion. By the activity of Paine and his adherents these were not only dispersed in the cottage and the work-shop, but found in great numbers of the public roads, and at the bottom of mines and coal-pits. At this crisis some persons of high eminence, both in church and state, prevailed on the Author to use her humble efforts to aim at counteracting these pernicious publications by Tracts of an opposite tendency. This little piece was hastily written, and many hundred thousand copies were circulated in a short time. The language was adapted to the readers for whom it was chiefly intended. Many of the terms, happily, will now be scarcely understood, but were then but too intelligible. The success of this little tract encouraged her to pursue the idea, and the establishment of the Cheap Repository was the consequence."[2]

The Cheap Repository Tracts are directed to the poor; written over a period of three years, and hugely successful, the volumes consist of stories, poems, and analyses of biblical stories and parables, all directed to making the poor more sober, industrious, pious—and politically inert. Most of the stories teach the poor how to make do within their poverty, and show the poor how very satisfied they should be with their place in society; a few of the tales illustrate how the poor man or woman can, by dint of application to a trade, actually move up in society, always, of course, without losing sight of the strict moral code that allowed him, or very occasionally her, this success. The goal of education for young girls, in general, is to make them into better servants and better wives for poor men; it is not meant to lift them from their poverty, or to give them any ideas about changing their social state. In fact, not only is such change for poor men and women not part of the agenda of the benevolent, but it would be rejected by the deserving poor if offered. Thus, the "deserving poor" man would be willing to accept enough help to arrange a subsistence for himself and his family, with a dry hovel to shelter them, but, to be deserving, he also should reject any suggestion of more aid.

These are the lessons of perhaps the best known of the Cheap Repository Tracts, "The Shepherd of Salisbury Plain," which begins with "Mr. Johnson, a very worthy charitable gentleman,"[3] coming upon a shepherd "busily employed with his dog in collecting together his vast flock of sheep" (398). Mr. Johnson notices immediately that the shepherd's clothes, while denoting his poverty, are well mended, patched, and cleaned, and he remarks to himself on the good housewife to whom the shepherd must be married. Mr. Johnson "perceived [the shepherd] to be a clean, well-looking, poor man near fifty years of age. His coat, though at first it had probably been of one dark colour, had been in a long course of years so often patched with different sorts of cloth, that it had now become hard to say which had been the original color. But this, while it gave a plain proof of the shepherd's poverty, equally proved the exceeding neatness, industry, and good management of his wife" (398–99).

The first lesson Hannah More will teach, then, is about how the good housewife, through her hard work and management, prevents her family's poverty from being a burden to them. The responsibility for decent living is hers; the question is not one of getting more, but of making do—and doing well—with what she has. So important is this lesson that it continues for two more paragraphs before we get back to the shepherd himself. Having described the shepherd's coat, More goes on: "His stockings no less proved [his wife's] good housewifery; for they were entirely covered with darns of different-colored worsted, but had not a hole in them; and his shirt, though nearly as coarse as the sails of a ship, was as white as the drifted snow, and was neatly mended where time had either made a rent or worn it thin" (399). Not yet satisfied that her lessons on the importance of "housewifery" for the poor have been adequately underscored, More continues, "This furnishes a rule of judging by which one shall seldom be deceived. If I meet with a labourer, hedging, ditching, or mending the highways, with his stockings and shirt tight and whole, however mean and bad his other garments are, I have seldom failed, on visiting his cottage, to find that also clean and well ordered, and his wife notable, and worthy of encouragement. Whereas a poor woman, who will be lying a-bed, or gossiping with her neighbors when she ought to be fitting out her husband in a cleanly manner, will seldom be found to be very good in other respects" (399). The irony that many feminist studies[4] discuss Hannah More as an early feminist is powerful, for More, of course, says that women, especially poor women, should be something quite close to the servants of their husbands. While the poor man should be happy with his subservient and often dependant state, the poor woman is doubly subservient, for she is at the disposal of her husband as well as of his masters. Her job is to "fit out her husband" and keep his cottage clean with whatever means she has.

These themes are repeated often in the Cheap Repository Tracts. The stories are directed to the poor primarily and to those better off who may come in contact with them. The stories tell the poor how to behave and those who would be their benefactors how to help them to be productive in their poverty. And so Mr. Johnson is "not more struck with the decency of [the shepherd's] mean and frugal dress, than with his open honest countenance, which bore strong marks of health, cheerfulness, and spirit" (399). The poor in More's stories generally exhibit good health and cheerfulness as long as they behave properly, that is, as long as they are satisfied with their poverty, work hard, give themselves no airs and have no pretensions to luxuries (or even necessities) above their station, and, of course, as long as they are good Christians. One of More's primary purposes in the Tracts is to foster appreciation of and belief in Christianity, and she ties poverty and belief together at every point. Belief supports poverty, making any burden not merely less irksome but simply not burdensome at all.

Thus "The Shepherd of Salisbury Plain" turns from the Shepherd's orderly outward appearance directly to that inner state so well represented by his outward demeanor. The shepherd, we are not surprised to hear, is fully satisfied with his lot in life, since this is what God has given him. Mr. Johnson remarks, "'Yours is a troublesome life,'" and the shepherd responds, "'To be sure, sir . . . 'tis not a very lazy life; but 'tis not near so toilsome as that which my GREAT MASTER led for my sake, and he had every state and condition of life at his choice . . . while I only submit to the lot that is appointed me'" (400–401). Not only is the shepherd happy to accept "the lot that is appointed to me," but he finds that, all in all, whatever he has turns out for the best. When Mr. Johnson comments, "'You are exposed to great cold and heat,'" the shepherd assures him that although that surely is true, on the other hand,

> "I am not exposed to great temptations; and so throwing one thing against another, God is pleased to contrive to make things more equal than we poor, ignorant, short-sighted creatures are apt to think. David was happier when he kept his father's sheep

on such a plain as this . . . than ever he was when he became king of Israel and Judah."

"You think, then . . . that a laborious life is a happy one."

"I do, sir; and more so especially, as it exposes a man to fewer sins." (401)

In fact, the shepherd goes on, "'I wonder all working men do not derive as great joy and delight as I do from thinking how God has honoured poverty. Oh! sir, what great, or rich, or mighty men have had such honour put on them, or their condition, as shepherds, tent-makers, fishermen, and carpenters have had?'" (402).

With the biblical references, More ties poverty to virtue, even to holiness. And how does the shepherd come by his knowledge of scripture? The shepherd tells Mr. Johnson, "'I learnt to read when I was a little boy; though reading was not so common when I was a child . . . [as] through the goodness of Providence and the generosity of the rich, it is likely to become now-a-days'" (403). The "generosity of the rich" is a theme that More comes back to over and over in these Tracts. Conveniently, this generosity costs very little and is directed to such "help" as keeps the poor "good" and working. More's concept of appropriate aid to the poor is directly tied to religion; it is through the lessons of religion that the poor shall be taught to be virtuous, and part of this virtue is to be happy in their poverty and grateful for such help as will make that poverty bearable. All More's lessons are directed to helping the poor to understand that poverty is a fine and respectable state; certainly the poor should not seek to gain more wealth and change their condition, a lesson that More inculcates in different ways in story after story.[5] We should note, too, the shepherd's apprecia-tion both for "the goodness of Providence" and for "the generos-ity of the rich," linking them almost as manifestations of the same power. As the story progresses, it becomes ever clearer that the small investment required to teach the poor to read enough so that they can read the Bible is an excellent investment in social harmony, although More presents it as an act of pure benevolence on the part of the better-off.

"'I believe there is no day for the last thirty years,'" the shep-herd earnestly tells Mr. Johnson, "'that I have not peeped at my Bible.'" Carefully, he explains that this reading never takes time away from his work (another theme repeated from story to story), for his reading—and thinking about the lessons to be found in the reading—takes place always in the interstices of work: "'I defy any man to say he can't find time to read a verse; and a single text, . . . well followed and put in practice every day, would make no bad figure at the year's end'" (403). As a shepherd, he often is obliged to be still "'while the flock is feeding, . . . and at such times I can now and then tap a shoe for my children or myself, which is a great savings to us; and while I am doing that, I repeat a bit of a chapter. . . . [I] have . . . often had but little to eat, but my Bible has been meat, and drink, and company to me'" (404).

Naturally, "'the promises of this book'" are a great comfort to the shepherd in his troubles which, although the shepherd says he has "'but little cause to complain, and much to be thankful'" (404), might seem significant to us. He, his wife, and his eight children live in a two-room hovel that barely has a chimney and the roof of which leaks prodigiously. But, the shepherd notes, "'many better men have been worse lodged'" (405)—in prisons and dungeons, for example—and his family doesn't need much of a chimney anyway, since "'we have seldom smoke in the evening, for we have little to cook, and firing is very dear in these parts'" (404). The only real problem is that his "poor wife is a very sickly woman," (404–5), and her health is not aided at all by the rain that beats through the thatch of the roof when she is in bed!

This exemplary woman, like her exemplary children, has no complaints. On the contrary, she repeats in several different contexts how blessed she is. The shepherd is very proud of her, for she is "'not only the most tidy, notable woman on the plain, but she is the kindest wife and mother, and the most contented, thankful Christian that I know'" (410). Struck by a "'violent fit of the rheumatism, caught by going to work too soon after her lying-in'" (410), she becomes paralyzed, losing all but the use of her hands. This is truly a blessing, as both she and her husband see the situation, for, not even able to "'turn in her bed,'" she can still "'contrive to patch a rag or two for her family'" (410). More emphasizes her point: "'She was always saying, had it not been for the great goodness of God, she might have had her hands lame as well as her feet, or the palsy instead of the rheumatism, and then she could have done nothing: but nobody had so many mercies as she had'" (410).[6]

And indeed, the "mercies" are many: a shilling from good Mr. Jenkins the minister allows the shepherd to "'buy a little ale and brown sugar to put into her water-gruel; which . . . made it nice and nourishing'" (414). And yet more wondrous, someone else bestows upon them "'two warm, thick, new blankets'" (415) and half a crown. The shepherd enthuses, "'Thus . . . have our lives been crowned with mercies. My wife got about again, and I do believe, under Providence, it was owing to these comforts; for the rheumatism . . . without blankets by night, and flannel by day, is but a baddish job, especially to people who have little or no fire. She will always be a weakly body; but, thank God, her soul prospers and is in health'" (415).

The humility and intense gratitude for any blessing that both the shepherd and his wife manifest are reflected in their children's behavior. As we have seen, the poor are supposed to work very, very hard for bare sustenance, and to be content—even to feel blessed—with whatever they have. More takes several pages of her story to delineate the proper attitudes of the deserving child who is poor. Not surprisingly, like his parents, the child is to work hard, be pious, and never question his or her own good fortune in whatever small degree that good fortune manifests itself. We first meet Molly, "a fine plump cherry-cheek little girl," as she happily runs to her father to show him "'how much I have got'" (407). Molly is ecstatic with her success, and her father is most pleased with her. The occasion of this mutual congratulation is "a small quantity of coarse wool" (407) that the child had managed to glean by "'finding what little wool the sheep may drop when they rub themselves, as they are apt to do, against the bushes. These scattered bits of wool the children pick out of the brambles; . . . they carry this wool home, and when they have got a pretty parcel together, their mother cards it'" (408–9) So even the children "'who are too little to do much work'" (408) can make themselves useful in the family economy. More footnotes this particular part of the story, assuring us that "This piece of frugal industry is not imaginary, but a real fact, as is the character of the shepherd, and his uncommon knowledge of the Scriptures" (408).

The mother cards the wool, "'for she can sit and card in the chimney-corner when she is not able to wash, or work about [the] house.[7] The biggest girl then spins it: "it does very well for us without dyeing, for poor people must not stand for the colour of their stockings. After this, our little boys knit it for themselves, while they are employed in keeping cows in the fields, and after they get home at night. As for the finer knitting the girls and their mother do, that is chiefly for sale, which helps to pay our rent'" (409).[8] The deserving poor, then, should be ready to work continuously, even in the interstices of other labor. No matter how sick or tired or young, the worker should be productively occupied. And by no means should he expect to keep the better parts of his craft: those should be sold to obtain money to keep himself afloat. The poor should be satisfied with the coarse, with the undyed stockings, while the nicer ones are sold to his "betters." Note too the emphasis on work for all the children, including even the very youngest.

Mr. Johnson, as he leaves the shepherd, "On the whole . . . was more disposed to envy than to pity the shepherd. 'I have seldom seen,' said he, 'so happy a man'" (415–16). Mr. Johnson attributes this contentment to religion: "'No, my honest shepherd, I do not pity, but I respect and even honour thee; and I will visit thy poor hovel on my return to Salisbury with as much pleasure as I am now going to the house of my friend'" (416). One of the recurring themes in eighteenth-century literature is this "respect" for the poor: the implication is that if we respect their situation, and of course if we pronounce them happy in it, we need do nothing to change it.[9] More's stories are meant to be explicitly didactic.

We should ask, then, what "The Shepherd of Salisbury Plain" is meant to teach. First of all, it teaches that those who are better off should feel no guilt about the poor; a small donation from time to time, perhaps, shows an admirable spirit of benevolence, but one wants to be careful not to be carried away and give enough significantly to change anything for the object of charity. This is intimately tied to More's equally important lesson: the poor should want no more than they have. The shepherd and his family, if they work really hard, can gather wool, card it, spin it and knit it until finally they have stockings. These are not the same stockings as the soft, dyed yarns the rich wear—but the poor should not want dyed stockings anyway. More surely does not suggest that anyone should attempt markedly to change the condition of the poor; the central comment of the story is when, as I noted earlier, Mr. Johnson explicitly says that he would not change the shepherd's lot in life. One of the remarkable aspects of eighteenth-century writing on the poor is that similar pronouncements can be found on both sides of the political spectrum. More's conservative coloring might prepare us for her bent, but surely no radical writer would insist on the glories of poverty?

Elizabeth Inchbald, member of the radical circle surrounding William Godwin, in her novel *Nature and Art* writes a scathing critique of the various corruptions in her society; among the most prominent of these is the mistreatment of the poor by the rich. Much of her novel documents these abuses. Yet, illogically, her novel ends with a paean of praise for poverty itself, a panegyric that contradicts all the social criticism in her novel. The three most appealing characters in the book, reunited at last after nineteen years of separation, sit together contentedly moralizing about rich and poor:

> "My son," said the elder Henry . . . "It is the want of industry, or the want of reflection, which makes the poor dissatisfied."
>
> "I once," replied the younger Henry, "considered poverty a curse—but after my thoughts became enlarged, and I had associated for years with the rich, and now mix with the poor, my opinion has undergone a total change". . . .
>
> "The worst is," said Rebecca, "the poor have not always enough."
>
> "Who has enough? Were we, my Rebecca, of discontented minds, we have now too little. But conscious, from observation and experience, that the rich are not so happy as ourselves, we rejoice in our lot. . . . I remember, when I first came a boy to England, the poor excited my compassion; but now that my judgment is matured, I pity the rich. I know that in this opulent kingdom, there are nearly as many persons perishing through intemperance as starving with hunger—there are as many miserable in the lassitude of having nothing to do, as there are bowed down to the earth with hard labour. . . . Add to this, that the rich are so much afraid of dying, they have no comfort in living."
>
> "There the poor have another advantage." said Rebecca, "for they may defy not only death, but every loss by sea or land, as they have nothing to lose.". . .
>
> "[T]he fault of education, of early prejudice," said the elder Henry, [is that] "our children observe us pay respect, even reverence to the wealthy, while we slight or despise the poor. The impression thus made on their minds in youth, they indelibly retain."

"Let the poor, then" (cried the younger Henry) "no more be their own persecutors—no longer pay homage to wealth—instantaneously the whole idolatrous worship will cease—the idol will be broken."[10]

The absurdities here are manifold: the comment about the poor defying death because they have nothing to lose is wonderful! Listen now to Inchbald's precisely opposite number on the political spectrum, More's friend Soame Jenyns, who in his *A Free Inquiry into the Nature and Origin of Evil* explains the advantages of poverty:

Poverty, or the want of riches, is generally compensated by having more hopes and fewer fears, by a greater share of health, and a more exquisite relish of the smallest enjoyments, than those who possess them are usually bless'd with. The want of taste and genius, with all the pleasures that arise from them, are commonly recompensed by a more useful kind of common sense, together with a wonderful delight, as well as success, in the busy pursuits of a scrambling world. The sufferings of the sick are greatly relieved by many trifling gratifications imperceptible to others, and sometimes almost repaid by the inconceivable transports occasioned by the return of health and vigour. . . . Ignorance, or the want of knowledge and literature, the appointed lot of all born to poverty . . . is the only opiate capable of infusing that insensibility which can enable them to endure the miseries of the one, and the fatigues of the other.

Like More, Jenyns would not have those better off meddle with the natural state of the poor. Ignorance "is a cordial administered by the gracious hand of providence; of which [the poor] ought never to be deprived by an ill-judged and improper education. . . . I have ever thought it a most remarkable instance of divine wisdom, that whereas in all animals, whose individuals rise little above the rest of their species, knowledge is instinctive; in man, whose individuals are so widely different, it is acquired by education; by which means the prince and the labourer, the philosopher and the peasant, are in some measure fitted for their respective situations."[11] The widespread agreement that there is nothing inherently wrong with poverty—that those better off may even find much to envy in the state of the poor—makes benevolence both easy and morally quite voluntary since if being poor is such a worthy state, those better off certainly need feel no guilt at the relative inequities in society. This is More's perspective.

The Tracts present a world of exemplary order in which it is by no means easier or more pleasant to be rich than to be poor, and in which virtue—especially Christian virtue—is itself sufficient organizing principle for all social and familial relationships. Everything is always for the best, because when bad things happen to bad people, justice is done, and when bad things happen to good people, it helps them to become even better Christians. Social hierarchy not only is recognized but applauded by More, for More sees satisfaction with one's lot as a sign of resignation to the will of God—and if God decided that someone is to be poor, then it is the poor man's duty to accept his place in the social hierarchy; even further, it is his duty to treat his betters as he would want to be treated were he in their place: he must be as honest and as productive as he possibly can be in the interests of those he serves. Much as children with parents, those in the lower reaches of society must work hard and obediently for their masters.

More insists that work, along with religion, is very good for the poor. Her preferred image of the poor is of constant work, even their "leisure" passed in work. Poor children should be set to work as soon as they are able to toil. Only this kind of poor family, More teaches in story after story, is worth the richer person's compassion and aid. Poor people who do not work all the time and who do not keep themselves and their (few) possessions in as good repair as possible, do not deserve and should not expect help from those above them. Thus in the story "Black Giles the Poacher: Containing Some Account of a Family Who Had Rather Live by Their Wits than Their Work," we know at once that "Poaching Giles" and his family can't be worth much because his is "that mud cottage, with the broken windows, stuffed with dirty rags. . . . You may know the house at a good distance by the ragged thatch on the roof, and the loose stones which are ready to drop out from the chimney."[12] More explains that "a short ladder, a hod of mortar, and half an hour's leisure time, would have prevented all this, and made the little dwelling tight enough" (IV, 115). But More is quite sure it is not carelessness only that makes Giles neglect his house. He thinks the appearance of disrepair and need will attract compassion. Not so, insists More. This kind of sloppiness only excites disgust in the rich. "Giles fell into that common mistake, that a beggarly looking cottage, and filthy ragged children, raised most compassion, and of course drew most charity. But as cunning as he was in other things he was out in his reckoning here; for it is neatness, housewifery, and a decent appearance, which draw the kindness of the rich and charitable, while they turn away disgusted from filth and laziness; not out of pride, but because they see that it is next to impossible to mend the condition of those who degrade themselves by dirt and sloth; and few people care to help those who will not help themselves" (116).

More's assumptions here are central to her view of the compact between rich and poor. For the rich aid to the poor is a "kindness" drawn forth by their own sense of the deserving nature of the individual case. People do not care to help those who do not seem to be making the maximum effort to help themselves. Thus, in the case of Giles and his children, the charity that they hope for is deflected by their own obvious unworthiness. Giles' "hovel" lies just near a gate through which carriages must pass as they travel from one moor to another. "To be sure it would be rather convenient when one passes that way in a carriage if one of the children would run out and open the gate"—but instead, "what does Giles do, but set all his ragged brats, with dirty faces, matted locks, and naked feet and legs, to lie all day upon a sand-bank hard by the gate, waiting for the slender chance of what may be picked up from travellers. At the sound of a carriage, a whole covey of these little scare-crows start up, rush to the gate, and all at once thrust out their hats and aprons" (116). This kind of behavior, enough to frighten the horses and certainly enough to frighten the passengers, More pronounces unacceptable. These "little idle creatures, who might be earning a trifle by knitting at home, who might be useful to the public by working in the field, and who might assist their families by learning to get their bread twenty honest ways" (117), merely lie about in the hope of a sixpence. More's language expresses contempt rather than compassion. These are "ragged brats," a "covey of . . . little scarecrows," "little idle creatures." These small children should be earning a living rather than hoping for charity. And so, "when the neighbouring gentlemen found out that opening the gate was the family trade, they soon left off giving any thing. And I myself, though I used to take out a penny ready to give, had there been only one to receive it, when I see a whole family established in so beggarly a trade, quietly put it back again in my pocket, and give nothing at all" (117). The lesson is clear: the poor by thrusting themselves in the way of the rich to demand charity will get nothing.

Thus begins More's tale of Giles the poacher, who will come to no good end, we may be sure. Giles and his family are to stand as lessons to the poor about how not to conduct themselves, but this story, like so many of the Repository Tracts, also aims to teach the rich how to act toward the poor. Thus More disapprovingly notes that Giles tries to train his children to "*tumbling* for the diversion of travellers," warning that only the "unthinking" traveler will respond to such behavior with "a reward instead of a reproof" (117–18). Even further, More wants "to put all gentlemen and ladies in mind that such tricks are a kind of apprenticeship to the trades of begging and thieving; and that nothing is more injurious to good morals than to encourage the poor in any habits which may lead them to live upon chance" (118).

Black Giles and his wife Tawny (!) Rachel are incorrigible. We know this because in addition to all the other bad things they do, not only do they not go to church, but they keep Sunday as a regular work day. In fact, since all good people are in church on Sunday, that day presents for Giles and his family an especially good opportunity to pilfer while property lies unguarded and vulnerable. Tawny Rachel uses Sunday as her one day for domestic work, washing and ironing on this day only: the rest of the week she too is busy at different scams. Giles and Rachel are thoroughly corrupt; she even steals a pair of shoes the kindly minister has given to her son Dick. Dishonest themselves—Giles as ratcatcher *plants* rats to make sure of an adequate population for him to catch—they train their children to be dishonest too. When that same kindly minister again shows favor to young Dick, this time giving him a job planting beans, Giles takes the beans from the contentedly working child and forces Dick to dump them on the ground rather than sow them—not forgetting to keep some for himself, however.

This is the man who turns in "poor Jack Weston, an honest fellow in the neighbourhood" (125), for poaching.

This part of the story is subtitled "The Upright Magistrate";

the magistrate is Mr. Wilson, who "was not only a pious clergy-man, but an upright justice" (124). In his character as minister, Mr. Wilson had been very kind to the needy Jack Weston. Desirous of somehow repaying that kindness, Jack in a moment of thoughtlessness knocks down a rabbit that crosses his path: he intends to present it to Mrs. Wilson who is, he knows, "fond of hare" (126). This best-case scenario—a good man poaching for a selfless reason—More takes as the occasion for a sermon on the evils of poaching. Motives are irrelevant, Justice Wilson tells Jack, as is character. The law makes poaching a crime; one who has committed a crime must be punished. Although Justice Wilson is "moved" and "touched" by Jack's story, "this worthy magistrate never suffered his feelings to bias his integrity: he knew that he did not sit on that bench to indulge pity, but to administer justice; and while he was sorry for the offender, he would never justify the offence" (126). More makes a pretense of doubting whether the poaching laws are just. ("'It is not your business nor mine, John [sic], to settle whether the game laws are good or bad. Till they are repealed we must obey them'" [127].) But it is clear that she indeed supports them: the respect for property, for More, is an absolute value. "'All property is sacred'" (128), Mr. Wilson, the justice and the minister, says flatly. More sees spiritual and temporal order as a continuum: Mr. Wilson says, "'On Sunday I teach you from the pulpit the laws of God, whose minister I am. At present I fill the chair of the magistrate, to enforce and execute the laws of the land. Between those and the others there is more connection than you are aware'" (126–27).

The smallest transgression against the laws of property is profoundly dangerous, for, unchecked, it will lead irrevocably to a criminal career: "'There is hardly any petty mischief that is not connected with the life of a poacher'" (124). Mr. Wilson explains to Jack, "'With poaching much moral evil is connected; a habit of nightly depredation; a custom of prowling in the dark for prey produces in time a disrelish for honest labour. . . . He who begins with robbing orchards, rabbit-warrens, and fish-ponds, will probably end with horse stealing or highway robbery. Poaching is a regular apprenticeship to bolder crimes. He whom I may commit as a boy to sit in the stocks for killing a partridge may be likely to end at the gallows for killing a man'" (127–28). Jack, then, is lucky to have been caught and punished and thus turned away from this evil course, for though it takes him nearly a year to work off the debts he incurs to prevent his going to prison, he "began to think more seriously than he had ever yet done, and grew to abhor poaching, not merely from fear but from principle" (129).

More is educating and warning the poor here, a stance that is typical of these tales. Throughout the Cheap Repository Tracts More's aim is to teach the poor how to behave so that they can be productive and decent citizens within their social level. Far better, she insists time and again, for the poor man to behave properly from his conviction that such behavior is moral; but always standing next to this moral suasion is the explicit threat of punishment from society if he transgresses. The nature of the social contract is absolute: it does not matter that Justice Wilson knows Jack to be of good character, nor even that the intention of Jack's action was itself benevolent. The law is the law. We should note too the degree of horror that More tries to inculcate for the specifically lower-class crime of poaching. As in her stories that deal with servants and their responsibilities towards their masters, More's point is always that the poor not only must respect but in fact should safeguard the property of their betters—Jack Weston learns his lesson and goes on to prosper. Black Giles dies in misery as the result of injuries he causes himself while attempting a robbery. Justice in the Cheap Repository Tracts is absolute.

But while punishment is inevitable, reform, especially for the not-yet-hardened reprobate, is possible. And it is the duty of the upper classes to attend to these reforms whenever a likely object presents itself. Thus Mr. Wilson repeatedly has given his attention to young Dick, one of Giles' children. This sort of intervention does work, even in the face of such a totally pernicious education in theft and immorality as Dick had received. Giles and his family pillage the orchard of a poor widow as she sits at church; when it seems likely that they will be caught, they cast suspicion on an innocent youth, Tom. Tom's well-known good character makes it unlikely that he had committed such a theft, yet the evidence of his guilt seems abundant. Dick, while not regretting his participation in the theft, yet feels pity for Tom, who had been kind to Dick on a number of occasions. Drawn the next Sabbath to the Sunday school where all the good boys are learning moral lessons along with their letters, Dick does not have the courage to enter.

Mr. Wilson encourages him to come in, and so Dick happens to be present when the schoolmaster takes for his subject matter the recent story of widow Brown and her stolen apples. When Mr. Wilson gets to the discussion of what punishment awaits Tom, the supposed thief, Dick can support his guilt no longer and to much applause cries out that "'it was father and I who stole the apples'" (144). Thus Dick shows that he can be saved. The story ends not with Giles' arrest but his death. Incorrigible, of course he must die. Jack Weston, the man we earlier saw repenting his unpremeditated poaching, ministers to the dying Giles, who had pulled a wall down upon himself in the course of a robbery. And so every aspect of the story instructs. More seems to have no sense of the heavy-handed nature of her moral tales. She sees herself in much the same role as that schoolmaster whose earnest peroration brings Dick to confess.

And so it is perhaps amusing in ending the discussion of the tale of "Black Giles the Poacher" to come back to More's description of the schoolmaster and his weekly "custom."

> It was the custom in that school . . . for the master, who was a good and wise man, to mark down in his pocket-book all the events of the week, that he might turn them to some account in his Sunday evening instructions; such as any useful story in the newspaper, any account of boys being drowned as they were out in a pleasure-boat on Sundays, any sudden death in the parish, or any other remarkable visitation of Providence; insomuch, that many young people in the place, who did not belong to the school, and many parents also, used to drop in for an hour on a Sunday evening, when they were sure to hear something profitable. (140–41)

More's tone of moral satisfaction is unmistakable: remarkable is the lack of compassion she shows for boys who drown in pleasure boats on Sundays. Such accidents provide useful instruction, indeed, pleasurable instruction, without the distraction of pity.

The continuation of the tale of Black Giles centers on his wife, "Tawney Rachel; or The Fortune Teller." Like the "Black" in Giles' name, "Tawney" here signifies moral defect, and indeed Rachel's story rings several of More's favorite themes. Repeatedly in these stories More evinces distrust of the poor: when these men and women travel through the countryside engaged in their small buyings and sellings, More recognizes a serious potential for the perpetration of various scams. Thus "Rachel travelled the country with a basket on her arm. She pretended to get her bread by selling laces, cabbage-nets, ballads, and history books, and used to buy old rags and rabbit skins. Many honest people trade in these things, and I am sure I do not mean to say a word against honest people, let them trade in what they will. But Rachel only made this traffic a pretence for getting admittance into farmers' kitchens, in order to tell fortunes" (148). The tacit warning is clear: itinerant peddlars may be honest, but there is a good chance that they may be up to no good. Fortune-telling clearly is to be frowned upon, and, even worse, the pretence of telling fortunes gives Rachel the chance to enter people's houses to steal from them. Just as a suspicion of poor people winds through these tales, so does a dubiety about the intelligence of women, especially about the ability of the good woman to see beyond the tricks of someone like Tawney Rachel who would try to take advantage of her.

The first episode of "Tawney Rachel" sees Rachel "contriv[e]" to enter a farmhouse "when she knew the master of the house was from home, which, indeed, was her usual way." The farmer's wife, Mrs. Jenkins, "was a very inoffensive, but a weak and superstitious woman" (149–50). Rachel convinces Mrs. Jenkins that if she lets Rachel leave five pieces of gold in a basin in the cellar for forty-eight hours, Mrs. Jenkins will find "a pot of money hid under one of the stones in your cellar" (150). Rachel steals the gold and is long gone by the time the scam is discovered. And how is it discovered? "When farmer Jenkins came home he desired his wife to draw him a cup of cider: this she put off doing so long that he began to be displeased" (151). As his wife continues to try to avoid entering the cellar to get his drink, he becomes really angry (More does not find his badgering of Mrs. Jenkins offensive), and Mrs. Jenkins finally tells him the story. "The farmer, who was not so easily imposed upon, suspected a trick. He demanded the key, and went and opened the cellar door: there he found the basin, and in it five round pieces of tin covered with powder. Mrs. Jenkins burst out a crying; but the farmer thought of nothing but of getting a warrant to apprehend the cunning woman" (151–52). The farmer, being male, is "not so easily imposed upon" (152) as his wife; while she stands helplessly and uselessly crying, his thought is practical. Good women, More shows, are often credulous, superstitious, and impractical. Tawny Rachel, in order to practice her nefarious tricks, knows to wait until the men have left home so that she can prey on the women.

More makes this point about weak-brained and weak-willed women often; if she cannot find a rational story line, she simply adds on episodes, as she does in the story of "Tawney Rachel" when the example of Mrs. Jenkins is followed by the story of poor Sally Evans. "Sally was as harmless a girl as ever churned a pound of butter; but Sally was credulous, and superstitious" (152). Sally attends to every omen. The moles on her cheek have meaning; the way a plant grows is significant. Her superstitions even impinge on her work, for "[p]oor Sally had so many unlucky days in her calendar, that a large portion of her time became of little use, because on these days she did not dare to set about any new work" (153). This inability to work properly is very important to More, who is always concerned that the poor can be distracted in one way or another from their labor. Sally allows Tawney Rachel to convince her that she is fated to marry not the upstanding young man who loves her and whom she loves, but a stranger whom she will know by a sign that she can learn (for money, of course) from Tawny Rachel. Sally pays and gives up her good young man for Rachel's partner. After he takes her money and deserts her, Sally falls into "a deep decline, and she died in a few months of a broken heart, a sad warning to all credulous girls" (161).

More's tales are full of warnings. One of her often repeated caveats is to stay away from ballad sellers: More finds these cheaply sold ballads a significant threat to the Christian ideology she is trying to inculcate. Naturally, then, along with Rachel's other wares, she hawks "very wicked ballads to . . . children" (161). The thoroughly corrupt Rachel can only come to no good, and More indeed provides a very satisfying ending for Rachel's story. Just as Mr. Wilson is about to reprimand Rachel for selling such ballads to children, a constable and several other people come up. Among them is farmer Jenkins, who as a good citizen has "taken pains to trace her to her own parish: he did not so much value the loss of the money, as he thought it was a duty he owed the public to clear the country of such vermin" (161). Note More's language. Earlier, farmer Jenkins had called Rachel an "old witch" and an "old hag" (161). We are to have no pity for such "vermin," and, indeed, the year's imprisonment for her theft of the five pounds does not satisfy More. Rachel is convicted of another of her robberies, and "she was sentenced for this crime to Botany Bay; and a happy day it was for the county of Somerset, when such a nuisance was sent out of it" (162).

More ends the story with an explicit summing up that emphasizes the didactic intention of her tale. "I have thought it my duty to print this little history as a kind warning to all you young men and maidens not to have any thing to say to *cheats, imposters, cunning women, fortune-tellers, conjurers,* and *interpreters of dreams.* Listen to me, your true friend, when I assure you that God never reveals to weak and wicked women those secret designs of his providence" (162). This personal appeal very much represents the wise upper-class mother speaking to her not very bright lower-class children. Much comment has been devoted to the paternalistic voice of eighteenth-century society, particularly as it is seen limiting women. It thus is especially interesting to find the same tone of benevolent authority *from* a woman, and we must wonder, then, if we have been seeing the terms of eighteenth-century "paternalism" somewhat wrongly. I would suggest that in view of More's and Edgeworth's and all the other didactic writers' "advice" books we might redefine our concept of eighteenth-century paternalism as being directed at (or against) women and see at least this part of its manifestation (the limitation and prohibition of behavior) as part of an overall didactic impulse—an impulse that Paul Hunter discusses so cogently in *Before Novels.*[13]

If Black Giles, Tawney Rachel, and all those credulous females Rachel victimizes do everything wrong, all the people in "The Happy Waterman" are models of good behavior. This includes both rich and poor; as usual, the lesson to be learned is that the poor must work constantly, save rigorously, and be scrupulously honest. The rich then will be disposed kindly toward them, and although, as always, the rich are not obligated to give these people anything, when they see such industry and responsibility in the poor, the rich will be happy under appropriate circumstances to help them. "The Happy Waterman" begins with "a GENTLEMAN and lady, walking on the bank of the river Thames" (365).[14] Many of the Repository's stories begin with upper-class people accidentally coming into contact with the poor. The presence of these members of the upper class signals a lesson in right behavior: the rich characters are themselves good, moral people who can recognize and appreciate good behavior in the poor. The rich are always benevolently interested in uncovering the details of the poor man's life: no one is going to cross class lines, but there can and should be conversation across the fence. In fact, such conversation itself constitutes a benevolent gesture by the rich. Thus the "*GENTLEMAN* and lady walking on the banks of the river Thames [see] a neatly-dressed Waterman" (365); already we know that the waterman is a good man from his proper appearance. It is this proper appearance in fact that draws the gentleman and lady to engage him in conversation.

The waterman's life does not sound so "happy," although this is "the title that he had given himself." He is the sole support of a wife, five children, and his wife's parents. Before his father's death, he had assisted his father in running a small ferry; "'on his death, it was necessary (in order to pay his just debts) to sell our boat'" (365–66). More has no special compassion for such a happening. The father's debts are "just," and they must be satisfied. No pity should be wasted on such a situation even if clearing the father's debt takes away a whole family's livelihood. And the young boatman feels no anger at his loss—only a firm determination to earn enough to buy back his boat. He tells the gentleman, "'the distress that I felt spurred me on to industry, for I said, I will use every kind of diligence to purchase my boat back again. I went to the person who had bought it, and told him my design; he had given five *guineas* for it, but told me, as I was once the owner, that I should have it whenever I could raise five *pounds*. "Shall the boat be mine again" said I; my heart bounded at the thought'" (366). This is More's ideal poor person.

And indeed he and his "'young, healthy, and industrious'" wife cheerfully labor incessantly, he "'as a day-labourer in the garden of our squire,'" and she either at the house or in "'needle work, spinning, or knitting at home; not a moment in the day was suffered to pass unemployed'" (366). Not only do these paragons labor without pause, saving whatever they can, they yet remember to give what they can spare to the poor around them. Any extra money they get by "'accident or charity'" they keep "'for the BOAT! . . . Our labour was lightened, by our looking forward to the attainment of our wishes'" (366–67). Just so should the poor behave: by setting goals, saving pennies toward those goals, and themselves finding a bit for those even worse off, the poor can keep themselves happy and look forward to greater comfort as they continue to work. Such behavior will attract aid—but not charity—as it becomes known.

Those always benevolent rich people of More's stories like to see the results of a poor family's struggle. Thus "'Our family indeed increased, but with it our friends increased also, for the cleanliness and frugality which furnished our cottage, and the content and cheerfulness that appeared in it, drew the notice of our rich neighbors; of my master and mistress particularly, whose rule was to assist the industrious, but not to encourage the idle. They did not approve of giving money to the poor; but in cold winters, or dear times, allowed us to buy things at a cheaper rate: this was *money to us,* for when we counted our little cash for the week's marketing, all that was saved to us by our tickets to purchase things at reduced prices, went into "our little box"'" (367). It is significant that these comments are made to come from the poor man's mouth—of course, he agrees fully that help should not be given to any but the industrious and sober poor, and he agrees as well that aid, but not charity, is the way such help should be administered. The poor should be honestly thankful for even the most limited recognition of their needs by those above them in the social hierarchy; and if, as happens in this story, the rich mistreat them, the poor are to be not only forgiving but, again, truly grateful when things are straightened out.

The waterman and his family save up through their unstinting efforts four of the five pounds. And then, one day on his way home from work, the waterman finds a pocketbook with pound bank-notes that he realizes belongs to the squire. His children are elated, assuming that they can keep the money since he had found it. Sternly he reprimands them, reminding them how they would feel if someone found their four pounds. Do unto others, he reminds them forcefully: More never seems to realize that this golden rule might go from poor to rich but also from rich to poor. The next morning the waterman takes the pocketbook with him to work, planning to return it "'as soon as the family rose'" (368). (The implicit assumption is that the poor would be at work long before the squire's household is even awake.) Unfortunately, he loses the money; worse, the appearance is that he had stolen it. He is immediately arrested "'and hurried away to prison! I protested my innocence, but I did not wonder that I gained no credit'" (369). The unfairness of being sent to prison with so little ground is neither remarked on by More nor resented by its victim. Only when another of the laborers is found to have taken the money is the waterman released.

The master, "'with many expressions of concern for what had passed,'" gives the money to the waterman: "'It is the best and only return I can make you, as a just reward of your honesty'" (371). The master is portrayed as acting more than handsomely; we are to learn the lesson here that honesty really is rewarded. Of course, if the waterman had not found the money, the bank bill would have been lost anyway, and, we might remember, the master had had our honest waterman unfairly arrested—but no mention is made of these things. Rather, the waterman is grateful to the master for all his concern: "'This kind and worthy gentleman interested himself much in the purchase of my boat'" (371), he sincerely assures his auditors.

The story reinforces the lesson that the rich are only likely to help the deserving poor. The waterman is pleased that he has the ability now himself to help the poor, "'for when a rich passenger takes my ferry, as my story is well known in the neighborhood, he often gives me more than my fare, which enables me to let the next poor person go over for half price.'" And indeed, "the lady and gentleman were extremely pleased with the waterman's story. . . . They passed over in his ferry-boat for the sake of making him a handsome present" (371–72). They are so pleased with him, in fact, that they in effect become lifelong patrons of this deserving man and his entire family: "And from this time, becoming acquainted with his family, they did them every service in their power, giving books and schooling to the little ones, and every comfort to the old father and mother-in-law as long as they survived" (372).

These principles of behavior for the poor are enunciated even more forcefully in the story of "The Lancashire Collier-Girl." For me, this is the most repugnant of the Cheap Repository's tales for the extraordinary lack of sympathy and common compassion it shows while purporting to be a most compassionate telling of the life of a poor but very good young girl. In Shirley Jackson's modern short story "The Lottery," one inhabitant of a small town is chosen each year to be stoned to death as a kind of ritual offering; the reader is horrified by the townspeople's willingness to accept such a horror year after year and is compelled to wonder how it can be that these people do not recognize the awfulness of what they do. "The Lottery" demands this response from the reader; so does "The Lancashire Collier-Girl," but in the case of the Cheap Repository tale, this result is clearly antithetical to the author's intention. We have seen in story after story More's insistence on the virtue of work for poor children. Here the premise is taken even further, as the story insists that work so brutal that it wrecks the health of the child is acceptable, even desirable. "The Lancashire Collier-Girl" serves to underline the fallacies to which More's morality is fatally vulnerable. Even allowing for the differences in social perspective between More's time and our own, the story's disregard for any aspect of its heroine's well-being except for her determination to stay off the parish rolls is remarkable. To get the flavor of its piety, it is necessary to quote at least the beginning of the story at length:

> In a small village in Lancashire there lived, a few years ago, an industrious man and his wife, who had six children. The man himself used to work in a neighboring colliery, while the wife took care of the family, attended also to their little farm, and minded the dairy, and when all her other work was done, she used constantly to sit down to spin. It will naturally be supposed that the children of such a mother, even when very young, were not suffered to be idle. The eldest daughter worked with her mother at the spinning-wheel, which she learned to think a very pleasant employment. . . .
>
> But the second daughter, of the name of Mary, is the chief subject of the present story. When this girl was nine years old, the honest collier, finding that he had but little employment for her aboveground, took her to work with him down in the coalpit, together with one of his boys, who was then no more than seven years of age. These two children readily put their strength to the basket, dragging the coal from the workmen to the mouth of the pit; and by their joint labors they did the duty of one of those men who are commonly called "drawers," clearing thereby no less than seven shillings a week for their parents. It must be owned, that they may have sometimes exerted themselves even beyond their strength, which is now and then the case with small children, through the fault of those who exact the work from

them; but since in this case the father had an eye on them during
the hours of labor, while they had a prudent and tender mother
also to look after them at home, there is no particular reason to
suppose, that at the time of which we are now speaking, they
were ever much overworked. (142–43)

These passages are meant to be read without irony. Quite
the contrary: the story celebrates the usefulness of the children
and the careful overseeing of their labor by the parents. We are
introduced first to the mother, who works constantly and teaches
her six children to do the same. "Naturally," the author emphasizes, the children "even when very young, were not suffered to
be idle." So the oldest girl spins by her mother's side, but for the
next child they can't find much employment "above ground" so
the good father takes her and the seven-year-old down to the coal
pits, where though sometimes they might have "exerted themselves . . . beyond their strength," we don't have to worry that
they "were ever much overworked"! "The Lancashire Collier-Girl"
insists that this situation not simply is acceptable but is ideal. The
money the children earn is welcome to the parents, and if the children are worked beyond their strength to earn it—well, "that is
now and then the case with little children."

To emphasize the idyllic nature of this happy family, the story
contrasts them with less wholesome families: "let us stop to remark how different was the case of this numerous family from
that of many others in the same humble situation of life. Mary
and her brother, so far from being a burden, were bringing a little
fortune to their parents, even when they were eight or ten years
old; all the family were getting forward by the help of these little
creatures, and their worldly comforts were now increasing on
every side" (143–44). Families in which children are not put to
hard labour are blameworthy; a family like Mary's that manages
to make of their children "a little fortune" instead of "a burden"
are admirable. The welfare of the children is clearly not part of
the calculation, for they are seen essentially as economic counters.
The implicit logic here is wonderfully comforting to the upper
class, for the story shows that no matter how poor a family is, no
matter how many children there are, as long as the parents run
their family economy correctly—that is, as long as all children
work, no matter how young, the family's "worldly comforts" will

increase nicely. Notice how neatly this schema puts all the responsibility for survival on the poor themselves: if they do not do well, the fault is not in a system that militates against them, but in their own laziness or misplaced conception of how to treat children. Incidently, in More's stories, children whose mothers do not want them to work or go to school (these are seen in the same frame) inevitably wind up on the gallows blaming those very mothers for bringing them up so badly.

But in "The Lancashire Collier-Girl" all is going well. Mary and her brother, properly brought up, work to and beyond the limits of their abilities. The problems only begin when, "on one fatal day," stones fall on the father's head, killing him instantly as his "children stand near him in the coal-pit" (144). The mother, hearing the news, "became disordered in her understanding, nor did she to the end of her life recover her senses. Being now rendered extremely helpless, she was separated from her children by the parish officers, who continued to take the charge of her for the space of five years" (145). The eldest daughter marries; the nine and seven year old boys "were bound apprentices by the parish, which also took the charge of two others, one three years old, the other an infant, until they should be sufficiently grown to be bound out also" (145).

The text explicitly emphasizes that taking such young children from their mother and siblings to be apprenticed is not cruel: on the contrary, the author interrupts the story to comment, "In this place I cannot avoid observing, what a blessing it is to poor people in this country, that parish officers are obliged, in all such cases of necessity as that of which I am now speaking, to give maintenance to those who apply to them" (145).[15] The parish's arrangements are seen as absolutely satisfactory; the only "pity" is "that this wise and merciful provision of our laws should ever be abused" (145). The onus is on the poor not to take more than they are entitled to from society. And indeed the rest of "The Lancashire Collier-Girl" details how the dutiful Mary, working double shifts in the coal pits, manages one by one to take her family members from the parish's support and to maintain them by herself.

Mary is "between eleven and twelve years old" when these disasters overtake her parents. "[H]aving already been trained to industry, [she] was by no means disposed to seek any unnecessary help from the parish . . . and determined to maintain herself, like a little independent woman, by her usual work in the coal-pit" (145–46). Within three or four years, she has increased her daily earnings to "no less than two shillings." Of course, she does not use this money to treat herself to a day or two off "because she had got enough for herself to live upon during the four or five working days" (146). Rather, at the age of sixteen, "she relieved the parish from the burden of maintaining her mother" (146). A little later, she also manages "the charge of one of her brothers, and continued to provide for him until he died[;] she afterwards undertook the maintenance of one of her other brothers, who remained with her during sixteen weeks' illness; at the end of which period she followed him to the grave, burying him at her own expense." Seven years later, when her mother dies, Mary buries her too, again, "without any assistance from the parish" (146–47).

Clearly Mary is a paragon. As a child of fourteen, Mary supports herself; at sixteen, she supports a whole family. It is entirely appropriate that society should bear no responsibility for such a child; moreover, it is most positive that the child herself takes the "burden" of her mother and brothers from the parish. Mary's health-threatening labors are to be applauded. The author is aware that Mary herself is still a child: "If any of my readers should here inquire, how it could be possible for so young a child to support all these relations, many of them being also occasionally very burdensome through their sickness; the answer is, that in the case of these extraordinary calls upon her, she used to betake herself to extraordinary labor, sometimes earning no less than three shillings and sixpence in the four and twenty hours, by taking what is called 'a double turn' in the coal-pits" (147).

More's expectation—or hope—that the poor should labor mercilessly carries throughout the Repository stories. Mary is a good girl because she is willing to work herself to and beyond the point of illness; if she were not ready to submit cheerfully to such labor, she would not be good. Using Mary, a female child, as its protagonist, "The Lancashire Collier-Girl" emphasizes this lesson perhaps even more strongly than if the child were male. Mary, following the scriptural injunction to obedience to one's parent, "cheerfully followed [her father] down into the coal-pit, burying herself in the bowels of the earth, and . . . without excusing herself on account of her sex, she joined in the same work with the miners" (148). Eventually, even Mary "began to be bowed down, in some measure, by the afflictions and labors which she had endured. It was evident that she had now been led to exert herself beyond her strength" (148–49). Actually, she suffers a complete mental and physical breakdown, hallucinating, "being both weak in body and sadly enfeebled in her mind" (151).

This breakdown provides an opportunity in the story to discourse at length on the great goodness of God and the all-too-frequent insubstantial complaints of the poor. "How lamentable" it is that while some people give themselves diseases "from the abundance of their riches" (149), there should be poor people like Mary who are bowed down and who could do with a bit of help from the rich—Mary being one of the few poor who would be a legitimate object of charity, unlike "so many poor people [who] are seen who are apt to complain too soon" (149). Piously, the author comments that it really is too bad that "there should be any [unlike that "many"] who do not tell their distresses to those who can help them till it is almost too late, which, I trust, however, does not often happen" (149)! But always in cases like Mary's, those "distresses" are all to the good, the "peculiar blessing of Heaven . . . these very afflictions will be made the means of increasing their trust in God, and prove, in the end, to have been entirely designed for their good" (150). The story tots up the score of Mary's "afflictions": watched her father die, watched her mother deteriorate, nursed two sick brothers and then buried them, lost her mind and her physical strength, was left all alone with no one to care for her or for her to care about. "It was at this period of her extremity that it pleased God to raise up for her some kind friends" (151).

The "kind friends" are a lady in the village and the family she has heard about that might need a servant. She "advised Mary, feeble as she was, to present herself" to these people "as a candidate to fill this comparatively easy and comfortable position" (151–52). Mary tells them about her former work and the current state of her health; although this disclosure was "much against her interest . . . it was perfectly right," for how can "any of us hope for the blessing of God . . . [if] instead of trusting in God, [we] trust to our own little frauds and crooked contrivances" (152)? Mary does not get the job.

She doesn't get the job because the prospective employers think she must be too rough to live in their house, given her background. Mary is not disappointed that she did not get the position, but she is horrified at "this unhappy suspicion against her character. . . . She walked very quietly away, with a downcast look, and with a mind quite broken down by this fresh affliction and disaster" (152). This is precisely the way she should react. Anger or disappointment would be unseemly and might indicate hubris; "her patient and silent grief" (153), on the other hand, speak well for her. The "gentleman," who had observed her as she walked away, goes to the colliery to inquire about her. He is so satisfied with the results of his "very minute and full examination" (153) that he hires her. Six years later, her "health is recovered, her habits of diligence are still very great, and she is said to be of a remarkably modest, humble, and contented spirit." Indeed, as a kind of final stamp of approval, it is this very gentleman who has "furnished all the materials of this story" (154).

These are the "useful lessons" with which the story ends:

> In the first place, I think it may teach the poor, that they can seldom be in any condition of life so low as to prevent their rising to some degree of independence if they choose to exert themselves; and that there can be no situation whatever so mean as to forbid the practice of many noble virtues.
>
> It may instruct the rich not to turn the poor from their doors merely on account of first appearances, but rather to examine into their character, expecting sometimes to find peculiar modesty and merit even in the most exposed situations.
>
> This story may also encourage the afflicted to serve and trust God in every extremity; and finally,
>
> It may teach all descriptions of persons who may have to pass through dangerous and trying circumstances, that they may expect the divine protection and blessing, provided they . . . endeavor, like Mary, "to learn and labor truly to get their own living, and to do their duty in that state of life which it hath pleased God to call them." (154–55)

The lessons pointed out in this instructive summation are not quite the ones we might note. For the primary lesson of "The Lancashire Collier-Girl," it seems to me, is that class absolutely delineates every aspect of the human being's experience, and that the lower-class person has no right even to think of aspiring to anything that would change his place in the social scale. To think otherwise is not only to go against the realities of the world as it is but, more important, against the perfection of a spiritual-experiential continuum that God himself has created. To wish to change one's allotted role in the world is to sin against a benevolent and assuredly all-knowing deity. For More it is class, not gender, that determines what is appropriate in life. Only within a given class might gender distinctions be important (the role of the Salisbury shepherd's wife is to enable him able to work rather than to earn the family's subsistence herself), but, as we see with Mary, gender is not a deciding factor even in wage earning. Character is a very important aspect of the poor man or woman, for of everything it is the aspect of life that the person can control. For the poor, character translates into a willingness to work without complaint even to the point of illness. The rich, on the other hand, are not obligated to help the poor, although it is nice if they do try, within limits, to aid them. Thus when Mary collapses, we cannot expect anyone to *give* her support, but it is an adequately benevolent gesture that someone bothers to tell her about a servant position open at a local house. Similarly, the rich family is presented as extremely responsible and benevolent for bothering to check out Mary's background and to let her work for them. No mention is made of a convalescence!

Before turning from "The Lancashire Collier-Girl" there is one further aspect of the story that bears attention. Surely, dear reader, you have been worrying about the virtue of a young girl alone in the mines with all those miners. The author knew that you would be wondering and assures the reader that, while these are "a race of men rough indeed," they are "highly useful to the community," and, further, "they have the character of being honest and faithful as well as remarkably courageous" (148). Indeed, there have been "some striking instances of their readiness to receive religious instruction when offered to them" (148). The condescension, not to mention suspicion, implicit in these remarks is striking; such workers are more than a little alarming, but they are, after all, useful, their courage making the comfort of other people's lives possible. The compliments to them are carefully hedged: there even have been cases in which these men could be trained to religion, we are told with unintentional irony. They may "take a cup too much" now and then, they may be "a set of coarse miners," but they have a "rule of decency and propriety towards young women" that could be a model for "some of those persons who are pleased to call themselves their betters" (153). "Among these men . . . Mary's honor was safe"; it is said that she even received help from them occasionally, help given "with great feeling and kindness" (148). Notice that among class equals, then, even among these "rough" men, the story shows common human sympathy, while between classes, it is enough for "a lady" merely to tell Mary about that job down the street. Note too that these men may be coarse, but even they respect the decent boundaries between men and women, which is sometimes more than can be said of those higher in the social scale, one of More's major points in the *Strictures*.[16]

Those higher in the social scale can be guilty of even more wide-ranging lapses of behavior than could be supposed possible in the mine pits, and these lapses, as More cautions in work after work, carry enormous social consequences. One of the principle snares for the upper class comes in the realm of misguided philosophical systems which can then lead to misguided actions. More is horrified by the new philosophy, that philosophy of individual liberty and personal responsibility that makes man the center of the ethical system and moves God and organized religion to the periphery of the shaping of human conduct. We need not wonder who she had in mind in writing "The History of Mr. Fantom, the New-Fashioned Philosopher, and His Man William." The story is an explicit attack on the radical formulations of such "new philosophers" as Tom Paine, that "Thomas Paine, whose 'Rights of Man' and 'Age of Reason' were widely circulated at this period, in cheap editions, by missionaries in the employ of seditious clubs and infidel societies," as one of More's early editors notes in a comment on the story,[17] and as such "The History of Mr. Fantom" represents a return to the beginning of More's pamphlet career, *Village Politics*.

This long narrative of Mr. Fantom marks something of a departure from More's usual purpose in these Tracts, which is to direct the behavior of the poor. Here, her focus is on the well-off Mr. Fantom and the deleterious effects of his new philosophy both for his family (especially his servants) and his community. More excoriates the ideas of men like Paine and other radicals like Godwin and his circle who were intent on creating a new philo-

sophical world that would rely for moral structure on man and
reason rather than on God and faith; we have seen the bitterness
of the discussions about Wollstonecraft between More and
Walpole, for example.[18]

More makes it clear that the new philosophy—with its questioning of Christianity and its emphasis on a secular system of
moral improvement and universal benevolence—is the sort of
system that would appeal only to cold hearts and shallow minds.
Mr. Fantom, as his name suggests, has no moral substance. A successful retail trader, he is "covetous and proud, selfish and con-
ceited";[19] he wants to set himself apart from his peers but does
not know how he wants to do it. He decides to join a club: "the
usual means of attaching importance to insignificance occurred
to him. . . . To be connected with a *party* would at least make him
known to that party, be it ever so low and contemptible" (III, 2).
More complains that this kind of affiliation "draws off vain minds
from those scenes of general usefulness, in which, though [such
people] are of more value, they are of less distinction" (III, 2).

The story of Mr. Fantom is to instruct us in the true meaning
of social usefulness and awaken us to the false, pernicious con-
ceptions of universal benevolence that More sees becoming increasingly prevalent as the thinking of Paine and his friends takes
hold. Mr. Fantom discovers "a famous little book written by the
NEW PHILOSOPHER, Thomas Paine, whose pestilent doctrines
have gone about seeking whom they may destroy" (III, 2). More
comments that such doctrines find fertile ground in a mind like
Fantom's, "at once shallow and inquisitive, speculative and vain,
ambitious and dissatisfied" (III, 2). Not very subtly, then, More
insists both on the evil of the new philosophy and the fault in the
kind of person who would be intrigued by it. Only a person of
immense vanity and no education would be taken in by such doctrines. Mr. Fantom, ready to be "a full-grown philosopher at once,
to be wise without education, to dispute without learning," has
found a way to "*distinguish himself*" (III, 3).

More pillories those who accept the "new doctrines," making fun of them as people for whom "almost every book [is] new";
Fantom "fell into the common error of those who begin to read
late in life, —that of thinking that what he did not know himself
was equally new to others [and that] he and the author he was
reading were the only two people in the world who knew any

thing" (III, 2–3). The effect of this exposure to new ideas is a pro-
clivity to question all the tenets of morality and civil responsibility understood by sober citizens. "Mr. Fantom believed, not in
proportion to the strength of the evidence, but to the impudence
of the assertion. The trampling on holy ground with dirty shoes,
the smearing the sanctuary with filth and mire, the calling proph-
ets and apostles by the most scurrilous names, was new, and dash-
ing, and dazzling. . . . he was the convert of a man who had written
only for the vulgar[,] . . . who had stooped to rake up out of the
kennel of infidelity all the loathsome dregs and offal dirt which
politer unbelievers had thrown away as too gross and offensive
for their better-bred readers" (III, 3).

More's prose is usually mild and lady-like, her writing persona sweetly reasonable, her voice that of reassurance and instruction. But in these passages More gives up all pretense of sweet
reasonableness and offers no balanced view. Paine's are the writings of the devil, and More's job is to make *her* readers impervious to his seductions. She begins with these vituperations and
then goes on to show the hideous effects on human lives of the
philosophical positions Paine and his followers espouse. The real
problem as she sees it is that although such evil ideas originally
are accepted by an empty-minded man like Fantom, because of
his social position, Fantom has the potential of infecting others.
Near the end of the story, Mr. Trueman tells Mr. Fantom that whatever sins a man could have, getting drunk every day and gaming
every night, "'they are not so bad as the pestilent doctrines with
which you infect your house and your neighbourhood. A bad action is like a single murder. The consequence may end with the
crime, to all but the perpetrator; but a wicked principle is throw-
ing lighted gunpowder into a town; it is poisoning a river; there
are no bounds, no certainty, no end to its mischief. . . . [S]ouls may
be brought to perdition by a wicked principle after the author of
it has been dead for ages'" (III, 32).

The wicked principles are "all the commonplace notions
against Christianity" mixed with the new "cant" of universal benevolence. Mr. Fantom "prated about *narrowness*, and *ignorance*,
and *bigotry*, and *prejudice*, and *priestcraft* and tyranny, on the one
hand; and, on the other, of *public good*, the *love of mankind*, and
*liberality*, and *candour*, and *toleration*, and, above all, *benevolence*.
Benevolence, he said, made up the whole of religion, and all the

other parts of it were nothing but cant, and jargon, and hypocrisy" (III, 4). Fantom conceives of benevolence as a thought system that will save the world: he is interested only in schemes that
will benefit hundreds, that will result in the amelioration of the
human condition. He is not willing to spare a guinea for an individual man.

Having retired to the country to philosophize, Fantom invites Trueman out as audience where they discuss the issues dear
to More's heart: the true function of individual benevolence and
the proper activities of a Christian—especially on a Sunday. The
enlightened Mr. Fantom is in favor of enjoying nature as well as a
drink and in general not abiding the old "vulgar prejudices about
the church and the Sabbath, and all that antiquated stuff" (III, 10).
Mr. Trueman, More's voice, insists on strict observance of the Sabbath. This is more important that we might think for, again, the
point is not just that the masters will go cavorting into the country, drinking and eating at public houses, or having people to dinner at home, but that all this sets a bad example for the servants if
it does not, as in the case of the dinner parties, actually prevent
their attendance at church.

And this moral slippage is symptomatic of further moral
decay. More advocates practical, individual charity; the new philosophy is for changing the world. More sees these grand schemes
as excuses for not doing one's part to help one's neighbors. This
debate between the grand scheme and the individual gesture forms
the core of "The History of Mr. Fantom." Within our discussion of
the poor it is of central import. Trueman believes in doing good
on an individual level, in helping actual people he knows or knows
about. He belongs to "the Sick Man's Friend, and to the Society
for relieving Prisoners for small Debts"; Fantom finds these "petty
occupations" (III, 11). But Trueman counters, "I had rather have
an ounce of real good done with my own hands, and seen with
my own eyes, than speculate about doing a ton in a wild way,
which, I know, can never be brought about." Fantom ridiculously
answers, "I despise a narrow field. O, for the reign of universal
benevolence! I want to make all mankind good and happy" (III,
11). When Trueman suggests that Fantom try his "hand at a town
or parish first," Fantom responds "I have a plan in my head for
relieving the miseries of the whole world. Every thing is bad as it
now stands. I would alter all the laws, and do away all the reli-

gions, and put an end to all the wars in the world. I would everywhere redress the injustice of . . . Providence. I would put an end to all punishments; I would not leave a single prisoner on the face of the globe . . . (III, 11–12).

Trueman is a little frightened at the idea of releasing all the prisoners and not at all impressed by the rest. The utmost extent [of Trueman's] ambition at present is "to redress the wrongs of a parish apprentice who has been cruelly used by his master" (III, 13). But Fantom, worried about "the Poles and South Americans," is not interested in "the petty sorrows of workhouses and parish apprentices. It is provinces, empires, continents, that the benevolence of the philosopher embraces; every one can do a little paltry good to his next neighbour" (III, 13). Mr. Trueman's response is clearly More's: if everyone did a little, the "grand ocean of benevolence would be filled with the drops which private charity would throw into it" (III, 13–14).

More's representation of the dichotomy between conservative and radical visions of benevolence is not an entirely accurate one, however. If we look back at Robert Bage's *Hermsprong,* we find the same terms set out for individual benevolence that More presents: on the morning after a great storm Caroline and Hermsprong are out among those who need help. Bage's second point would not suit More, however: the clergyman, Dr. Blick, whose job such aid and comfort ought to be, lies comfortably abed, while the agnostic hero Hermsprong energetically dispenses charity. The radical Holcroft, too, in *Anna St. Ives,* emphasizes in tableau after tableau the importance of individual benevolence. This theme goes across the political spectrum of novelists: the quite conservative Fanny Burney in *Evelina* makes much the same sort of references to individual benevolence that the radical novelists make twenty years later. More, however, sees morality as connected to ideology. Fantom's portrait is without shading. His radical notions are clearly wrong. He is a hypocrite; while he wants to save the world—and money of course means nothing to him—he will not give a single guinea to help get his "poor old friend, Tom Saunders" (III, 14) out of jail, where he languishes because of a debt that he was powerless to avoid.

Many of More's favorite themes are rung in "The History of Mr. Fantom." Repeatedly she stresses the importance of Christianity, a Christianity undiluted and unquestioned. Part of the defense of this Christianity lies in spreading its doctrines through educating the poor enough so that they can participate in the religion, specifically so that they can read the Bible. We saw the importance of this theme in "The Shepherd of Salisbury Plain"; here it arises again when Trueman comments that he wants "the true light . . . to reach the very lowest, and I therefore bless God for charity-schools, as instruments of diffusing it among the poor" (III, 15). One measure of Fantom's fault is that he will not give his servants time or opportunity to "be taught a little. The maids can scarcely tell a letter, or say the Lord's Prayer" (III, 16), his wife diffidently reminds him. Naturally, his zeal for doing good does not extend to anything so practical as educating his servants or subscribing to the local Sunday school.

Trueman sums up Fantom's character: "To love mankind so dearly, and yet avoid all opportunities of doing them good; to have such a noble zeal for the millions, and to feel so little compassion for the units. . . . Surely none but a philosopher could indulge so much philanthropy and so much frugality at the same time" (III, 17). If the absence of any positive good were the sole outcome of such hypocrisy, Fantom's posturing would be relatively harmless. But the example he sets destroys others. More's case in point is the servant, William. William, when he worked in a "sober family" (III, 6), was responsible, properly religious, and of course law-abiding. Fantom lures William away from his employer with the promise of higher pay. In the Fantom household, with the model of Mr. Fantom before him, William's behavior degenerates.[20] He becomes lazy and turns to drink. When reprimanded, he tells Fantom that "'if I do get drunk now and then, I only do it for the good of my country, and in obedience to your wishes. . . . I have often overheard you say to your company, that private vices are public benefits; and so I thought that getting drunk was as pleasant a way of doing good to the public as any, especially when I could oblige my master at the same time'" (III, 28–29).

Fantom throws William out; he does not pay him his wages. William, on his side, departs with three new spoons. All Mr. Fantom's old port is gone too. From here, in More's view, it is only a short step to murder. Some weeks later, Mr. Fantom receives a letter from William, who awaits his execution for murder the very next day (More seems to forget the long wait for trial that eighteenth-century justice usually implies). William accuses Fan-

tom of making him "'a drunkard, a thief, and a murderer. . . . Sir . . .
from you I learned the principles which lead to those crimes. . . . I
should never have fallen into sins deserving of the gallows, if I
had not overheard you say there was no hereafter, no judgment,
no future reckoning'" (III, 38). Thus in his dying speech William
attributes his own fall to the bad example set by his master. A
master who does not allow his servants time for church, who himself does not pray, and, worst of all, who discusses the new, anti-
religious notions of the day in the hearing of his servants, incites
those servants to lose not only their own religious principles but
their very souls. "'A rich man, indeed, who throws off religion,
may escape the gallows, because want does not drive him to commit those crimes which lead to it; but what shall restrain a needy
man, who has been taught that there is no dreadful reckoning?'"
(III, 41) William rhetorically asks from the gallows.

More constantly links religion, proper conduct, and benevolence. Mr. Fantom's benevolent projects can have no validity because they are based in rejection of religion, and, indeed, we see
that his projects are the product of mere posturing. He will never
do actual good to anyone; his philosophical stance—universal
benevolence without the steadying base of religious commitment—only harms those it touches. Mr. Trueman, a man of firm
religious principle and belief in the amelioration of individual
need, represents More. And since benevolence is tied to religion,
the saving of souls is at least as valuable as the supplying of bread
or shelter. Thus Trueman sends Fantom home from the prison,
ironically urging him to go home "'and finish your Treatise on
Universal Benevolence and the Blessed Effects of Philosophy'"
(III, 39), while Trueman stays the night with William in the prison,
helping him to prepare his soul for the following day's execution.
The structure and development of "The History of Mr. Fantom"
may be more sophisticated than those of *Village Politics*, but the
thrust of More's argument has not changed at all.

As we will see in the next chapter, More wrote continuations
of several of her stories, so that the stories in effect became serials.
Most of these continuations were written and published within
short chronological intervals. The continuation of Mr. Fantom's
story, however, comes almost twenty years later, long after the
end of the Cheap Repository project. "The Death of Mr. Fantom,"
even more obviously than the earlier part of the story, is a direct

attack on Thomas Paine, but this time More virtually gives up the pretence of a narrative line. The tale reads as a simple wish fulfillment—More's wish fulfillment—as we see Mr. Fantom die a lingering, horrible death in the throes of his remorse for having caused so much evil in propagating the horrendous ideas of that Thomas Paine. In contrast to the earlier story, where Paine was named directly only once and other references to him were oblique, here Paine is mentioned by name repeatedly.

Mr. Fantom, dying of a series of strokes, sees himself as "a miserable wretch" (III, 48). His political activities were subversive not only of order in this world but in the next. He "would have overturned the peace of society," he laments. He "would have rooted up the very foundations of religion and government" (III, 48). What is the connection he makes between the religious and the secular? To More, the connection is seamless: Fantom understands now that "'*No tyranny* was our motto. And what does that imply? No king on earth, no God in heaven'" (III, 48). This is a direct reference to Paine's *Rights of Man* which, we remember, mocks the concept of kingship, seeing the king and his supporting cast simply as a drain on the economy.

We learn more about Fantom's past in this sequel to his "History." Fantom himself is the victim of his own disillusionment. Apprenticed to a "professor of religion," he watched as the man used his supposed good character to flog inferior goods. The professor employs Fantom "'in many illegal practices. This contradiction between principle and practice laid the foundation of all the corruptions of my own character; for the effect produced on my mind was not so much that my master was a bad man, and made use of a show of religion to cover his vices, as that religion itself was an imposture'" (III, 49). Having been disillusioned and corrupted by his master, Fantom was vulnerable to being further misled. "'Just about this time Thomas Paine published his two well-known works, the one intended to overturn all governments, the other to abolish all religion. I was just in that state of mind ready to be acted upon by such books'" (III, 50). The implication here is that only someone already corrupted could be attracted to the "'presumptuous falsehoods'" of such works; thus do the pernicious effects of Paine's works spread, as the initially vulnerable disseminate in ever-widening circles the seductive pseudo-logic of Paine's writing. Fantom explains that the "'road to glory now seemed to lie open before me. As I was sober, and not openly immoral, I maintained for a time that degree of character which may be preserved without a single good principle. I became an infidel from the same cause from which I became a jacobin; that is, hatred of every thing greater than myself, whether in heaven or earth, in church or state, in rank or fortune'" (III, 50–51).

Fantom underscores the tie between corrupt political values—that is, disrespect for the institutions of government, especially for the monarchy—and corrupt moral values, or a lack of religion. "'Pure jacobinism would never have maintained its ground in this country had it not been accompanied, and even introduced, by impiety. In the party I joined, superstition, bigotry, and priestcraft were the watchwords for destroying Christianity, as oppression, injustice, and tyranny were for overturning government'" (III, 51). More's references to Paine's two works hardly could be clearer. Where Paine sees a release from the tyrannies of state and religion, More sees invitations to political anarchy and moral decay. I have alluded repeatedly in this book to More's emphasis on a divine order that is based in a social, political, and religious continuum; Paine's challenge to this construct for More implies not just a decay of the social order but an implosion of the moral order as well. Paine's new social order in fact is premised on the destruction of religion. Fantom laments that "'Our leaders knew mankind too well not to know that our surest road to success was to begin by extinguishing all sense of religion; to make them believe that Christianity was a fable, the Saviour an impostor, and the church an engine of superstition and spiritual tyranny'" (III, 51).

Fantom heaps scorn not only on his own ill-conceived ideas but on those who had listened to them: they are "'silly boys . . . and men who . . . like parrots, . . . pronounce[d] certain words of which they did not know the purport. Annual parliaments, universal suffrage, elective franchise, were to them terms without a meaning. They only inferred, from *their* being directed to echo them, that they promised plenty without working; vice without restraint; liberty without a superior; plunder without a prison to punish it; and a jovial course of sin on earth without any dread of a hell hereafter'" (III, 52). Fantom's evil is that to satisfy his own ambition he furthered a course that he himself understood to be harmful; if his ignorant listeners only saw in these new philosophies the way to a free and easy life without social or moral consequences, Fantom, more intelligent than those he was corrupting, did indeed know what he was promulgating. And now he suffers the torments that More feels would be just for all such infidels.

In the throes of the spiritual upheaval that accompanies the knowledge of his imminent death, Fantom is sure "'that nothing should ever tempt me to return to those principles and habits which have undone my soul'" (III, 53). If he could, he would undo the damage he has caused, but this damage basically is irreparable since the many men he has "'led from the sober duties of life'" cannot be given back that which he has taken from them. "'What restitution can I make them for loss of time, of character, of principle, perhaps of life? How can I restore, by my remorse, seditious subjects to their king, rebels to submission to the laws, atheists to the blessings of religion. . . . I can only bequeath my dying advice to those whom I have deluded; tell them of my deep remorse'" (III, 59). As the servant William did in "The History of Mr. Fantom," here Fantom asks only that after he dies his "solemn recantation" be published for the guidance of the living.

While Fantom is repenting, the evil of his former party goes on; one Saunders comes to the house looking for Fantom: money is owed for payment of bills having to do with their work. Specifically, Saunders presents to Trueman an itemized list of expenses for which he is expecting payment from Fantom. Included in the list are charges for, among other things, "cockades," "paying for signatures from unwilling, but distressed persons," "supplying hawkers with tracts against religion and government," "supplying ditto with a few godly tracts to put at the top of their baskets, to conceal the others [!]," and so on.

Trueman tells Saunders about Fantom's dire condition. Saunders, supposedly Fantom's comrade in the political wars, shows absolutely no interest in Fantom's illness; he is, however, most anxious for the money. His lack of compassion is noted by Trueman, and Saunders makes no pretense of denying it. "'It would be absurd in me to affect feeling for a worthless individual,'" he says, sounding precisely like Fantom in his own earlier, unregenerate days, "'when I have the cause of a whole kingdom at my heart, and in a good measure, indeed, on my hands'" (III, 63). The debate between Trueman and Saunders continues for some pages, with Trueman, as More's voice, lamenting the evil that men such as Saunders cause, and Saunders simply dismissing Trueman for being "'ignorant of politics.'" Trueman's answer is that, along with Locke, he finds that all men should be acquainted with their own business and their own religion, but that the study of politics should be left to those wise enough to comprehend it properly: "'I myself have heard sensible men say— that to understand politics, it is necessary to understand many other things, more than are to be picked up in a Saturday's Register'" (III, 65).

Fantom, as he lays dying, repents all his misplaced political enthusiasms. Trueman suggests to him an appropriate expiation: "'Allow me to recommend to you to do, without loss of time, what the Ephesian sorcerers did when they began to feel the guilt and danger of sin. *They burnt their books,* their magical books, with which, like you, they had bewitched the people'" (III, 70). Fantom is only too happy to acquiesce in this plan and orders the servant to bring in three large trunks of books. "When they were brought in, he desired Mr. Trueman to take out the contents. The first he opened was nearly filled with *Paine's Age of Reason,* and the *Rights of Man.* 'There,' said Fantom, 'there is the seed-plot, there is the prime dunghill from which all our noxious weeds have sprung up in such abundance'" (III, 70–71). The second and third trunks are filled with assorted subversive pamphlets, including one trunk full of Fantom's own writings. All these he orders publicly burned. As Fantom looks on from his window, Trueman sees to the assembling of the huge pile of papers, "and with his own hand set fire to this combustible heap. It was an affecting sight" (III, 72). And so, with the burning of books, "The Death of Mr. Fantom" comes to its climax. More clearly sees none of the implications of book burning that might trouble at least some of her readers. So hateful are Paine's ideas, even these many years later, that More would support whatever it takes to root them from men's minds— and their libraries.

# Seven

# Economic Circumstances

## More's Cheap Repository Tracts

MOST OF THE CHEAP REPOSITORY TRACTS contain economic as well as moral lessons for the poor; many include advice to the better off about helping the poor to manage their finances. But some of the Tracts, especially those written by More herself, focus on the specifics of getting ahead in terms of the attitude and skills needed by the poor man or woman if he or she is to make significant economic progress. More writes in story after story, beginning with *Village Politics*, about the wonderful and reliable help to the poor that the parish system provides for them in times of need, and she is equally enthusiastic about the potential that it provides for the young poor person through the apprenticeship apparatus for joining the nation's economy and thus enjoying the profits that that economy holds out for those who work hard and with honesty. More is so certain in her belief that a young person who approaches his training seriously and who applies himself earnestly one day can be an independent master workman that she actually explains in detail the way to go about this training and then the building of the business! Such a rise in social standing, not to mention economic well-being, seems to conflict with the very clear belief in most of More's tales that the poor man should be content with what he has and should not, under any circumstances, harbor even the desire to change his social place. This template for social and spiritual behavior we have seen most forcefully enunciated in "The Shepherd of Salisbury Plain," perhaps the most typical of More's stories for the Cheap Repository. But More makes a distinction between the poor who labor on the land or as servants, where in reality there is little room for economic advancement, and those who labor in business, where serious application judiciously expended has the potential to produce real goods that add real value to the economy. In other words, it seems to me that More is not being inconsistent in the very different attitudes toward the poor that she manifests in stories such as "The Shepherd of Salisbury Plain" and, for example, "The Two Shoemakers." The sober, diligent man with a good trade does, in More's reckoning, stand a fair chance of rising well above his initial condition.

Like many of More's stories, this one begins with a family situation that almost guarantees the misfortune and ultimate failure of one of the paired protagonists of her tale. For "The Two Shoemakers," not surprisingly, will chronicle the careers of two young men as they pursue their training and then set up in business.[1] The first of the two seems to have all the advantages. The son of a well-off farmer, Jack will be sent as apprentice to Mr. Williams, the shoemaker in a small town in Oxfordshire. Because Jack is "a wild, giddy boy, whom his father could not well manage or instruct in farming, his father thought it better to send him out to learn a trade at a distance, than to let him idle about at home."[2] So this eldest son, instead of becoming the heir to a good farm, must go out to learn a trade because his father cannot, or will not, train him at home to take over the family farm.

And why is Jack such a troublesome lad? It's his mother's fault, of course. For as we have seen in so many of More's stories, the mother who is too indulgent to her child, especially to her son, will ruin him. He "might have turned out well enough, if he had not had the misfortune to be his mother's favourite" (441). The farmer, to obtain peace in the family, gave up the discipline of his son to his wife, and thus "gave up the future virtue and happiness of his child." The farmer was a hardworking man, "but he had no religion," and "his wife managed him entirely" (441). Marvelously, now we see yet another reason for a man to have religion: he must be able to manage his wife! He does not look beyond the present, and since his wife manages her own farm responsibilities efficiently, the farmer does not worry about such future problems as the result of neglecting the children's morality. Rather, the wife's bad temper and her mismanagement of the children send the farmer out to drink, even though he does not even particularly like to drink! Like many other men in More's stories, the farmer turns to the public house because his own home is not made pleasant by his wife. Almost every character defect of both husband and child is the fault of the imperfect wife and mother. Jack's mother wants him to go to school to save him from the fatigue of work (she has not "sense enough to value" learning). The "foolish woman" (442) wants him to be a parson so that he will be a gentleman; she gives no thought to his fitness for a religious post.

The father just hopes the boy unfit for the life of a farmer might be good enough for trade, but he does not choose carefully in finding a master for the child; he does not look for a "sober, prudent, and religious" (442–43) man to guide his son but simply takes the master whose business goes well and, in deference to his wife, the man who has a reputation for not being strict. By not looking out for a master who properly would give his son moral as well as work guidance, the farmer has made himself "in a great measure answerable for the future sins and errors" (443) of his child. So here we have the case where father and mother, although well enough off financially, do not provide adequate moral guidance or proper parental model to their son. The reader already can make a good judgment as to how Jack will turn out.

What of the financially poor boy who has received adequate moral tutelage? James Stock is the son of a laborer in the next village. He is bound out by the parish because his own father is too poor to make provision for him. "James was in every thing the very reverse of his new companion. He was a modest, industrious, pious youth; and though so poor, and the child of a labourer, was a much better scholar than Jack, who was a wealthy farmer's son. His father had, it is true, been able to give him but very little schooling, for he was obliged to be put to work when quite a child" (444). James sounds much more promising than Jack in terms of character, and we can be assured that that promise will fulfill itself as the two boys are put apprentice to the same master. We see the roots of James' future success in his childhood. He voluntarily does errands for the curate, his neighbor Mr. Thomas, and Mr. Thomas in return often sends for the child after James has finished his work in the field to teach him "to write and cast accounts, as well as to instruct him in the principles of his religion" (444). There is no suggestion that the child might wish to pass his evenings after work in any other manner. Indeed, the curate decides to lavish these favors on James after noticing him with a new Bible purchased with a whole year's savings of single half-pence earned one at a time for favors to Mr. Thomas: "in all that time he had not spent a single farthing on his own diversions" (445). One of More's favorite lessons for the poor child is that he should work continuously and should use any bits of money he comes by for worthwhile things like buying religious books. Mr. Thomas is sure that James will do well in life.

As the child grows older, he can do more services for Mr. Thomas, and as he earns more, he saves more. Eventually, James even can buy shoes and stockings; all the money he earns at his day job in the fields, naturally, goes to his mother to buy bread for the family. When the time comes for him to be apprenticed, the parish puts James out and pays for him. It is clear that James' father would have preferred a more responsible master; unlike Jack's father, who does have the choice of master but does not have the good sense to choose well, the poor man must take what is given him. So only James' good sense and good moral training will stand to protect him from the errors his insufficient master will make. Off he goes with his remade old coat and waistcoat to begin his apprenticeship.

Jack is a smart boy but has no self-discipline; as soon as he is distracted, he drops his work and goes off in search of entertainment.[3] Because his "ill-judging mother" privately sends him pocket money, "that deadly bane to all youthful virtue" (448), he can indulge his desires as much as he pleases. But even worse than wasting his own money, he wastes his master's time. Since in all these stories More sees her mission as in part teaching the poor how to act properly in terms of their economic interactions with others (much as our contemporary "workfare" is supposed to teach the poor how to function in the workplace and thus secure them from needing welfare), this point about wasting the master's time, time that the apprentice in effect is stealing from the master, is underscored. James, the good boy, points out this flaw to Jack repeatedly. When Jack tells him that the waste of his time is his own business, James "fetched down their indentures, and there showed him that he had solemnly bound himself, by that instrument, not to waste his master's property." The apprentice's time "is a very valuable part of [his] master's property" (448). Wedgwood in his *Address to the Young Inhabitants of the Pottery* does not say it much differently.

As we would expect, Jack's love of amusement leads him on into ever more dangerous paths to the place "to which all these fiddles and shows naturally lead,—I mean, the *alehouse*" (449). The bad people he gets to know bring him into more and more vicious behavior, until the idle pastimes he took up as a boy "soon led to the destructive vices of the man" (449). A large part of this degeneration is due to the slackness of the master, whose job it is to teach proper values to his young charges. But he himself is not a "sober nor a steady man," and he spends much of his time at the tavern too. In fact, he is disposed to value Jack more than James because Jack came from a family with more money. James is taught little of his trade, and his time is taken up with running errands for the mistress of the house.

More interrupts her narrative here, as she does in many of her stories, for a direct explanation of how things should be done. In this case, she defines the respective responsibilities of master and apprentice: "And here I must remark, that though parish apprentices are bound in duty to be submissive to both master and mistress, and always to make themselves as useful as they can in a family, and to be civil and humble; yet, on the other hand, it is the duty of masters always to remember, that if they are paid for instructing them in their trade" (450), they should do so and not just use the apprentices for housework, thus depriving them of the opportunity to learn a trade. This is a most interesting observation in a number of ways. More's unembarrassed didactic pause here emphasizes that she sees her role as that of instructress; further, she is instructing both the lower and higher classes. Each person, as we have seen so often, has a place and a duty in life that is dependent on his station and his relative position vis-à-vis those with whom he is interacting. Thus the apprentice has his duty to be as helpful to the family as possible, and the master, too, has his own proper role to play. More makes no attempt to make such commentary part of the flow of her tale.

When she gets back to the story, we find Mr. Williams in some difficulty: he is too drunk to make out a customer's bill. Jack is useless—no amount of tutoring has taught him the elements of arithmetic. James "with great modesty" asks if he might have the privilege of helping his master, and Mr. Williams finally notices that it is James who is the valuable apprentice. James takes on the management of the accounts, and all the customers are "well pleased" since the overcharges for which the shop had been known are no more. James goes on to become the shop's best workman, and he also goes on to become its critic. For there are many things he disapproves of in both shop and family. "Some of the journeymen used to swear, drink, and sing very licentious songs. All these things were a great grief to his sober mind: he complained to his master, who only laughed at him. . . . What grieved him most was the manner in which the Sunday was spent" (451–52), either in lying abed or in doing business: the apprentices were expected to deliver shoes on Sunday morning. James, with tears in his eyes, begs to be excused from this Sunday work, but he is laughed at. The best he can do is to repeat his psalms and chapters as he walks to and fro, and then to go twice to church after his business is done.

James, no matter how hard he works, cannot keep the shop in order, and all his protestations to Mr. Williams fall on deaf ears. In fact, the master takes to spending more and more time at the tavern, while his wife spends money as fast as she can at home. Finally, one morning, James is summoned to the tavern where his master lies dying. Williams begs comfort from James; and "James spoke kindly to him, but was too honest to give him false comfort, as is too often done by mistaken friends in these dreadful moments" (457). Painting a pathetic deathbed scene, More shows us one of her favorite images, the dying profligate, repenting all as he goes into "an awful eternity" (457). There is, however, profit to be taken here, and James prays that so terrible a lesson will enable him to live "in a constant state of preparation for death" (458).

Then he goes home to deal with the affairs of disbanding the business. He is so good at settling these affairs that the business' creditors ask him to take over the shop. They volunteer to advance him the money for the business with no security but his bond, trusting him to repay them in a given number of years. James, through his own efforts, is now the master of his own shop. More posts the moral: "other apprentices will do well to follow so praiseworthy an example, and to remember, that the respectable master of a large shop and a profitable business was raised to that creditable situation without money, friends, or connections, from the low beginning of a parish apprentice, by sobriety, industry, the fear of God, and an obedience to the Divine principles of the Christian religion (460).

The first part of "The Two Shoemakers" chronicles the rise

of James from parish apprentice to business owner. Part two, "The Apprentice Turned Master," is a how-to guide for running a small business; More teaches the up and coming entrepreneur how to build clientele and reputation. First of all, she underscores the dignity of the business owner: James will "hereafter" be referred to as "Mr. James Stock." The change in his status is itself a trial for him, for he must remember to remain humble and not let his new position go to his head. Some folks "no sooner get a little power than their heads are turned . . . so that one would think that with their poverty they had lost their memory too" (461). James, however, ruled always by religion, remembers to be responsible for those over whom he has power and responsible to those in whose debt he works. In fact, "he worked with double diligence in order to get out of debt, and to let these friends see he did not abuse their kindness." More comments that "such behaviour as this is the greatest encouragement in the world to rich people to lend a little money. It creates friends, and it keeps them" (462). We have seen similar advice from More on how to get rich people to help poor ones in many of her tales, among them "Black Giles." But she does not stop at general advice here, going on to explain in detail how James builds up the business.

> His shoes and boots were made in the best manner—this *got* him business: he set out with a rule to tell no lies and deceive no customers; this *secured* his business. He had two reasons for not promising to send home goods when he knew he should not be able to keep his word. The first, because he knew a lie was a sin; the next, because it was a folly. There is no credit sooner worn out than that which is gained by false pretences. After a little while no one is deceived by them. Falsehood is so soon detected, that I believe most tradesmen are the poorer for it in the long run. Deceit is the worst part of a shopkeeper's stock in trade. (462)

Since work on Sunday is one of More's absolute bugbears, she emphasizes that James never makes deliveries on that day— and that he loses nothing for his good behavior, since his customers "liked Saturday night just as well" (463). His treatment of his apprentices, similarly, is morally and economically sound: his kindness to and careful monitoring of the young men results in a

disciplined and honest workforce. He oversees their morality as
well as their work. Sunday evenings they "divert themselves with
writing out half-a-dozen texts of Scripture in a neat copy-book
with gilt covers." More reminds her reader that "You may have
the same at any of the stationers; they do not cost above four-
pence, and will last nearly a year" (464). There is no hint that such
activities could be less than perfect as a way for the apprentices to
spend their free time. And when one of the apprentices plays and
wastes time, James brings him into line not with punishment but
with religion: "He showed him what was meant by *being obedient to
his master in singleness of heart, as unto Christ,* and explained to him
with so much kindness what it was, *not to work with eye-service as
men-pleasers, but doing the work of God from the heart,* that the lad said
he should never forget it; and it did more towards curing him of
idleness than the soundest horse-whipping would have done" (464).
Thus, More would use Christianity to keep the workers in line; we
remember her invocation of the Bible as a guide to the duty to pay
taxes in *Village Politics.* Obedience to secular masters, whether employer or state, for More is part of the poor man's Christianity.

So, too, with business practices: moral characteristics that
make a good Christian also make for good business. James develops a reputation for skill in his trade, and he has more work than
he can take on. He pays all debts promptly, especially the interest
due his creditors. Soon he begins to pay off the principle. "His reason for being so eager to pay money as soon as it became due" was
that if a tradesman keeps the money he owes to others in his pocket,
he can soon forget that that money belongs not to him but to his
creditors. If the money is paid out directly, this temptation does not
arise. "This [principle] might help to prevent many a bankruptcy"
(465), More proclaims. These principles are so important that even
charity should never be allowed to interfere with them: PAY OFF
THY CREDITORS FIRST seems almost a commandment to More.

And so when a starving child appears before James—it tran-
spires that he is the son of James' old master, now fallen into des-
perate poverty through the wastefulness of his mother—James,
although he wants to help the boy, knows that the product of his
work must go to pay off his debts. In the chapter titled with one
of More's very favorite concepts, "HOW MR. STOCK CON-
TRIVED TO BE CHARITABLE WITHOUT ANY EXPENSE,"
James contrives to find a way to help little Tommy Williams with-

out taking anything from the creditors. He decides that he works twelve hours for them; if he works another hour after that, those proceeds can go to care for the child. He will give the child a year's board and schooling; the only condition is that Tommy may not visit his mother in the parish poor-house where he would be exposed to all the wrong ideas. There is no question in More's mind that in order to give the child a chance, he must—and should—be taken from his mother, a woman who is a model of how not to behave.

In a year or two James is out of debt. It is now time for him to look for a wife. There are lots of girls around, but they are all empty-headed lasses in "tawdry finery." Some, like Nancy, the tanner's daughter, come with significant dowries. But James chooses Betsy West, a quiet, modest girl who has been caring for her invalid mother; Betsy will have nothing after her mother's death. James "was almost sorry that he had not in this case an opportunity of resisting his natural bias, which rather lay on the side of loving money. 'For,' said he, 'putting principle and putting affection out of the question, I shall do a more *prudent* thing by marrying Betsy West, who will conform to her station, and is a religious, humble, industrious girl, without a shilling, than by having an idle dressy lass, who will neglect my family, and fill my house with company'" (474–75).

There is nothing wrong with having a natural bias on the side of loving money. Loving money, as long as it is done in the right spirit (if I may pun) is a very good Christian principle of behavior, for it leads one to be prudent and financially responsible. The eighteenth-century stereotype of the profligate woman who spends far more than her husband earns and thus is instrumental in the ruin of the family shows up often in More's work; the master's wife Mrs. Wilson will be reflected in many of the rejected women in *Coelebs*. It is an important principle for More that a wife must conform to her husband's station, doing the very best she can within the limits of that station to make life pleasant and wholesome for her family. In this regard, the shepherd's wife in "The Shepherd of Salisbury Plain" serves as the model for all wives; whatever her class, whatever resources her husband can give her, a wife's role is basically the same. The religious, industrious Betsy is precisely the girl James needs as a helpmate. And just as one should choose wisely in taking a wife,

More cautions, so should one take equal care in choosing . . . a business partner!

"And here, by-the-by, let me drop a hint to other young men who are about to enter into partnership. Let them not do that in haste which they may repent at leisure. Next to marriage, it is a tie the hardest to break" (477–78)! As so much in this story is meant as direct advice for success in business, this injunction is meant to be taken very seriously. Men much better off than James Stock still need to heed More's warning. Jack, the boy who had been James' fellow apprentice, wants to become his partner; Jack's family is willing to pay handsomely for the privilege. But James is not to be taken in: he "reflected that a young man who has his way to make in the world must not only be good-natured, he must be prudent also. 'I am resolved,' said he, 'to employ none but the most sober, regular, young men I can get. . . . That which might be kindness to one, would be injustice to [the others in the house and shop], and therefore a sin in myself" (III, 478). Jack's family, enraged, sets him up in competition with James, and in the process they do everything wrong. These images too are meant to be caveats for the would-be young businessman. Jack's mother gets him a showy, expensive house; she advises him to undersell his competition, buy low quality goods, and employ cheap workmen.

Jack's goal is to ruin James; James, generously, tries to teach Jack how to be successful. He actually gives Jack "ADVICE TO YOUNG TRADESMEN." More clearly means this paragraph to apply to any and all businesses. Note that More has no hesitation in giving business advice; in contradiction to modern critics who sometimes insist on seeing eighteenth-century women as segregated from mainstream eighteenth-century life, women such as More rather obviously felt no such separation. And so she instructs young tradesmen to "*Buy the best goods; cut the work out yourself; let the eye of the master be every where; employ the soberest men; avoid all the low deceits of trade; never lower the credit of another to raise your own; make short payments; keep exact accounts; avoid idle company, and be very strict to your word*" (480–81). These are the tenets by which James prospers; the disregard of these precepts means that Jack will fail. He makes promises he has no intention of keeping; he produces shoddy goods which, though cheaper than James's, don't last. His customers soon leave him, and he finds himself in debt to his landlord, his workers, and his suppliers. Still he spends what money he has on amusements, always putting off payment until the specter of prison sends him begging to James Stock. Stock and some friends loan Jack the money for the rent; Jack manages to lose it. The way down is quick and inevitable, although More manages to spread Jack's ruin through twenty pages. Finally, ill and crippled from jail fever, he is released because when his father died intestate, James inherited some money; this inheritance, however, is barely adequate to pay his debts, and so Jack ends his days in the parish workhouse, "which, he said, was a far better place than he deserved" (513). From here he is regularly wheeled to church in a sort of barrow contrived for this purpose. As I have mentioned in other contexts, justice in More's Tracts is absolute, and we see that justice reflected in all aspects of a life, including not only the spiritual but the business success of the individual. This is the lesson of "Betty Brown the Orange-Girl," a story that depicts not the full promise of the young apprentice but the very lowest case of a poor, deserted child of the streets.

"Betty Brown, the Orange Girl, was born nobody knows where, and bred nobody knows how."[4] Betty had no other skills than to drive her barrow; she could not sew, spin, wash, or read. "She came into the world before so many good gentlemen and ladies began to concern themselves so kindly that the poor might have a little learning. There was no charitable society then, as there is now, to pick up poor friendless children in the streets, and put them into a good house, and give them meat, and drink, and lodging, and learning, and teach them to get their bread in an honest way, into the bargain. Whereas, this now is often the case in London, blessed be God" (99–100)! So poor Betty must make shift for herself, both in terms of keeping her body alive and her morals in order. Unfortunately, without guidance, the one is often in conflict with the other, although Betty herself has not enough moral training to understand that what she does is wrong. A hard-working girl, she soon catches the eye of a certain cook in her neighborhood; the woman pilfers bits and pieces from her employers, using Betty to sell them for her to Mrs. Sponge, who deals in such dubious goods. This Mrs. Sponge sets Betty up in business: she will give Betty start-up money to buy a barrow and some fruit. Betty will repay her a bit at a time from her profits, as well as paying room and board as a lodger in her house. All of these services are highly overpriced, and Betty becomes in effect an indentured servant; the more she works, somehow, the more she owes. Mrs. Sponge also instructs her eager pupil in ways of getting rid of rotten fruit and bad six-pence pieces. Betty is too morally ignorant to be put off by these nefarious practices and too naive to understand the monetary arrangement into which she has entered.

Luckily, she happens to meet a kindly "lady." As we have seen, the poor always are fortunate when they have the opportunity to be singled out by those in the upper classes. So when Betty drives her barrow through a street near Holborn, and a lady cries through her window that she wants some oranges, Betty's life changes. The lady begins to talk to Betty and finds out about Betty's arrangement with Mrs. Sponge. And "the lady, whose husband was one of the justices of the new police, happened to know more of Mrs. Sponge than was good" (107). She explains to Betty that she has already paid for the initial loan of five shillings the sum of £7, 10s. The lady gives Betty a crash course in economics; if she stops eating and drinking at Mrs. Sponge's house, Betty will soon have saved the amount she owes. Within a year, the £7, 10s she would have given to Mrs. Sponge in interest will belong to her: "Only oblige yourself to live hard for a little time, till you have saved five shillings out of your own earnings. Give up that expensive supper at night, drink only one pint of porter, and no gin at all. As soon as you have scraped together the five shillings, carry it back to your false friend; and if you are industrious, you will, at the end of the year, have saved £7, 10s. . . . judge how things will mend when your capital becomes your own. You will put some clothes on your back; and by leaving the use of spirits, and the company in which you drink them, your health, your morals, and your condition, will mend" (108). As in all these stories, the "lady" could give Betty the money, but she thinks it will be better for Betty to earn it herself. And so Betty, apparently with no ill effects, gives up her supper. More is always ready to see the poor go without food or clothing or heat in the service of building their character.

When Betty goes back to Mrs. Sponge with the five shillings, she is shocked to hear that she supposedly owes her money for all sorts of things. Mrs. Sponge takes everything Betty has and then threatens to call the police. Betty runs away and tells her new friend what has happened. The lady's husband, the justice, has long had Mrs. Sponge in sight as a receiver of stolen goods; he explains to Betty—and the reader—the very severe consequences of Mrs. Sponge's little scam. The justice notes that "if one of these female sharpers possesses a capital of seventy shillings, or £3, 10s with fourteen steady regular customers, she can realize a fixed income of one hundred guineas a year" (110) in addition to what she forces them to pay for food, lodging, and drink. He asks Betty to point out some of these victims so that he "can endeavour to open their eyes on their own bad management" (110). As an astute member of the upper class, one of the kindest things he can do for the poor is to teach them how to manage better—a familiar lesson in these stories. "It is one of the greatest acts of kindness to the poor to mend their economy, and to give them right views of laying out their little money to advantage. These poor blinded creatures [!] look no further than to be able to pay this heavy interest every night, and to obtain the same loan on the same hard terms the next day. Thus are they kept in poverty and bondage all their lives" (110–11). He is as good as his word. Mrs. Sponge is forced to return Betty's money, and then she is sent to jail for various other offenses.

Betty, put on the right road, does well. She gives up drink—and can buy shoes in a fortnight! The lady gives her a new gown and hat, only requiring that she go to church, where, of course, Betty first learns that she is a sinner. But before Betty is committed to a moral makeover, More has underscored the material benefits to be accrued if the poor person commits herself to a frugal lifestyle, especially if she gives up drinking alcohol. Religion for More always is valuable in itself, but she often presents morality to the poor as attached to real-world advancement. It takes Betty only two weeks of "leaving off spirits" before she has a new pair of shoes to show for her good behavior.

And the more areas of life that good behavior shapes, the more prosperous, materially and spiritually, Betty will be. Take a room in an honest house, the lady tells Betty, and keep your Sundays for church and the Bible. "A barrow-woman may pray as heartily morning and night, and serve God as acceptably all day, while she is carrying on her little trade, as if she had her whole time to spare," the lady tells Betty. "To do this well, you must mind the following 'RULES FOR RETAIL DEALERS'" (113). The rules are a straightforwardly didactic list of injunctions for the honest course of business; God and commerce go hand-in-hand.

*"Resist every temptation to cheat."*
*"Never impose bad goods on false pretences."*

*"Never put off bad money for good."*
*"Never use profane or uncivil language."*

Somewhat less important (this rule is not underlined), "Never swear your goods cost so much, when you know it is false." The "lady" comments that "to break these rules, will be your chief temptation. God will mark how you behave under them, and will reward or punish you accordingly." And then she notes, "These temptations will be as great to you, as higher trials are to higher people; but you have the same God to look to for strength to resist them, as they have" (113).

That the "trials" of the rich are somehow quite different from those of the poor (an idea we remember from Soame Jenyns) seems to More self understood. Naturally, the class implications of these distinctions do not disturb Betty, who breaks into tears of "joy and gratitude" at her lucky chance. The tale ends with one more quick lesson: there is no such thing as luck, the lady tells Betty; it is all God's will. "Betty Brown the Orange-Girl" makes it clear to the poor that their good behavior is a part—a large part—of their duty to God. Honest business practices not only will keep them from want but will keep them from God's direct punishment. The reverse is very frightening, and More means her poor auditors to be scared into the appropriate paths for selling oranges and for offering prayers. Not least of the lessons to be learned in this tale is that if the poor person is good, those better off will help him or her. Betty never would have become self-sufficient if it had not been for the kindly intercession of the lady and the justice. Certainly those closer to Betty in class, like Mrs. Sponge and the drinking companions Betty picks up both at the house of Mrs. Sponge and at the tavern, are a source of danger rather than comfort. This lesson might be less than palatable to those More is addressing, and she makes it rather more subtly than her other lessons.

Somewhere between the decent beginnings of both boys in "The Two Shoemakers" and the utter destitution of the poor "St. Giles Orange Girl" is Tom White at the beginning of "Tom White the Postilian." "Tom White" is actually the first story published in the Repository series, and in its outlines we can see a great many of the elements that will appear in the stories that follow. Tom comes from a simple but decent family. To help his family to manage financially, he leaves home as early as he can to make his own way. He is fortunate to find employment that gives him respectable work all week and that requires him to spend his Sundays, although he is an adult, attending Sunday school. On Sunday evening, "after he had served his cattle," the worthy farmer who employs Tom "always made him read his Bible."[5] But Tom is seduced by the bright livery of the postboys, and he gives up his job as the farmer's waggoner "to drive a chaise, to get money, and to see the world" (2).

Given his motives for the change, the reader already can guess that this decision will not have positive results. Tom is exposed to "evil company," and although for a time his "good education stood by him" (IV, 2), after awhile he too succumbs to the temptations that surround him. He begins by being shocked at the swearing of his fellows; too soon, he imitates their nasty language. This misconduct is the first in a series that brings him to the very depths of degradation. More, as we so often have seen, is a great believer that there is a slippery slope to evil. Tom begins by swearing at his horses; this first step is soon followed by taking to drink. Tom does not even like drinking, but he is following his peers. He works on Sunday, and soon "did not know Sunday from Monday" (4). He earns a great deal but spends all of it. Tom is well on the way to trouble. And the trouble indeed finds him. Somewhat drunk, he one day challenges another driver to a foolish race; there is an accident, and Tom is seriously injured. "Tom was taken to one of those excellent hospitals with which London abounds" (6). Horror-stricken at the state he finds himself in both spiritually and physically, Tom is forced to face his errors and vows to reform.

We have noted More's habit of inserting little sermons into the texts of her stories. Here in this early story she sets the pattern by interrupting her tale with a salutary commercial for the great social services that England provides for the poor. The moral is that those poor and laboring men should be grateful and docile citizens in return for the remarkable support and benevolence that their government provides. The year of "Tom White" is 1795, and growing unrest had been agitating Britain at least since the late 1780s. The second part of this tale, with no subtlety, is titled "The Way to Plenty; or, the Second Part of Tom White. Written in 1795, the Year of Scarcity." More notes that although Tom's broken bones and high fever were very serious, "By the blessing of God on the skill of the surgeon" (6), Tom soon grew better. And then she simply halts her narrative: "And here let me stop to remark what a mercy it is that we live in a Christian country, where the poor, when sick, or lame, or wounded, are taken as much care of as any gentry; nay, in some respects more, because in hospitals and infirmaries there are more doctors and surgeons to attend than most private gentlefolks can afford to have at their own houses, whereas THERE NEVER WAS AN HOSPITAL IN THE WHOLE HEATHEN WORLD. Blessed be God for this" (6–7). With no transition, she then simply rejoins Tom, who could not be moved from his bed for eight weeks: "This was a happy affliction; for by the grace of God, this long sickness and solitude gave him time to reflect on his past life" (7).

As in "The Shepherd of Salisbury Plain," this formulation about "happy afflictions" seems to have been part of a pattern of thought current in More's circle. Here in "The History of Tom White," More makes a most convincing case for the positive side of Tom's accident. Tom resolves to reform, and although he goes back to the same job, he no longer is tempted by any follies. He has studied his Bible and his catechism diligently during his long recovery, and all the lessons serve him well upon his return to the rough and tumble of his world. He finds ways to adapt his work life so that he still can live up to the moral measure he has set himself. Perhaps most distressing to him is that he must drive on Sundays; after much thought, he realizes that while waiting for his fares to return, he can go to church in any town. And if prayers are over, perhaps he can still hear the sermon. He keeps his chaise neat and takes good care of his horses. As the word gets around about Tom, many patrons request only his services. "Tom soon grew rich for one in his station; for every gentleman on the road would be driven by no other lad if *careful* Tom was to be had. Being diligent, he *got* a great deal of money; being frugal, he *spent* but little; and having no vices, he *wasted* none" (11).

From here Tom climbs steadily upward,[6] for More shows that just as vice leads to ever greater degradation, good behavior draws attention to itself and accrues more and more spiritual and worldly profit. When after a few years Tom takes a vacation and goes home to his native village (his father is dead, but Tom's contributions kept him off the parish during his last serious illness), Tom finds that his "good character" (12) has preceded him. His first employer, Farmer Hodges, in the meantime has "grown old and infirm" and wants to retire. Finding that Tom has some money, as well as knowledge of the business, "he offered to let him a small farm at an easy rate, and promised his assistance in the management for the first year, with the loan of a small sum of money, that he might set out with a pretty stock" (12). Tom thanks him and goes back to take leave of his current master, who is so aware of Tom's contribution to *his* business that he gives Tom a cart and a horse as a parting gift. Tom works diligently at his new profession, and the farm is soon brought "to great perfection" (13). Tom is transformed into the respectable "Mr. Thomas White." Successful Farmer White finds that he needs a wife: "Farmer White soon found out that a dairy could not well be carried on without a mistress, and began to think seriously of marrying: he prayed to God to direct him in so serious a business" (13). He finds a "prudent, sober, industrious, and religious" (13) girl to wed, and they live happily ever after.

The moral to part one of "Tom White" is made explicit in the first sentence of part two: "Tom White, as we have shown in the first part of this history, from an idle post-boy was become a respectable farmer. God had blessed his industry, and he had prospered in the world" (17). This result was in no way inevitable and, in fact, had Tom not had his fortunate accident, he might have frittered his time away in the worst activities of a postboy's life. But now Tom has achieved the substantial station of farmer; he has married prudently, and he lives a serious, properly religious life. His hard work is rewarded, but More makes a point of insisting that the flowering of Tom's pursuits is not due only to his own efforts, for hard work alone without God's blessing does not guarantee success. This is important, because connected with this idea is the concept that hardship, too, is good for the individual. In this "Year of Scarcity" 1795, that precept seems a particularly useful one for the upper class to promulgate among the lower classes.

Tom realizes "that a time of public prosperity was not always a time of public virtue" (18), so that "when he lately saw signs of public distress coming on, he was not half so much frightened as some others were, because he thought it might do us good in the long run; and he was in hopes that a little poverty might bring on a little penitence" (19). The whole of the second part of "Tom White" is intended to teach the poor to appreciate their good fortune in the face of whatever hardship God chooses to give them. More believes strongly that recipes for cheap dishes will help a great deal! But the recipes (similar to those we shall see in the next story I look at, "A Cure for Melancholy," often called "The Cottage Cook") come after other practical lessons for managing in these hard times.

Do the laborers complain that they can't afford a bit of meat? That problem can be solved if they will just work on their holidays. Farmer White explains patiently to Tom, a thatcher who interrupts a job he was doing to take Easter Monday and Easter Tuesday off, that if Tom works these two days he will earn four shillings. Should Tom stay with his mates during these days, he would spend three shillings on drink. Seven shillings! Gently, Farmer White chides Tom, "'Tom, you often tell me the times are so bad that you can never buy a bit of meat. Now here is the cost of two joints at once; to say nothing of the sin of wasting time and getting drunk'" (23–24). The advice doesn't stop there: a shoulder of mutton left over from Saturday's market will come cheaper than normal; directions for the cooking are to bake the meat in a "'deep dish of potatoes. . . . [Y]ou need not give the mutton to the brats; the potatoes will have all the gravy, and be very savoury for them'" (24). Advice also is given about home brewing, another of More's favorite topics, for beer brewed at home will keep men away from the local tavern.

And so the hardness of the times can be finessed quite easily—just brew at home, work on holidays and remember to give the "brats" only a potato and gravy. This is the sort of advice that More is very fond of: she never seems to be aware that her ideas for helping the poor could be less than generous. And so "Mrs. White was so considerate, that just at that time she lessened the number of her hogs, that she might have more whey and skimmilk to assist poor families; nay, I have known her to live on boiled meat for a long while together, in a sickly season, because the pot-liquor made such a supply of broth for the sick poor" (28–29). Mrs. White's munificence in giving the water in which she boiled her meat to the sick poor is, for a modern reader, less than overwhelming. But that Mrs. White consistently eats meat while the poor get the cooking water does not seem in any way uncomfortable to More.

The second part of "Tom White" is in fact straightforward propaganda designed to keep the poor from rising up to attack those better off. More's message is based without any subtlety on the dual platforms of reward and punishment: do what the rich expect and demand of you, she tells the poor, and they will help you as much as they can within the limits of the current economic situation; do not behave precisely within the guidelines set up by your betters, and you can expect no help at all. And, as always in these tales, the message is that society owes the poor very little; any aid the poor man gets must be well earned, and even then, he should be markedly grateful for it. More makes overt references to those who would use these difficult times as an impetus to revolt; it is absolutely clear that listening to any such counsels will be catastrophic for the poor since by so doing they will lose all hope of aid and comfort from those with any power to provide help. Besides, More makes clear, God would not like such behavior by the poor.

God does everything for a reason, and so if there is not enough to eat, that is God's will, although it is man's responsibility to "hope for a good day" while preparing as best he can "against an evil one" (30). The responsibility of the better off is, in large part, to provide hope for the poor, and so the rich should be careful not to manifest public pessimism. At the same time, "in case the corn *should* fail" (30), the farmers should allow their laborers to plant potatoes or, even better, turnips (which take up less room) in the waste corners of the fields. The good farmer will resist the possibility of selling his harvest at "an extravagant price" (30) but should sell at decent, even below market prices, to his own neighboring poor. And further, the rich in More's stories, as here in "Tom White," are shown as always concerned with "the best method of further assisting the poor" (32). When the crops do come in better than expected, for example, the farmers get together a plan "to subscribe for a large quantity of rice, which was to be sold out to the poor at a very low price, and Mrs. White was so kind as to undertake the trouble of selling it. After their day's work was over, all who wished to buy at these reduced rates were ordered to come to the farm on the Tuesday evening" (33). This gesture is clearly more political than not, for More makes it very clear that such aid is entirely dependent on the good behavior of the poor. Political unrest—riot—will close off the channels of benevolence.

The threat is explicit. During this time of hardship, "There

are some idle, evil-minded people, who are on the watch for public distresses; not that they may humble themselves under the
mighty hand of God, which is the true use of be made of all
troubles, but that they may benefit themselves by disturbing the
public peace." Those who incite or participate in "riot and drunkenness, double the evil which they pretend to cure" (33). The threat
is overt: riot will only make things worse. "Riot will complete our
misfortunes, while peace, industry, and good management, will
go near to cure them" (33–34).

In addition to the problem of unrest, which in itself More
implies somehow calls forth misery for the poor, many of the problems that the poor face are due to their own mismanagement. And
so More's story gives explicit lessons about how to manage better. The minister takes the occasion of having essentially a captive
audience—the poor women have come after work to collect their
ration of rice—to tell them just that: "My good women, I truly
feel for you at this time of scarcity; and I am going to show my
good will, as much by my advice as my subscription. It is my
duty, as your friend and minister, to tell you, that one half of your
present hardships is owing to *bad management*" (34).

What are these women doing wrong? Their children are bare-
foot, but they get three servings of white bread each day. They eat
their bread hot out of the oven. The minister, with the help of
Mrs. White (clearly meant to be More herself), will teach them
how to do better.[7] Mix the grains to make your bread, and make
your bread part of a leak or onion porridge. Put a little oatmeal,
an onion, a bit of salt and some bread together for a breakfast that
will feed your whole family cheaply. Make a stew with some cheap
cut of meat, "a sheep's head, or any such thing" (35), she tells
them. Actual recipes for "rice milk" and rice pudding, parsnips
the first day and the second ("warmed in the frying-pan, and a
little rasher of pork or bacon will give them a nice flavour" [37]),
cheap mutton stew, pickled herring and potatoes—the threat about
the riots is followed by page upon page of benevolent suggestions to the poor for making-do with what they have.

And in case in the course of appreciating all this good advice the poor have lost awareness of the stick just behind the carrot, the end of the story again emphasizes explicitly that any
actions by the poor that do not have the approbation of the rich
immediately will result in the forfeit of all aid. This misbehavior

comes in the two categories we already have seen defined, mismanagement and rebellion; of the two, it is clear that rebellion is by far the worst mistake and, therefore, it is only to be expected that any untoward actions of this sort on the part of the poor will be met with the most serious sanctions by their superiors. More makes the assumption that social or political "riot" is most likely to be manifested by the men, as, lower on the scale of misdeeds but still very serious, is an over zealous appreciation of the local pub. The two kinds of bad behavior in fact seem somewhat connected in "Tom White." In real life, of course, since so much of the political discussion of the working men and so much of the attempt to radicalize them took place in the public houses, More's linking of the two warnings reflects the dangers that many in her class perceived in these institutions. We have seen in previous chapters with what seriousness More and her friends viewed these interactions.

And so the narrative in "Tom White" turns from the mismanagement of the female poor, which generally manifests itself in such ways as feeding their children too much white bread or not knowing how to prepare cheap nourishing food, to the potentially more serious issues that involve the men: "'Sir,' said Farmer White, 'I beg leave to say a word to the men, if you please, for all your advice goes to the women. If you will drink less gin you may get more meat. If you abstain from the ale-house, you may, many of you, get a little one-way beer at home.'"

In any case, "'The number of public-houses in many a parish brings on more hunger and rags than all the taxes in it, heavy as they are. All the other evils put together hardly make up the sum of that one'" (39). This is really a brilliant argument: the poor should not blame their economic troubles on external burdens, on taxation, for example, but on their own indulgence. The specific remark about taxes needs to be emphasized here, for as I showed in my discussion of Paine's *Rights of Man*, one of the principle arguments of the radicals is that the tax burden—both direct and indirect—is the cause of virtually all the economic ills in the nation. More is answering that claim here, and I think that her reference specifically is to the arguments that she and her class see as so dangerous in their appeal to the poor.

More's next comments make the link explicit between the poor man's social obedience and his well being: if he does not act in precise accord with what his betters see as appropriate behavior, he will get none of their help. Farmer White says, "'We are now raising a fresh subscription for you'" (39), but he immediately states the conditions to which the poor must accede if they are to partake of this charity. "'This will be our rule of giving,'" he says, and then he proceeds to list his conditions, conditions which the entire upper-class community is enforcing. Note that the list of prohibitions begins with moral and behavioral issues; it ends, significantly, with an unambiguous prohibition against political, communal rebellion. "'We will not give to sots, gamblers, and Sabbath-breakers. Those who do not send their young children to work on week-days, and send them to school and church on Sundays, deserve little favour. . . . Such as come to the vestry for a loaf, and do not come to church for the sermon, we shall mark; and prefer those who come constantly whether there are any gifts or not'" (39–41).

And then the tone changes. The prohibitions take on, as it were, a harder, more ominous aspect. "'But there is one rule from which we never will depart. Those who have been seen aiding or abetting any riot, any attack on butchers, wheat-mows, mills, or millers, we will not relieve; but with the quiet, contented, hard-working man, I will share my last morsel of bread'" (41). This very firm reference to the social and political unrest, including food riots, that I discussed in chapter three is coldly threatening. The gentle persona of the kindly helper of the poor that Hannah More becomes so very famous for in her lifetime is underlaid by an unforgiving foundation of social pragmatism. In her own way, she is perhaps no less rigid in her social stance than the wretches she condemns for their violence in France.

So blatant is the threat expressed here at the end of "Tom White" that More attempts to soften it somewhat in her last sentences. The softening, however, itself is in no way a backtracking. "'I shall only add,'" Farmer White says, that "'though it has pleased God to send us this visitation as a punishment, yet we may convert this short trial into a lasting blessing, if we all turn over a new leaf'" (41). The fault, you see, is in both rich and poor; the poor, like the rich, just have not been using their resources as well as they ought! "'Prosperity has made most of us careless. The thoughtless profusion of some of the rich could only be exceeded by the idleness and bad management of some of the poor'" (41). So the only people who have been more profligate than the rich

are . . . the poor! The only logical conclusion, then, is that they all
"'adopt that good old maxim, *Every one mend one*'" (41). And on
that happy thought, all the poor people go off contentedly to make
their lovely rice pudding: "The people now cheerfully departed
with their rice, resolving, as many of them as could get milk, to
put one of Mrs. White's receipts [recipes] in practice,—and an
excellent supper they had" (41).

The following year (1797), More writes the very long three-
part tale of "A Cure For Melancholy: Showing The Way To Do
Much Good With Little Money, Written During The Scarcity Of
1794," which becomes "The Sunday School," and then "The History Of Hester Wilmot," in which all the lessons of "Tom White"
and "Betty Brown" are repeated and expanded. The first part, "A
Cure For Melancholy," spends even more time than "Betty Brown"
on the good the upper classes can do the poor; wonderfully, this
good need not cost a shilling. At the center of the story is Mrs.
Jones, who had been a great merchant's wife. She always had given
money to the poor, but without much thought. Poor Mr. Jones
suffers terrible reverses in his business, and as the business fails,
it destroys his health and he dies. Mrs. Jones retires with a "very
narrow income"[8] to a small village and becomes something of a
recluse, indulging her sorrow. Mr. Simpson, the vicar of her local
church, finds her in tears after one of his sermons on the good
Samaritan. She regrets, she tells him, that she has so little now to
give the poor. Mr. Simpson assures her that it is not money only
that the poor need from people like her. He has been surprised, in
fact, that she has not made herself more useful. She replies that
she has stayed away from the poor since she has nothing to give
them. "'Nothing! madam?' replied the clergyman: 'do you call
your time, your talents, your kind offices, nothing? . . . You,
madam, I will venture to say, might do more good than the richest man in the parish could do by merely giving his money. Instead of sitting here brooding over your misfortunes . . . bestir
yourself to find out ways of doing much good with little money;
or even without any money at all. You have lately studied economy
for yourself; instruct your poor neighbors in that important art.
They want it almost as much as they want money'" (274–76).

As we just have seen in "Tom White," this is one of More's
axioms for the poor: they don't necessarily need more money or
goods, they just need to learn to manage better, and one of the

greatest kindnesses their better-off neighbors can give them is the skill to live better with what they already have. It is also a wonderfully easy road for the better-off to take, since often, no matter how much they own, they are reluctant to part with their resources. But "influence," for example, is another matter. If Mrs. Jones does not have money herself to give to the poor, she still has "'influence with the few rich persons in the parish'"; she is admonished to "'exert that influence'" (276). More goes on to give us character sketches of the two richest men in the district, Sir John and the squire. Sir John is a good sort of man, but thoughtless. He does not hesitate to lay out money, but it is not always done in the wisest way: he is ready to give the poor drink at Christmas time, to give them "bell-ringing and bonfires . . . but he thought it was folly to teach them, and madness to think of reforming them" (277). The squire, on the other hand, is willing to help Mrs. Jones in all her plans as long as it does not cost him anything, "so she showed her good sense by never asking Sir John for advice, or the Squire for subscriptions, and by this prudence gained the full support of both" (278).

One of the useful things Mrs. Jones can do is to take on the role of social activist. She notices that the loaves in her village seem quite small. When she sends for a loaf from the town, and compares the weights, she finds the town loaf a full two pounds heavier than those that can be bought from the local baker for the same shilling. "This was not the sort of grievance to carry to Sir John; but luckily the Squire was also a magistrate, and it was quite in his way. . . . He told her he could remedy the evil if some one would lodge an information against the baker" (278–79). Mrs. Jones goes to the blacksmith and asks him to inform against the baker; although he has just been complaining about the short measure, the blacksmith nevertheless is shocked at the idea that he should be an informer. A very long discussion about the duty of people to inform against law-breakers convinces him, and the machinery of justice is set in motion. The dishonest baker Crib is fined and his bread given away free to the poor. "Thus had Mrs. Jones the comfort of seeing how useful people may be without expense; for if she could have given the poor fifty pounds, she would not have done them so great, or so lasting a benefit, as she did them in seeing their loaves restored to their lawful weight: and the true light in which she had put the business of *informing* was of no small use" (281).

She convinces the poor not to deal with shopkeepers who do business on Sunday. She convinces the rich to leave the coarse pieces of meat so that the poor can buy them. Poor women are taught to bake wholesomely and cheaply at home and to brew their own beer too. (Mrs. Jones has found means to have two of the local taverns shut down.) The brewing supplies yeast for the bread, and a communal oven allows for the baking. A lack of milk is fixed by convincing a local woman to keep cows just for the purpose of selling small amounts of milk at a time. The woman also sells rice cheaply, "so that with the help of the milk and the public oven, a fine rice pudding was to be had for a trifle" (287)— a formula familiar to us from "Tom White." Mrs. Jones has done a great deal of good for the poor without spending any of her own, or, except for the funds to build the oven, anyone else's money (the squire subscribed to the oven "because he thought every improvement in economy would reduce the poor's rate" [286]); More shows that such basic services for the poor more than pay for themselves in reducing the dependency of the poor on public aid. What else needed to be done?

How about the education of girls to be workers? The girls' school in the parish had fallen into disrepair; the local gentry have been neglecting their duty to have their "grown-up daughters . . . inspect the instruction of the poor" (287). Mrs. Jones restores the school. The girls and their mothers are taught how to make and mend, wash and iron. Once a week she teaches the poor "how to dress *one cheap dish*" (288). When the squire happens by, he is disturbed to find Mrs. Jones not teaching the girls manufacturing trades. She answers that theirs is not a manufacturing county, but that she does indeed teach them a bit of spinning and knitting so that they can make stockings for their families. Far more important, she tells the squire, is that she is carrying on now a "'manufacture [such that] I know of none within my own reach which is so valuable.' — 'What can that be?' said the squire. — '*To make good wives for working-men*'" (288), answers Mrs. Jones. She goes on at length:

> "Is not mine an excellent staple commodity? I am teaching these girls the art of industry and good management. It is little encouragement to an honest man to work hard all the week, if his wages are wasted by a slattern at home. Most of these girls will

probably become wives to the poor, or servants to the rich; to
such the common arts of life are of great value: now, as there is
little opportunity for learning these at the school-house, I intend to propose, that such gentry as have sober servants shall
allow one of these girls to come and work in their families one
day in a week, when the housekeeper, the cook, the house-maid,
or the laundry-maid, shall be required to instruct them in their
several departments. This I conceive to be the best way of training good servants." (288–89)

More's implication here, not surprisingly in view of what
we already have seen in stories such as "The Shepherd of Salisbury
Plain," is that the wife of a poor man essentially takes the role of
his servant; the skills the poor girl needs, whether she marries or
goes out to service, are the same. We should note too that More's
scheme of education for girls is designed to give them practical
skills. Poor men need useful wives, and the upper classes need
good servants. This practical emphasis is in line with More's larger
schemes for the education of the poor in her charity schools: we
remember her insistence that her plan includes reading but no
writing, for writing is a skill that might give the poor ideas for
advancement beyond their station. In this passage in "A Cure For
Melancholy" it is clear that the education these girls receive is
meant to fit them for their present life; it is by no means intended
to help to raise them out of their current situation. In More's reckoning, a poor girl's most likely options for economic survival are
either marriage within her class or life as a servant. The economic
and social movement that More posited in "The Two Shoemakers" for a hardworking poor man who through an apprenticeship
can rise well beyond his starting point does not seem to have been
a possibility in More's scheme for women.[9]

But making do with that which is available to the poor
woman does seem perfectly adequate—for the poor—to More.
When the good squire happens on Mrs. Jones' cooking lesson, he
is most surprised, "'for your pot really smells as savoury as if Sir
John's French cook had filled it'" (289). More provides an advertisement for her own Cheap Repository books; the recipe, Mrs.
Jones says, came out of one of these books. These recipes are all
good, and every Friday she and another of her friends come to
the school to show the women "'how it is done, and learn to dress

it at their own houses. I take home part of my own dinner, and what is left I give to each in turn. I hope I have opened their eyes on a sad mistake they had got into, *that we think any thing is good enough for the poor.'"* And she goes on—More is oblivious to the double meaning here—that she does "'*not* think any thing good enough for the poor which is not clean, wholesome and palatable, and what I myself would not cheerfully eat, if my circumstances required it'" (290). It is that last phrase that rings somewhat hollow, for while the sentence seems to say that the poor are entitled to food that is more or less the same as other people's, it says the opposite. Again, the poor are being told that, being poor, they must make do. Those better off are willing to help them to manage better, but this in no way implies that the poor should have access to a higher level of meat, for example. More, I think, cannot hear her own implication, for to her the kind of interventions Mrs. Jones makes are truly a help and a kindness to those in need. The squire, after all, not only tries the soup but likes it so much that he asks for the recipe.[10]

The second part of "A Cure For Melancholy" is called "The Sunday-School." This is the story of how Mrs. Jones went about setting up her school, and it details not only her philosophy for such schools but the hazards and hassles that such projects present to their initiators. The story conforms precisely to Hannah More's accounts in her letters and Patti More's descriptions in the *Mendip Annals* of the processes and trials they encountered in this work. "The Sunday-School" is in effect More's homage to her own efforts in the schools, although surely she would have seen the story as a guide and an inducement to those who would carry on such work themselves. Mrs. Jones simply is a pseudonym for Hannah More herself.

Mrs. Jones, we are told, did not much fear not being able to raise the money for the project; the real problem is in finding appropriately capable and religious people to run such a school. Not, she says, that "I would discourage those who set them up, even in the most ordinary manner, and from mere views of worldly policy" (293), for it is always "something gained to rescue children from idling away their Sabbath in the fields or the streets. It is no small thing to keep them from those tricks to which a day of leisure tempts the idle and the ignorant. It is something for them to be taught to read; it is much to be taught to read the Bible; and much, indeed, to be carried regularly to church" (293). But for the thing to work properly, it requires good teachers, "and a diligent attention in some pious gentry to visit and inspect the schools" (293)—gentry, of course, such as herself and her sisters.

Such "gentry" must first of all have good judgment, she says. Recommendations will come in from all sources for people to take over the school, but these recommendations must be carefully sifted: too often, the people being proposed are not qualified for the job but, in fact, represent someone else's problem—a cook who can't cook, a family living at the parish's expense that could be taken off the rolls if employment were found for them. Mrs. Jones is not surprised to find that it is difficult to find a good mistress for the school, one with sense, piety, and energy, but finally she does discover just such a woman, Mr. Edwards' housekeeper Betty. Betty even has some training in teaching children; for years each Saturday evening she has been examining the poor children of the neighborhood in their catechism when they come to the parsonage for a dole of broth. Mr. Edwards remarks that "'she is just and fair in dealing out the broth and beef, not making my favour to the parents depend on the skill of their children'" (297). Betty's cast-off caps and ribbons, her old clothes, become presents for the children. Such charity, which itself costs nothing and yet demands diligent attention, even work, from the poor, is More's favorite kind of benevolence. The lesson is explicit: "'it is not necessary to be rich in order to do good; a religious upper servant has great opportunities of this sort, if the master is disposed to encourage her'" (297–98). Having solved the problem of finding a mistress for the school, Mrs. Jones must convince the mothers to send their children. This she does simply by telling them that if the children do not attend Sunday school, they will be doomed to "sin and hell" and will curse their mothers ever after. This mild argument works wonders, and all the mothers are convinced. As in More's Mendip schools, the older children are required to attend before the younger are admitted; Mrs. Jones, like More in real life, will not allow her school to become a baby-sitting institution.

Now, Mrs. Jones is faced with getting support for her school. As More did, Mrs. Jones finds a combination of parsimony and scepticism among the better-off farmers and the neighboring squires and tradesmen. Most, however, do subscribe something, until she comes to the richest farmer in the parish, farmer Hoskins.

He does not want to subscribe, complaining that between tithes and subscriptions he loses too much. I've worked hard, he says; let others do the same. He is especially vehement against a school for the poor. "'[T]eaching the poor to read'" is the very worst sort of idea. Mrs. Jones voices More's own philosophy: "'to teach good principles to the lower classes is the most likely way to save the country'" (IV, 302). This is the bedrock on which all of More's work with the poor is founded, and again we see the identity for More of appropriate moral stance and appropriate allegiance as a citizen. The education of the poor to the end of creating good Christians also, and not less importantly, will produce loyal citizens supportive of the structures of the state. You save the country by teaching the proper principles to the lower classes; "'in order to [do] this, we must teach them to read'" (IV, 302). When farmer Hoskins argues that such teaching does more harm than good, Mrs. Jones admits that of course mischief is possible if you teach the poor to read but neglect to give them suitable materials to read. This caveat also comes with a commercial: the footnote to this sentence tells us that "it was this consideration, chiefly, which stimulated the conductor of the Cheap Repository to send forth that variety of little books so peculiarly suited to the young. She considered that by means of Sunday Schools multitudes were now taught to read, who would be exposed to be corrupted by all the ribaldry and profaneness of loose songs, vicious stories, and especially by the new influx of corruption arising from jacobinical and atheistical pamphlets; and that it was a bounden duty to counteract such temptations" (302).

More is horrified by the penny literature that was virtually ubiquitous; her job, as she saw it, in large part was to counteract the pernicious influences of the profane writing that was all too available to the poor. Far better that the poor should be exposed to writing that would teach them to think properly—and not simply in religious but in acceptable political terms. This is the argument Mrs. Jones makes to farmer Hoskins: proper books are a means of social control. For farmer Hoskins fears that the ability to read will make his workers unruly. "'I am afraid my own workmen will fly in my face if once they are made scholars; and that they will think themselves too good to work'" (303).[11] Patty More recounts just this type of dialogue in the *Mendip Annals*.

The fictional Mrs. Jones answers farmer Hoskins with More's

precise explanation of her project to Dr. Beadon in 1802, when he became bishop of Bath and Wells, an explanation repeated in letters to several of her friends: "'Now, the whole extent of learning which we intend to give the poor is only to enable them to read the Bible'" (303). Mrs. Jones insists that religion taught the right way promotes social order: "'The knowledge of that book, and its practical influence on the heart, is the best security you can have both for the industry and obedience of your servants. Now, can you think any man will be the worse servant for being a good Christian?'" (304). Even further, she asks rhetorically, "'Are not the duties of children, of servants, and the poor, individually and expressly set forth in the Bible?'" (304). The Christian religion teaches the poor to know their place and to work willingly for their masters. People are more likely to work well from "'those religious motives, which are backed with the sanction of rewards and punishments, of heaven or hell. . . . Will your property be secured so effectually by the stocks on the green, as by teaching the boys in the school, that *for all these things God will bring them into judgment?*'" (304). Farmer Hoskins is convinced and offers up half a guinea; he raises it to a whole guinea when Mrs. Jones lets slip that his neighbor, who is only a renter, already has given the smaller sum. And so, More shows, between logical argument and social rivalry well exploited, the project is brought forward by Mrs. Jones.

But Mrs. Jones is not through yet with farmer Hoskins, for in addition to his subscription, she tells him that his further support will be crucial to the success of the school. He must insist his workmen send their children, and he himself should look into the school from time to time to make sure that things go as they should, with rewards coming as appropriate. "'The most zealous teachers will flag in their exertions, if they are not animated and supported by the wealthy; and your poor youth will soon despise religious instruction, as a thing forced upon them, as a hardship added to their other hardships, if it be not made pleasant by the encouraging presence, kind words, and little gratutities from their betters'" (305). More from time to time was accused of using bribery (dinners, small presents) to make her instruction palatable to the poor; she would always insist, as here, that "little gratuities" are simply part of the machinery of instruction. And as in her schools, More here in the story suggests that older children, and, finally, their parents, all have a place after work hours and on Sunday evenings being instructed: "And it was observed that as the school filled not only the Fives-court and public houses were thinned, but even Sunday gossiping and tea visiting declined" (309).[12]

It only remains to show in detail the kind of changes that such a school makes in the lives of the poor, and this More does in the last part of "A Cure For Melancholy," titled "The History of Hester Wilmot." Hester is Rebecca Wilmot's daughter, and Rebecca does not want her child to go to the school. Rebecca does everything wrong, even the things that might seem right. She is very clean and tidy, but she carries her cleanliness to the point of making her family miserable, especially her husband. As all unhappy husbands do in More's stories, he finds refuge in the local tavern where he learns to drink, to stay away from his family, and generally to lead a disreputable and irresponsible life—all due to his unhapppiness at home. Hester learns all that she should learn at the school, and by her example, she even reforms her mother and father. The father, having borrowed and then lost the money Hester painstakingly had saved for a new gown for the May celebration at the school, watches his uncomplaining daughter as she shines through the children's competition even in her old frock. Moved by her devotion, both to her studies and to him, father gets religion too. Mother, noting all the good that her daughter and husband have brought into the house, herself embraces religion and learns to value important things and to ignore her vanities. Needless to say, everyone lives happily ever after, all due to the wonders of Mrs. Jones' school.

Eight

# Conclusion

## The Power of the Printed Word:
## Hannah More and
## Mary Wollstonecraft on Reading

THE EXTRAORDINARY BELIEF in the power of the printed word, especially its danger, that we have remarked in so many aspects of More's life and work, in her commitment to fighting the pamphlet war against the radicals, in her careful calibration of the amount of education her poor people should have and the kinds of materials to which they should be exposed, seems almost as if it should be sui generis to this one writer, so strong is the impulse. But we know that this is not the case; she begins her pamphlet-writing career, after all, in direct response to Tom Paine, and he, in turn, is writing in response to Burke. The belief that the printed word can change society is equally powerful on both sides of the political gate, as we have seen. And at both ends of the political spectrum this particular perspective sometimes results in very similar pronouncements coming from sources that we might be surprised to see line up so identically: for example, it was contemporary comment that first noticed the remarkably similar curves of the education tracts published by Wollstonecraft and, later, by More. The period's fascination with conduct manuals is part of the same impulse to control behavior with words; so too is the ubiquity of didactic fiction, from Defoe to Richardson through the radical novelists at the end of the century such as Holcroft, Godwin and Bage. Reading, and the appropriate authors to read, is itself a significant theme of eighteenth and early nineteenth-century writing. The conduct manuals, especially all those "Thoughts" on the education of females, refer to particular works that should be read; there are also remonstrances against authors and specific works or classes of writing (large swathes of the stage, for example) that are seen as corrupt and corrupting. Novelists too make frequent allusions of all these kinds to a wide variety of contemporary writing. One of the interesting aspects of this topic is that so many of the references indeed are to contemporary fare, yet another manifestation of the sense among these writers that they are engaging in a direct dialogue—in many cases, as we have seen, a direct confrontation—with other authors, and that the results of these contests are of enormous significance to the well-being not just of the individual but also of society.

Some authors seem ubiquitous. Everybody read, or at least talked about, Rousseau. John Locke provides salient examples for just about all social commentators, as does Edmund Burke—what the examples represent varies, of course, with the political stance of the writer pointing to them. After the publication of *Rights of Man*, it is difficult to avoid notice of Paine. And of course the Bible provides a major source for discussion especially, not surprisingly, in conduct manuals. Here I am going to turn to Hannah More and Mary Wollstonecraft as authors of conduct manuals—we will see between these writers, so opposite in their politics, an entire uniformity of respect for the extraordinary power they attribute to the printed word. And remarkably, we shall see too a virtually identical social perspective. I have suggested repeatedly in this book that the very conservative ideas of More with respect to the poor and the place of the poor in man's society and in God's order are part of the core set of beliefs of her time. How better underscore this centrality than to see these same ideas set forth—at times with even stronger bias—in Wollstonecraft's work as well?

Hannah More's *Strictures on the Modern System of Female Education* went through seven editions in the year it was published, 1799. It is, as its subtitle states, "A view of the principles and conduct prevalent among women of rank and fortune," and is clearly, as the title of the first chapter asserts, an "Address to women of rank and fortune, on the effects of their influence on society."[1] That influence, as More's two substantial volumes explain, is primarily a moral one, exerted on all those around her in the example set by the actions of the woman as well as by the education that she gives her daughters and, as well, her sons. Throughout, as we would expect from the author of the Cheap Repository

Tracts, More emphasizes the *Christian* context for these principles. As in the Tracts, More assumes a highly structured society, with each person defined not only by gender but by class. Woman, then, has a specific role as woman, just as the poor have their own delimited role. The role for "women of the higher class . . . is influence" (I, 1). More finds that "The general state of civilized society depends . . . on the prevailing sentiments and habits of women, and on the nature and degree of the estimation in which they are held" (I, 2).

But these are times of "alarm and peril," and so she "would call on [women] to come forward, and contribute their full and fair proportion towards the saving of their country" (I, 4). She calls on them "to raise the depressed tone of public morals [by] awaken[ing] the drowsy spirit of religious principle. [The] virtue and happiness, nay, perhaps the very existence, of that society" (II, 4–5) depends on the moral tone women bring to it by their influence. This is exactly the role More sees for herself. The woman must bring to those around her the example of her own upstanding Christianity to help the young, male and female, not only to "see through the miserable fallacies of the new philosophy" (I, 14), but to counter those forces in the fashionable world that "blight the first promise of seriousness" (I, 15): More would have them saved from that "cold compound of irony, irreligion, selfishness, and sneer which make up what the French (from whom we borrow the thing as well as the word) so well express by the term *persiflage*" (I, 15). We have seen these sentiments—equally forcefully expressed—in her tract "The History of Mr. Fantom" and other earlier works. Women, she notes, can undermine men's religion if women treat religion disrespectfully; this harm largely comes about because women too often subsume moral and intellectual characteristics under that which is merely "pleasant" (I, 18). "[W]omen of rank and influence" (I, 31) must repress everything that leads to such public corruption. These threats include science, philosophy, and romance.

This then is the context for an extraordinary and lengthy diatribe. More finds that modern literature, especially those horrid productions from France and Germany, can have extremely deleterious effects on the morals of those without adequate defenses— that is to say the young— because the immoral, unchristian lessons it teaches are presented in the guise of freeing the reader from prejudice and enlisting his sympathy for characters whose actions actually should evoke horror and disgust in a good Christian. The most abhorrent and apparently the most dangerous of these authors is Rousseau, whose pernicious message challenges the values of chastity and virginity and would destroy marriage itself by making adultery sympathetic. We remember that More's fear that French thought could pose a threat to good, stable English marriage goes all the way back to *Village Politics*.[2]

The literary menace is particularly insidious because it comes cloaked in false premises. More begins her attack on Rousseau by first attacking all literature that does not promote Christianity; indeed, she argues, the problem chiefly is that "by assuming the plausible names of Science, of Philosophy, of Arts, of Belles Lettres," these books are dangerous just because people would not be on their guard had the poison "been labelled with its own title" (I, 31). But, she demands, "who suspects the destruction which lurks under the harmless or instructive names of *General History, Natural History, Travels, Voyages, Lives, Encyclopedias, Criticism,* and *Romance*?" (I, 31). These works, she says, undoubtedly "contain much admirable matter, . . . [b]ut while 'the dead fly lies at the bottom,' the whole will exhale a corrupt and pestilential stench" (I, 32). And thus do we get to "Novels, which chiefly used to be dangerous in one respect" and are "now become mischievous in a thousand" (I, 32). More directs her attack in a number of directions: the radical political novels are dangerous, as are novels of sentiment. Rousseau, whose work combines both of these aspects, is especially despicable because he presents "profligacy" as a proof of reason and liberty. Modern novels, More warns, "diffuse destructive politics, deplorable profligacy, and impudent infidelity. Rousseau was the first popular dispenser of this complicated drug" (I, 32).

Rousseau's effectiveness, as More sees it, depends on his redefinition of virtue. His evil ideas are all the more dangerous because they are presented in the guise not of an attack on Christian morality but as an expansion of personal liberty and responsibility: "he does not attempt to seduce the affections but through the medium of the principles" (I, 32). By redefining virtue he changes the nature of actions; what should inspire horror and pity in a reader inspires instead respect and admiration. If the value of chastity is questioned and then denied, the unchaste heroine will appear even more attractive just because she is not chaste. More discourses on this very central problem at length. Rousseau, she says, "Does not paint an innocent woman, ruined, repenting, and restored; but with a far more mischievous refinement, he annihilates the value of chastity, and with a pernicious subtlety attempts to make his heroine appear almost more amiable without it. He exhibits a virtuous woman, the victim not of temptation but of reason, not of vice but of sentiment, not of passion but of conviction; and strikes at the very root of honour by elevating a crime into a principle" (I, 32–33). What Rousseau essentially is doing, according to More, by making chastity a choice rather than a necessity for women, is to convince them that they have the same options as men. "With a metaphysical sophistry the most plausible, he debauches the heart of woman, by cherishing her vanity in the erection of a system of male virtues" (I, 33). She begins even to think, to act, according to these guidelines, and as she is "tempted[ed] . . . to aspire" to such a male way of life she neglects the virtues "that are her more peculiar and characteristic praise" (I, 33). More is absolutely horrified by the idea that women should act the same as men and should have the same rights and freedoms that men assume. Rousseau, who in this and other issues challenges the God-given order by "corrupting the judgment and bewildering the understanding," has found "the most effectual way to inflame the imagination and deprave the heart" (I, 33).

Rousseau is especially dangerous because he appeals particularly to young, moral, sensitive people whose very thoughtfulness and concern for morality and truth leave them trustingly open to the twisted lessons of the person they see as an honest preceptor. Rousseau cloaks truth in falsehood, so that those "who love truth but . . . whose principles are not yet formed" (I, 34) are seduced.

> He allures the warm-hearted to embrace vice, not because they prefer vice, but because he gives to vice so natural an air of virtue; and ardent and enthusiastic youth, too confidently trusting in their integrity and in their teacher, will be undone, while they fancy they are indulging in the noblest feelings of their nature. Many authors will more infallibly complete the ruin of the loose and ill-disposed; but perhaps . . . there never was a net of such exquisite art and inextricable workmanship, spread to entangle

innocence and ensnare inexperience, as the writings of Rousseau: and, unhappily, the victim does not even struggle in the toils, because part of the delusion consists in imagining that he is set at liberty. (I, 34)

More expands her attack on Rousseau to include both the novel of sentiment and the politically radical novels, all of which she sees as "adopt[ing] and enlarg[ing] all the mischiefs" (I, 35) of Rousseau. More's complaint is that these novelists exalt duties and virtues that ignore, even contradict, the traditional Christian ones. Benevolence, for example, is raised to a great virtue—but without reference to other duties that might relegate such practice of benevolence to a much lower moral rung. When these novelists insist that the poor and downtrodden should be raised up, that insistence for More reeks of antichristian bias, for God in his wisdom created those very poor and downtrodden people whose state these novelists are trying to change; we have seen repeatedly in the Tracts that such tampering with the will of God for More is immoral, not to mention dangerous.

She insists that the "principal evil arising from [these novels] is, that the virtues they exhibit are almost more dangerous than the vices" (I, 35). Their characters "practice superfluous acts of generosity, while they are trampling on obvious and commanded duties" (I, 35). Duty is seen as emanating from the individual rather than from a higher source, leaving the door open to what seems to More like moral anarchy. These novelists raise passion to a virtue, instead of discussing how to subdue it. "They teach, that chastity is only individual attachment; that no duty exists which is not prompted by feeling; that impulse is the main spring of virtuous actions, while laws and religion are only unjust restraints; the former imposed by arbitrary men, the latter by the absurd prejudices of timorous and unenlightened conscience. Alas! they do not know that the best creature of impulse that ever lived is but a wayward, unfixed, unprincipled being! that the best *natural* man requires a curb; and needs that balance to the affections which Christianity alone can furnish, and without which benevolent propensities are no security to virtue" (I, 35–6).

More's horror at the challenge to the rules of God and man, to religious constraints and legal constraints, is manifest. When these books teach that chastity is only a choice, that duty is only a function of feeling, and that law and religion are only "restraints," they attempt to destroy the natural relationship of God to man. For More, these arguments against social and legal systems that appear unjust in fact are calls to challenge religion itself. Without Christianity, "benevolent propensities are not security to virtue." Without Christianity, that is, in More's definition, when human beings take it on themselves to challenge what they deem inequitable or harmful in society, there can be no good result.

> In some of the most splendid of these characters compassion is erected into the throne of justice, and justice degraded into the rank of plebeian virtues. Creditors are defrauded, while the money due to them is lavished in dazzling acts of charity to some object that affects the senses; which paroxysms of charity are made the sponge of every sin, and the substitute of every virtue: the whole indirectly tending to intimate how very *benevolent people are who are not Christians*. From many of these compositions, indeed, Christianity is systematically, and always virtually, excluded; for the law, and the prophets, and the gospel *can* make no part of a scheme in which this world is looked upon as all in all; in which want and misery are considered as evils arising solely from human governments, and not from the dispensation of God; in which poverty is represented as merely a political evil, and the restraints which tend to keep the poor honest, are painted as the most flagrant injustice. (I, 36–7)

The works which she is attacking are not named (except for Mary Wollstonecraft's *Maria, or the Wrongs of Woman,* to which specific reference is made a bit later), but it is clear that More has in mind the writing of William Godwin and others in his circle, perhaps Robert Bage and Thomas Holcroft as well as Wollstonecraft. Surely it is Godwin who is accused of treating marriage as an "unjust infringement on liberty, and a tyrannical deduction from general happiness" (I, 38). Godwin's comments on marriage in *Political Justice* certainly would have been anathema to More as, clearly, were all the references to the unjust nature of English law to be found not only in his *Political Justice* and *Caleb Williams* but in the novels of Holcroft, Bage, and Elizabeth Inchbald as well.

Having dealt with the homegrown vipers, More turns once again to the devils abroad, "those swarms of publications now

daily issuing from the banks of the Danube, which, like their rav-
aging predecessors of the darker ages, though with far other arms,
are overrunning civilized society. . . . [T]he Huns and Vandals
[are] once more overpowering the Greeks and Romans. . . . These
compositions terrify the weak, and disgust the discerning" (I, 40).
More footnotes this part of her discussion to remark, with evident disgust, that "The newspapers announce that Schiller's Trag-
edy of the Robbers, which inflamed the young nobility of Germany
to enlist themselves into a band of highwaymen to rob in the for-
ests of Bohemia, *is now acting in England by persons of quality! (I,
40). Some years earlier, it seems, the French had been the problem: "The writings of the French infidels were . . . circulated in
England with uncommon industry, and with some effect," but,
fortunately, "the plain good sense and good principles of the far
greater part of our countrymen resisted the attack" (I, 40). The
offending "doctrines and principles," More asserts, have had such
"dreadful consequences" not only in France but wherever in Europe they have been adapted, that those consequences serve as a
warning to other nations. Luckily, in England "the subject is now
so well understood, that every thing that issues from the *French*
press is received with jealousy; and a work, on the first appearance of its exhibiting the doctrines of Voltaire and his associates,
is rejected with indignation" (I, 41).

Sadly, however, "the modern apostles of infidelity and immorality . . . have indeed changed their weapons, but they have
by no means desisted from the attack. . . . Deprived of the assistance of the French press" (I, 41), they are now using German literature! "Poetry as well as prose, romance as well as history,
writings on philosophical as well as on political subjects, have
thus been employed to instil the principles of *Illuminatism*, while
incredible pains have been taken to obtain able translations of
every book which was supposed likely to be of use in corrupting
the heart or misleading the understanding. In many of the translations, certain bolder passages, which, though well received in
Germany, would have excited disgust in England, are wholly
omitted, in order that the mind may be more certainly, though
more slowly, prepared for the full effect of the same poison to be
administered in a stronger degree at another period" (I, 42–3).

These "poisons" come chiefly in the form of attacks on chastity and fidelity. More attributes the political developments in

France to "the effect which female infidelity produced" (I, 43). Those who would destroy English society through the importation of foreign ideas, having learned their lesson in their failure with French ideas, now with the German are addressing themselves to attempting to influence women instead of men. "For this purpose, not only novels and romances have been made the vehicles of vice and infidelity, but the same allurement has been held out to the women of our country, which was employed by the first philosophist to the first sinner—Knowledge. Listen to the precepts of the new German enlighteners, and you need no longer remain in that situation in which Providence has placed you! Follow their examples, and you shall be permitted to indulge in all those gratifications which custom, not religion, has tolerated in the male sex!" (I, 43–44). And women, merely by reading, by being "inquisitive after these monstrous compositions," by allowing their minds to come in contact with such contagious matter, . . . are irrevocably tainting them" (I, 44–5).

More's abhorrence of "German *writings*" extends to the imports of German drama as well—drama may be even more dangerous since "because there are multitudes who seldom read" (I, 45), the drama can reach those who would not be tainted by print sources. More turns to a spectacularly dangerous play, *The Stranger*, to show how this evil influence works. It is a play in which not only is there an adulteress, "but she is presented to our view in the most pleasing and fascinating colours" (I, 46). The adulteress has forsaken her perfectly nice husband to live with "her seducer." When she repents, her husband promises to forgive her and to offer her his protection and fortune—but he refuses to allow her to resume her place as his wife. More is shocked by the author's insistence that it is the husband who is wrong: "The talents of the poet . . . are exerted in attempting to render this woman the object not only of the compassion and forgiveness, but of the esteem and affection of the audience" (I, 46–7). It is the husband who is "a savage," although his resolution not to take his wife back is one that "every man of true feeling and christian piety will probably approve" (I, 47).

If More reacts with such horror to this *German* play, how could we then expect her to respond to an English woman's "direct vindication of adultery" (I, 48)? More's discussion of *The Stranger* leads into a relatively short but quite vicious attack on Mary

Wollstonecraft's *Maria, or the Wrongs of Woman*. More cannot actually bring herself to name Wollstonecraft; instead, she refers to "a professed admirer and imitator of the German suicide Werter" (I, 48), thus, not incidentally, making her tie between the damaging German writers and what she sees as their homegrown collaborators. *"The Female Werter*, as she is styled by her biographer"— More cannot bring herself to publish Godwin's name either— "asserts, in a work intitled 'The Wrongs of Women' [*sic*], that adultery is justifiable, and that the laws of England constitute one of the *Wrongs of Women"* (I, 48). Maria, the heroine of the novel, is locked up in a madhouse by her husband because she would not allow him to sell her to a colleague in payment of a debt; in the madhouse she meets Darnford, who also has been imprisoned unjustly. They escape together. Maria's husband has Darnford imprisoned for wife stealing, and Maria defends her lover before the court. *The Wrongs of Woman* catalogues an enormous list of offenses legally perpetrated against women, and men, by society. We have seen above More's response to the novel.

Interestingly, Wollstonecraft herself in her own *Thoughts on the Education of Daughters, With Reflections on Female Conduct in the More Important Duties of Life,* published twelve years earlier than More's *Strictures* (1787), says very much the same things about women in society; these similarities are so striking that they already were being commented on by contemporary readers.[3] A girl should have a becoming modesty, "which being accustomed to converse with superiors" will give her, Wollstonecraft counsels, and "The first things . . . that children ought to be encouraged to observe, are a strict adhherence to truth; a proper submission to superiors; and condescension to inferiors."[4]

By 1787 Wollstonecraft showed no sign of that later social consciousness so abhorred by More, a social consciousness that demands society's reassessment not only of the rights of women but of the poor. Even More in her *Strictures* demands that the young be taught to see that servants are people too, and that, for example, young people must be taught to respect their servants' off-duty times. But the Wolstonecraft who, in *The Wrongs of Woman,* would present such harrowing pictures of the travails of poor working women, in her *Thoughts on the Education of Daughters* neither shows nor counsels much respect for "inferiors." Children should not be "left entirely to the nurse's care" because "[t]hese women are of course ignorant, and to keep a child quiet for the moment, they humour all its little caprices" (5). When children are left with servants, "the first notions they imbibe . . . are mean and vulgar. They are taught cunning, the wisdom of that class of people, and a love of truth, the foundation of virtue, is soon obliterated from their minds" (13). Children must be kept "out of the way of bad examples" (14) she goes on, and "Art is almost always practiced by servants, and the same methods which children observe them to use, to shield themselves from blame, they will adopt. . . . [C]unning is so nearly allied to falsehood, that it will infallibly lead to it. . . . The riot of the kitchen, or any other place where children are left only with servants" (19), is to be avoided, Wollstonecraft strenuously insists. So servants are all stupid and lying, vulgar and riotous. Cunning is the wisdom of "that class of people," and "that class of people" can only provide bad examples for their employers' children. Wollstonecraft's contempt for the vulgarity of "those people" is extraordinary viewed, as it normally would be, through the perspective of her later, better known works. In the context of a discussion of More, however, Wollstonecraft's thought here serves to underline yet again how representative of her age's assumptions More really is. Wollstonecraft devotes an entire chapter to "the management of servants" because it is "a great part of the employment of a woman's life; and her own temper depends very much on her behavior to them" (118).

"Servants," she pronounces simply, "are, in general, ignorant and cunning" (118). They must be treated with forbearance, that is, as children would be treated. Kindness, she says, must be shown. Why? Perhaps because we feel sorry for their harder lot in life? "Kindness must be shewn, if we are desirous that our domestics should be attached to our interest and persons" (120). It is, after all, "pleasing . . . to be attended with a smile of willingness" (120). But above all, as More will say repeatedly not only in her *Strictures* but in so many of the stories in the Cheap Repository Tracts, masters should give servants "a good example" in religion. "The ceremonials of religion, on their account, should be attended to" (121) because servants otherwise will neglect proper observance. "We cannot make our servants wise or good," cautions Wollstonecraft, but we may teach them to be decent and orderly; and order leads to some degree of morality" (121). The "Observance of Sunday," then, deserves a whole chapter because the keeping of the sabbath, as More insists in virtually every one of the Tracts, is "of the utmost consequence to national religion" (124). For the "vulgar," going to church is absolutely necessary, for they are "so lost in their senses, that if this day did not continually remind them, they would soon forget that there was a God in the world" (125). And so Wollstonecraft explains that for the sake of the "minds of children and servants, who ought not to be let run wild, nor confined too strictly" (125), a wholesome passing of the sabbath must be shown by the example of the masters, lest the weak-minded servants, without their labor on a Sunday, fall into the wrong pleasures. This means, as it does in More's writings, that the lady of the house and her spouse must set an example for the servants by not going out, not playing cards, and so on.

As More does, Wollstonecraft sees dangers all around to the proper intellectual upbringing of young ladies, many of them though "improper books." One of the problems with boarding schools, for example, is that "a sensible governess cannot attend to the minds of the number she is obliged to have," and so "Improper books will by stealth be introduced, and the bad example of one or two vicious children, in the play-hours, infect a number" (58–59). For Wollstonecraft, "Those productions which give a wrong account of the human passions, and the various accidents of life, ought not to be read before the judgment is formed, or at least exercised. Such accounts are one great cause of the affectation of young women" (50). Like More, Wollstonecraft attacks sensibility, finding it harmful both in terms of the behavior it calls forth and the misperceptions it engenders in the minds of the susceptible young.[5] In these books "Sensibility is described and praised, and the effects of it represented in a way so different from nature, that those who imitate it must make themselves very ridiculous" (50). These are "superficial performances, which obtain their full end if they can keep the mind in a continual ferment. Gallantry is made the only interesting subject with the novelist" (50–51).

Wollstonecraft's objection to these kinds of productions is more complex than More's, for Wollstonecraft worries not just about the effect of this sort of literature upon the actions of young women but on their taste—and she sees both problems as equally serious. "Reason strikes most forcibly when illustrated by the brilliancy of fancy," she insists, and the important thing is for the mind to be opened so that it can continue to grow. "The mind set to work," she says, "it may be allowed to chuse books for itself, for every thing will then instruct" (51–52). Later she expands on this idea: "I recommend the mind's being put into a proper train, and then left to itself. Fixed rules cannot be given, it must depend on the nature and strength of the understanding; and those who observe it can best tell what kind of cultivation will improve it. The mind is not, cannot be created by the teacher, though it may be cultivated, and its real powers found out" (54). Interestingly, Wollstonecraft holds aside the Bible as a teaching tool; unlike More, who especially in the Cheap Repository Tracts sees the Bible as virtually the only worthwhile text (especially for the poor), Wollstonecraft believes that "so sacred a book" (54) never should be used as a means merely to learn reading.

Wollstonecraft's own reading included Locke on education, of course ("To be able to follow Mr. Locke's system . . . the parents must have subdued their own passions" [11], she cautions); she read Rousseau's *Emile* and other fashionable sentimental novels, as Moira Ferguson reminds us.[6] Of course, she challenged Edmund Burke. Ferguson also notes that Wollstonecraft "[k]new of women like Mary Astell, Lady Mary Wortley Montagu, and Catherine Macauley" who had written on women and society. But perhaps even more important than knowing what Wollstonecraft read is looking at the use she makes of that reading in the book that was clearly to be her all encompassing statement on the life of a woman in society, *Maria, or the Wrongs of Woman*. *The Wrongs of Woman* is full of books. If society has failed women as a source of support and comfort, the one steady friend is literature. Remarkably, considering Wollstonecraft's repeated contemptuous dismissals of servants as stupid in *Thoughts on the Education of Daughters*, in *The Wrongs of Woman* not only are working women among the most sympathetic of characters, they are also among the most sensible of the wonders of the written word.

From the beginning of the novel we are aware of the solace to be found in books: "Maria endeavoured to soothe, by reading, the anguish of her wounded mind" (30), begins chapter two. She "devour[s]" the books she has; she finds in them her only "resource to escape from sorrow" (30). When sometime later Jemima, Maria's keeper in the madhouse, brings her "a fresh parcel of books," Maria, who had "relapsed into despondency," is "cheered" (34). Maria is full of emotion before she even has read a word, for the books represent to her an intense relationship with whoever had last read them: "Maria took up the books with emotion. . . . Her heart throbbed with sympathetic alarm; and she turned over the leaves with awe, as if they had become sacred from passing through the hands of an unfortunate being oppressed by a similar fate" (34). The books themselves are a mixed selection of old and new; the modern texts are not named although older ones are: "Dryden's Fables, Milton's Paradise Lost, with several modern productions, composed the collection. It was a mine of treasure" (34).

Maria's response to the books is itself part of her characterization—her love of literature marks her as an intelligent, sensitive, and rational human being. Significantly, Wollstonecraft chooses Dryden and Milton for Maria's perusal, authors impeccable in reputation and serious in intent. Maria is delighted not just with the texts themselves but with the marginal notations made by the last reader, the mysterious male inmate from whom Jemima has borrowed the books. His comments "caught her attention: they were written with force and taste; and, in one of the modern pamphlets, there was a fragment left, containing various observations on the present state of society and government, with a comparative view of the politics of Europe and America. These remarks were written with a degree of generous warmth, when alluding to the enslaved state of the labouring majority, perfectly in unison with Maria's mode of thinking" (34). We must note first of all that Maria, as a woman, *has* a "mode of thinking" about these social issues, and we must note as well that her understanding clearly is the equal of the sophisticated male whose jottings she so much enjoys. When Maria and Darnford are first attracted, it is their intellects that meet. Each time Maria reread the marginal notations, "some fresh refinement of sentiment, or accuteness [sic] of thought impressed her" (35).

Among the other writings Maria has available to her is "a book on the powers of the human mind" (Locke?) and Dryden's Guiscard and Sigismunda; she turns to Dryden when "her attention strayed from the cold arguments on the nature of what she felt, while she was feeling" (35). Wollstonecraft focuses, then, on Maria's sensibility. Maria's intellectual ability, already firmly established, is emphasized by the fact that she is capable of reading in French; underlining her intellectual compatibility with the mysterious stranger whose books Maria has been borrowing, he too can read in another language: Jemima brings Maria Darnford's copy of Rousseau's *Heloise* in French, and Maria "sat reading with eyes and heart, till the return of her guard to extinguish the light. . . . She had read this work long since; but now it seemed to open a new world to her—the only one worth inhabiting" (37). If for Hannah More Rousseau represents everything that is subversive to morality and dangerous to the good order of society, for Wollstonecraft "'Rousseau alone, the true Prometheus of sentiment, possessed the fire of genius necessary to pourtray [*sic*] the passion, the truth of which goes so directly to the heart'" (38). The unhappy Maria "[flies] to Rousseau" for solace; when she "had finished [reading] Rousseau, [she begins] to transcribe some selected passages[,] unable to quit . . . the author" (38). Maria's passion for Rousseau represents Wollstonecraft's own feeling for the author; Rousseau is the only writer discussed at such length in *The Wrongs of Woman*; these quotations represent only a sample of Wollstonecraft's allusions to him.

Throughout the novel the value of writing and books is a constant theme. All three of the main characters, Maria, Darnford, and Jemima, are touched and changed by books. Darnford talks about his restless and unfocused youth: when he is wounded and forced into inactivity, "'Confined to my bed, or chair, by a lingering cure, my only refuge from the preying activity of my mind, was books'" (44). But it is Jemima's response to literature that is at once most touching and most surprising. After a horrendous childhood and young womanhood she takes a place as companion to a rich, old, rather strange man who, however, is an author. It is in his house that the heretofore uneducated Jemima "'now began to read, to beguile the tediousness of solitude, and to gratify an inquisitive, active mind.'" She had always, it seems, had an innate need for this sort of stimulation, even risking punishment "'often, in my childhood, [for following] a ballad-singer, to hear the sequel of a dismal story'" (61). Although in adulthood Jemima at first "'could just spell and put a sentence together,'" she listens to and learns from the literary discussions she hears at her master's table.[7] "'But my fondness of reading increasing, and my master occasionally shutting himself up in this retreat, for weeks together, to write, I had many opportunities of improvement'" (61). Her

master, finding in her an intelligent and receptive auditor, sometimes "'would read to me his productions, previous to their publication'" (62).

When he dies suddenly and Jemima is thrust back into the
"'lowest vulgarity,'" from which she had escaped during this period, she finds her situation virtually unbearable. And a large part
of the horror is the loss of "'the graces of humanity,'" for "'I had
acquired a taste for literature, during the five years I had lived
with a literary man, . . . and now to descend to the lowest vulgarity, was a degree of wretchedness not be imagined unfelt'" (63).
These are extraordinary sentiments to come from a character like
Jemima who, in the midst of the attempt literally to keep from
starving, feels the lack of intellectual life as keenly as the lack of
material support. For Wollstonecraft, literature itself, reading itself, is virtually a necessity of life. Note how Wollstonecraft has
changed her mind about the sensibility and the intellectual potential of the poor in a way that More never did, even in the face
of the genius of Yearsley. There is no sense in Wollstonecraft's
*Wrongs of Woman* that a woman like Jemima who reads so sensi-
tively is a freak of nature, which indeed is precisely how More
and Walpole saw Yearsley.

One of the main reasons for the enormous difference of opinion between Wollstonecraft and More on Rousseau, in addition to
More's hatred of anything French and radical, is More's intense
suspicion of sentiment, which she sees not as a mind-set that
should be encouraged but as something that needs to be reined
in. Clearly swiping at Rousseau and writers like him, More in
*Strictures* attacks the "class of contemporary authors [who] turned
all the force of their talents to excite *emotions*, to inspire *sentiment*,
and to reduce all mental and moral excellence into *sympathy* and
*feeling*. These softer qualities were elevated at the expence of principle" (I, 73).

Allied to the miseducation of women in terms of the emphasis on refining their feelings is the emphasis on refining their artistic talents—too much attention, More says, is paid to dance
lessons, and music lessons, and drawing. . . . These are not, she
insists, trivial complaints, for "Before the evil is past redress, it
will be prudent to reflect that in all polished countries an entire
devotedness to the fine arts has been one great source of the corruption of the women" (I, 81)! And since, as she had shown earlier,

women's influence is one of the primary shaping forces of society, corrupt habits of female education can bring down the state. "And while this corruption, brought on by an excessive cultivation of the arts, has contributed its full share to the decline of states, it has always furnished an infallible symptom of their impending fall. The satires of the most penetrating and judicious of the Roman poets, corroborating the testimonies of the most accurate of their historians, abound with invectives against the general depravity of manners introduced by the corrupt habits of female education" (I, 83). More is not alluding solely to ancient history: the recent events in France serve as adequate warning to British women. And while British ladies on the broader scale bear this heavy responsibility, that responsibility largely is played out in the domestic arena. The "true end of education [is not] to make women of fashion *dancers* [and] *singers*" (I, 106). Just as men prepare for a single profession, and not just a little of everyone's, "the profession of ladies to which the bent of *their* instruction should be turned, is that of daughters, wives, mothers, and mistresses of families" (I, 107). The irony of these goals, in the context of More's own career as a writer, does not seem to have occurred to the author.

More is very much aware of the figure of the contemporary female author, and in general she disparages these

ever multiplying authors, that with unparallelled [*sic*] fecundity are overstocking the world with their quick-succeeding progeny[.] They are NOVEL-WRITERS; the easiness of whose productions is at once the cause of their own fruitfulness, and of the almost infinitely numerous race of imitators to whom they give birth. Such is the frightful facility of this species of composition, that every raw girl, while she reads, is tempted to fancy that she can also write. And as Alexander, perusing the Iliad . . . felt himself the hero he was studying; and as Corregio, on first beholding a picture which exhibited the perfection of the graphic art, prophetically felt all his own future greatness, . . . so a thorough-paced novel-reading Miss, at the close of every tissue of hackney'd adventures, feels within herself the stirring impulse of corresponding genius, and triumphantly exclaims, "And I too am an "author" [*sic*]. (I, 191–92)

Ladies, More says, use novel writing as psychological therapy when they are not using it as a gentle form of extortion. A little "distress of mind" (I, 192) is soothed by writing a novel. "[D]epression of circumstances" (I, 193)? She can fix her economic problems through a subscription. And when the lady author succeeds in publishing, it only incites her to publish more: "Capacity and cultivation are so little taken into the account, that writing a book seems to be now considered as the only sure resource which the idle and the illiterate have always in their power" (I, 193).

These are not affairs pernicious just to the writers of these novels, for More sees far-reaching deleterious social effects across all classes from this proliferation of ladies' novels. In fact, "the corruption occasioned by these books has spread so wide, and descended so low, as to have become one of the most universal . . . sources of corruption among us" (I, 193). Labor is lost when in trades where numbers of girls work together, such as milliners and mantua-makers, "the labor of one girl is frequently sacrificed that she may be spared to read these mischievous books to the others" (I, 194). Even "in the wards of our Hospitals" these books are "greedily read" (I, 194). This horrendous fact brings More to emphasize again the importance of making sure that the poor are supplied with appropriate books as well as the instruction that will make them "abhor corrupt books." She emphasizes that the solution here is not to keep the poor in ignorance but to educate them properly, for "Those who cannot *read* can *hear*, and are likely to hear to worse purpose than those who have been better taught." We know how dangerous "that ignorance" can be, as "the late revolts in more than one country [France, of course], remarkable for the ignorance of the poor, fully illustrate" (I, 194).

What then should women read, and what defines an appropriate attitude towards reading? Women need to act practically in the world; they must maintain the moral economy of their households, be helpmates to their husbands and instructresses to their children. "The chief end to be proposed in cultivating the understandings of women, is to qualify them for the practical purpose of life. Their knowledge is not often like the learning of men, to be reproduced in some literary composition, nor ever in any learned profession, but it is to come out in conduct" (II, 1–2). This is no minor purpose, for as the essential arbitor of society's morals, woman has a serious responsibility. Before she can shape the morals of others, a lady must first shape her own, and so "she is to read the best books, not so much to enable her to talk of them, as to bring the improvement which they furnish, to the rectification of her principles, and the formation of her habits" (II, 2). In fact, "That kind of knowledge which is rather fitted for home consumption than foreign exportation, is peculiarly adapted to women" (II, 3). The well-regulated mind will produce "the best regulated family" because "a sound oeconomy is a sound understanding brought into action" (II, 5–6). Men of sense, in fact, should not be "inimical" (II, 15) to learning in women because men themselves benefit from it, not least because the more a woman knows, the more she understands her place in the domestic order.

More's belief in a God-ordained order, whether it is the social order or the domestic, is reflected in her discussion of women's education, which focuses on the importance of women understanding their place and staying in it: women are "lawful possessors of a lesser domestic territory" (II, 24). More insists that education—appropriate education—is necessary for women because education significantly contributes to moral excellence: "to women moral excellence is the grand object of education" (II, 156). She dismisses the idea that women are led astray by education, arguing that "sound knowledge" actually "would remove that temptation to be vain which may be excited by its rarity" (II, 159). She notes, with some irony, that "the husband of a fashionable woman will not often find that the library is the apartment the expenses of which involve him in debt or disgrace" (II, 158).

While More argues that women should understand their proper domestic role and not be led to desire or aspire to the positions men take in society, she at the same time is insistent that women be educated and that their education must go further than most contemporary female education does to challenge and develop their minds. She explores repeatedly the idea that it is not possible really to know what women's minds are capable of because, without a systematic education, women's minds simply have not had the training that men take for granted. She does see differences between the female and the male understanding— "women are little accustomed to close reasoning on any subject; . . . they are not habituated to turn a truth round, and view it in all its varied aspects and positions" (I, 188)—but female education in its current mode exacerbates rather than ameliorates this bent. Everything in a woman's life, More argues, militates against the development of her ability to undertake "serious study[,] . . . to religious reading, to active business, to sober reflection, to self examination: whereas to an intellect accustomed to think at all, the difficulty of thinking seriously is obviously lessened" (I, 189–90).

Unfortunately, "the taste of general society is not favourable to improvement" (II, 54). Women all too often do not "live or converse up to the standard of their understandings," and thus "The mind, by always applying itself to objects below its level, contracts its dimensions, and shrinks itself to the size, and lowers itself to the level, of the object about which it is conversant" (II, 54). Men expect women not to be particularly smart. The society of ladies is "a scene in which [men expect] to rest their understandings, [not] to exercise them" (II, 43), and women, desiring to please, trim their understanding to fit this image. The loss, More finds, is not just to women but to society as a whole. On the other hand, lest this discussion misleadingly shape the image of a feminist More crusading for the opening of the minds of her sex, we should remember that, firstly, all this intellectual development is meant to be channeled specifically to the moral improvement of the woman and her society, and, secondly, More certainly is not celebrating an incipient growth of female genius—women "vain" of their female genius, in fact, are even worse than women vain of their beauty: for while the beautiful woman is satisfied to have others praise only her, "she who is vain of her genius . . . is jealous for the honour of her whole sex, and contends for the equality of their pretensions, in which she feels that her own are involved" (II, 16). The next several pages of this chapter on "Female Knowledge" are devoted to an extended putdown of those vainglorious women intellectuals of the sixteenth century who, not satisfied even with the equality that it seemed to them they possessed, found that "nothing short of the palm of superiority was at length considered as adequate to their growing claims" (II, 18). More finds them ridiculous.

Also ridiculous are the contemporary ladies who, thanks to "the swarms of *Abridgments, Beauties,* and *Compendiums*" (I, 180) currently available, pretend to a knowledge that they don't have, and affect a wide awareness of literature when, in effect, all they've read are summaries.[8]

The *names* of the renowned characters in history thus become familiar in the mouths of those who can neither attach to the ideas of the person, the series of his actions, nor the peculiarities of his character. A few fine passages from the poets (passages perhaps which derived their chief beauty from their position and connection) are huddled together by some abstract-maker, whose brief and disconnected patches of broken and discordant materials, while they inflame young readers with the vanity of reciting, neither fill the mind nor form the taste: and it is not difficult to trace back to their shallow sources the hackney'd quotations of certain *accomplished* young ladies, who will be frequently found not to have come legitimately by anything they know. (I, 180–81)

Not only is the taste of one who dabbles in these volumes seriously compromised, but so is the development of her understanding and, further, her ability to commit herself to serious study. More is so disgusted by these "crippled mutilations" (II, 58) that she returns to the subject of abridgments again in her second volume. Reading "abridgments from larger works," she insists, "makes a readier talker, but a shallower thinker, than the perusal of books of more bulk" (II, 58). Although not as bad as excerpts, the reading of "short writings of the essay kind . . . when it comprises the best part of a person's reading, makes a smatterer and spoils a scholar; for though it supplies current talk, yet it does not make a full mind" (II, 59). Along the same lines, More warns that merely attending "a course of lectures," if it is not "furthered by corresponding reading at home," results in a mere "affectation of skill" (II, 55). And poets, of course, "are always ready to lend a helping hand when any mischief is to be done" (II, 135).

More's prescribed course of reading for women is precisely a kind of "bracing" medicine for the mind. "The instructor . . . would do well to prohibit relaxed reading for a mind which is already of too soft a texture, and should strengthen its feeble tone by invigorating reading" (II, 185). And so she would "recommend books . . . such as exercise the reasoning faculties, teach the mind to get acquainted with its own nature, and to stir up its own powers" (I, 185). The "strong meat" she recommends is such as "Watt's or Duncan's little book of Logic, some parts of Mr. Locke's Essay on the Human Understanding, and Bishop Butler's Analogy" (I, 186)—she would like to substitute such fare for "English Sentiment, French Philosophy, Italian Love-Songs, and fantastic German imagery and magic wonders" (I, 186). Other authors mentioned with approbation in the *Strictures* are Alexander Pope and Oliver Goldsmith.

Finally, a significant portion of More's text is devoted to educating women of the higher class to take their place in society. We have seen More's emphasis on the importance of a woman understanding her place as a woman in both her own domestic and in the larger economy. Since More sees everyone in society as belonging to a given position on a social grid—a grid that has been laid down by no authority less than God himself—it is natural that women have a fixed role vis-à-vis men in the same way that, logically enough within such a construct, the poor have their place in the larger scheme of existence. Just as women should not challenge this God-given order for themselves, as we have seen, to challenge it on behalf of others, specifically of the poor, is virtually blasphemy. Part of More's energies in the *Strictures*, in fact, goes to argue against the challenge that her radical contemporaries address to the social status quo, while, having illustrated the divine wisdom in creating the poor—the social necessity for the poor—she also instructs the upper-class woman of firm morality in how to deal with those poor to make them more comfortable and productive without, in fact, changing their poverty. These of course are precisely the lessons of the Cheap Repository Tracts.

# Notes

## Preface

1. S. G. Goodrich, *Recollections of a Lifetime, or Men and Things I have Seen*, vol. II (New York and Auburn: Miller, Orton and Mulligan, 1857), pp. 163–68.

## One. Introduction

1. Since the *DNB* does not update its entries once they appear, the original sources for each biography are especially important. The Folger Shakespeare Library has a late nineteenth-century edition of the *Dictionary of National Biography*, ed. Sidney Lee, vol. xxxviii (London: Smith, Elder, & Co., 1894), pp. 414–420, for the More entry; it is rather amusing to see how well the late-Victorian language of the biography fits there, as opposed to its rather dusty aura in more modern reprints of the *DNB*.

2. Henry Thompson, *The Life of Hannah More: with Notices of Her Sisters*, 2 vol. (Philadelphia: E.L. Carey & A. Hart, 1838). All further references to Thompson are to this edition; quotations without page numbers are from his preface, l, pp. v-x. Among the most recent modern critics who devote a good deal of attention to the details of More's biography are Patricia Demers, *The World of Hannah More* (Lexington: The Univ. of Kentucky Press, 1996) and Charles Howard Ford, *Hannah More: A Critical Biography* (New York: Peter Lang, 1996). Ford's book, although often rather naive in its judgments, does have a wealth of factual material.

3. It is amusing to note how great a proportion of eighteenth-century girl children apparently were precocious in their intellectual development, if we are to believe both contemporary and modern commentators. For discussion of this issue, see my review of *The Feminist Companion to Literature in English* in *The Age of Johnson*, vol. 5, ed. Paul J. Korshin (New York: AMS Press, Inc., 1992), p. 397.

4. Somewhat distorting the facts of the incident, Elizabeth Kowaleski-Wallace, *Their Fathers' Daughters* (New York: Oxford Univ. Press, 1991), p. 30, sees in the failure of the engagement the "exacerbation" of More's "fixation with older men." Kowaleski-Wallace incorrectly notes that More's sisters "insisted that she break the engagement and arranged for an annuity of 200 pounds in recompense." Ford, *Hannah More*, p. 15, develops a quite unsupported story about the engagement falling apart because "Turner had second thoughts about a woman who approximated the usually unattainable ideal of feminine sexual frigidity." Demers, pp. 6–7, rather more accurately,

and sensibly, recounts that "Turner postponed the wedding three times over six years; finally and without Hannah's knowledge, Dr. James Stonehouse intervened, with the result that Turner settled an annuity of £200 on Hannah and bequeathed her £1,000. They remained friends. . . . The effect of these canceled marriage plans is unclear. . . . Speculation about the grave or minor consequences of this disappointment and theorizing about the jilted bride or frustrated prude are quite empty."

5. *Mendip Annals: or, A Narrative of the Charitable Labours of Hannah and Martha More in their Neighbourhood. Being the Journal of Martha More.* Ed, with additional matter, by Arthur Roberts (New York: Robert Carter & Brothers, 1859).

6. More describes a tea-party, preceded by a visit to church. She and a group of her friends meet, as promised, with a group of their Cheddar clients. They set off first for church,

> the ladies in white, and many of the savages in white also; the whole preceded by the Sunday-school children. The bells were set a-ringing, the singers assembled, and a band of musicians very gallantly stepped forward, and played 'God save the King' before us. After service was over, and Mr Jones had preached a sermon, we returned in the same order, dismissing the younger part of the company. . . . After tea (during which, to do them justice, they all behaved incomparably, and I believe *this day's associating with their betters,* as it is called, *has brought them forward at least ten years in civilisation*), we read them a little exhortation, explaining to them the contrast between their situations and blessings now, and what they were two years before. *They have so little common sense, and so little sensibility, that we are obliged to beat into their heads continually the good we are doing them;* and endeavouring to press upon them, with all our might, the advantages they derive from us. It is really true, and oftentimes it is with difficulty we can keep from downright laughing" (italics mine). (*Mendip Annals,* 66–67)

7. *Mendip Annals* pp. 6–7.
8. *Mendip Annals* p. 17.
9. *Mendip Annals* p. 13.
10. *Mendip Annals* p. 21.
11. For a fuller discussion of this incident see my *Social Protest in the Eighteenth-Century English Novel* (Columbus: Ohio State Univ. Press, 1985), pp. 93ff.
12. See my discussion of More's coaching of Sarah Trimmer in *her* dealings with her publisher, in chapter four.
13. Bishop Dol was one of those executed at the guillotine. See Thompson, l, 168.
14. Demers, p. 88.

## Two. Conservative Contexts

1. Patricia Demers, *The World of Hannah More* (Lexington: Univ. Press of Kentucky, 1996), p. 3.
2. Mitzi Myers, "Hannah More's Tracts for the Times: Social Fiction

and Female Ideology" in *Fetter'd or Free? British Women Novelists, 1670–1815*, ed. Mary Anne Schofield and Cecilia Macheski (Athens: Ohio State Univ. Press, 1986), p. 264.

3. New York and Oxford: Oxford Univ. Press, 1991. For discussion of the "grotesque body" see pp. 76ff.

4. The following discussion of the history of poor relief largely is based on E. M. Leonard's classic *The Early History of English Poor Relief* originally published in 1900 by Cambridge Univ. Press and reprinted in 1965 by Barnes & Noble, New York. All references to Leonard are to this edition.

5. Mark Neuman, "Afterword" to *A Dissertation on the Poor Laws By A Well-Wisher to Mankind* by Joseph Townsend (Berkeley: Univ. of California Press, 1971), with a foreword by Ashley Montagu, p. 70. All references to Townsend are to this edition.

6. I have chosen to analyze in some detail Townsend's *Dissertation* because it so clearly states the premises that More's stories illustrate repeatedly. The structural problem here is difficult: to place my analysis of Townsend *after* the discussions of More is to lose him as a context *for* More. I have chosen, then, to examine the *Dissertation* at this point in my book, and to make brief references to More that will be illustrated in considerably greater detail in later chapters.

7. Neuman, "Afterword," *Dissertation*, p. 75.

8. E. P. Thompson, *Whigs and Hunters: The Origin of the Black Act* (New York: Pantheon, 1975), p. 21.

9. Montague, in his "Foreword" to the *Dissertation* notes that "In the Book of Books it is written that 'the poor shall never cease out of the land' . . . a station to which God had called them, just as he had called the rich man to his. This thought is engagingly expressed in a hymn that must have been sung by millions of English-speaking people" (p. 5); the end of the hymn is quoted above.

10. Dorothy Marshall, *English People in the Eighteenth Century* (Longmans, Green and Co.: London, New York, Toronto, 1956), p. 180.

11. We remember in the *Essay on Man* the critical insistence on hierarchy; why does the spider have so developed a sense of touch, the fly such fine eyesight? Everything is tightly organized, and even to question this organization is to doubt God's will. What sensible being, Pope asks quite rhetorically, would want to smell so intensely that he would "Die in pain of an aromatic rose"? Just so, the poor man would not want the richer man's burdens along with his pleasures, and the rich man. . . .

12. Oddly, Dorothy Marshall in her otherwise most sensible book seems to hint at something of the same "satisfaction" conditioning the poor's sense of their own place in society. Having just detailed some of the food riots of the later eighteenth century, she ends the chapter with the following:

> Certainly when pushed too far the eighteenth-century English-men, and women, lacked neither courage nor initiative, and if they took a modest view of their rights, and demanded little beyond a roof for their heads, sufficient food to fill their bellies, and clothes that would cover them, with a sauce of drink and idleness to give a relish to the monotony of life, when these things were jeopardized their protests were vigorous enough. That they should have been so sporadic, tak-

ing place only in times of sudden worsening of conditions or when the mob to satisfy some political rancours had been stirred to life by its betters, *is some indication that in ordinary times the mass of the labouring poor felt no great sense of injustice against the social order of their age* (my italics). (196–97)

It is interesting to contrast this analysis with the disaffection among those same laborers that E.P Thompson discerned. See the following chapter for extended discussion of this issue.

13. See both Montague's and Neuman's essays in *Dissertation*.

## Three. Radical Contexts

1. Donna Landry, *The Muses of Resistance: Laboring Women's Poetry in Britain 1739–1796* (Cambridge: Cambridge Univ. Press, 1990), p. 16.

2. Olivia Smith, *The Politics of Language 1791–1819* (Oxford: The Clarendon Press, 1986), p. 90.

3. Jonathan Wordsworth, "Introduction" to Hannah More, *Village Politics* (Oxford: Woodstock Books, 1995). I will discuss the contexts of these negotiations at length in the next chapter. The quotations are from pages 1 and 4, respectively.

4. E. P. Thompson, *The Making of the English Working Class* (New York: Vintage Books, 1963); Isaac Kramnick, *Republicanism & Bourgeois Radicalism: Political Ideology in Late Eighteenth-Century England and America* (Ithaca: Cornell Univ. Press, 1990).

5. The first of the acts made it a treasonable offense to incite by speech or writing against the king and the government; the second made it illegal to hold a meeting of more than fifty persons without notifying a magistrate. Thompson, p. 145.

6. Hannah More explicitly addresses the situation of 1795 in her tract "The Way to Plenty; or, the Second Part of Tom White," advising the starving workers that just a little better management on their part would pretty much fix the situation: if they don't take off holidays and don't drink, they can buy two joints of meat with the money they accrue in the two days that they otherwise would miss from work. See chapter seven.

7. Thomas Paine, *Rights of Man, Common Sense and Other Poltical Writings* (Oxford: Oxford Univ. Press, 1995), ed. Mark Philp. All references to Paine's work are to this edition. Paine alludes repeatedly to "Mr Burke's Pamphlet," *Reflections on the Revolution in France*, first in the "Preface to the English Edition" of *Rights of Man* and then at the beginning of his text: "Among the incivilities by which nations or individuals provoke and irritate each other, Mr Burke's pamphlet on the French Revolution is an extraordinary instance" (89). A few sentences later, however, he remarks that "Every thing which rancour, prejudice, ignorance, or knowledge could suggest, are poured forth in the copious fury of *near four hundred pages*" (89; italics mine).

8. Paine's is not, of course, the only reply to Burke, nor even the earliest. James T. Boulton's analysis of the responses to Burke's *Reflections* in *The Language of Politics in the Age of Wilkes and Burke* (Westport, Conn.: Greenwood Press, 1963; repr. 1975) remains one of the most useful sources for background and explication of these pamphlets. He documents the extraordinary

# Notes

233

sales of Burke's work, sales which in turn were to be dwarfed by the sales of Paine's response (pp. 80–82). The controversy produced at least seventy pamphlets: "Within a fortnight of the appearance of the *Reflections* the first answer was on sale—*A Letter to the Right Hon. Edmund Burke, in Reply to his 'Reflections on the Revolution in France,' &c. By a Member of the Revolution Society.* Before the end of the year ten further replies were published" (p. 83). Boulton notes that common features of "literature addressed to the uneducated" are "protests against the economic system . . . which caused hardship" and "appeal[s] to prejudice against the privileged classes; . . . In most writings for the same audience the connection between economic and political evils is particularly stressed" (pp. 86–87). Similarly, the "overthrow of priestcraft" (91) is stressed in a number of these responses to Burke, especially those of the Dissenters. But it is Paine who puts together these themes in so compelling an argument, and it is Paine—and the overwhelming response to his *Rights of Man*— who is seen as a dire threat by the upper classes.

9. It is interesting that the attack on the limitations of the parish system comes from both sides of the political spectrum; we have seen Townsend's denunciation of the distortion in the labor market that he attributes to the parish system.

10. Kramnick discusses the extraordinary impact of this relatively small group of men as well as the political ramifications of the industrial revolution in *Republicanism and Bourgeois Radicalism*; see especially chapters 2, 3, and 4.

11. Keane notes that "What alarmed Burke, in short, were the attempts by Price and Paine to link English politics to the American and French Revolutions—spread talk, as Paine had put it, of 'the contagion' of revolution." *Tom Paine: A Political Life* (Boston and New York: Little, Brown and Company, 1995), p. 288.

12. Keane, 289.

13. Keane, 305.

14. David Freeman Hawke, *Paine* (New York and London: Norton, 1974), p. 223.

15. Hawke, 223, and Keane, 305.

16. Moncure Daniel Conway, perhaps Paine's earliest biographer, discusses the publication of the first part of *Rights of Man* at length; see pp. 116–117 of his *The Life of Thomas Paine* (New York: Benjamin Blom, Inc., 1972), first published 1892, for Holcroft's response to this episode.

17. Keane, 307.

18. Hawke, 223; Keane, 309.

19. Keane, 307–308.

20. Quoted by Keane, 310. Keane also quotes, p. 592, note 129, from a letter Paine wrote to George Washington in which he says that he intends to "make a cheap edition, just sufficient to bring in the price of printing and paper, as I did by *Common Sense.*" Boulton, p. 88, notes that Part One was "first published in February 1791 at half a crown—half the cost of the *Reflections*" by J. Johnson; "it lacked Paine's preface which was included in the edition published by J. S. Jordan in March 1791 at a cost of 3s."

21. Keane, pp. 324–327, provides details of all these transactions; especially interesting is the story of how Chapman, having decided that he was afraid to publish the work, managed to slip out of the problem by using

Paine's own behavior (he had been intoxicated and argumentative) as his excuse.

22. Boulton, 140–41.

23. Boulton, 138.

24. Thomas Holcroft, *Anna St. Ives* (London: Oxford Univ. Press, 1970), p. 383. For a full discussion of this novel see chapter four of my *Social Protest in the Eighteenth-Century English Novel* (Columbus: Ohio State Univ. Press, 1985).

25. Quoted by Wordsworth, p. 1.

26. Hannah More, *The Works of Hannah More. A New Edition , with Additions and Corrections, in Eleven Volumes,* vol. III (London: T. Cadell, 1830), pp. 365–66.

## Four. "The Pen That Might Work Wonders"

1. Hannah More, *Memoirs of the Life and Correspondence of Mrs. Hannah More* by William Roberts, Esq., 4 vol. (London: R.B. Seeley and W. Burnside, 1834), I, vi. Roberts notes that "no pains were necessary, had it been his object, to extend this work to an unreasonable or inconvenient length. His difficulty has consisted in reducing his materials within the present compass." Interestingly, he insists "that all the proceeds of the sale of the copyright, beyond the costs and charges incident to the preparation of the work for the press, are destined to charitable purposes, and will be so applied" (vii). The Folger Shakespeare Library has a good number of manuscript letters, as do the Huntington and the Clark libraries. Mitzi Myers, "'A Peculiar Protection'": Hannah More and the Cultural Politics of the Blagdon Controversy," note 14, p. 255, in *History, Gender & Eighteenth-Century Literature,* ed. Beth Fowkes Tobin (Athens, Georgia: The Univ. of Georgia Press, 1994) asserts that "The printed correspondence is not only limited but also censored and Victorianized;" this assumption is echoed by a number of modern critics. My examinations of the letters, however, have not led me to such a harsh verdict of Roberts: More sounds very much the same speaking through his edition, in the Walpole letters, and in the various manuscript letters I have cited. It is not Roberts' voice, or editing, that make More sound "Victorian"; her attitudes *were* after all very much what later would be called Victorian, and the Roberts *Life* remains a most useful source. All further references to the *Memoirs* are to this edition.

2. Henry Thompson, as I mentioned in the introduction to this book, says that there were two poems to be published in a small quarto; in any case, what is significant is Cadell's decision to pay More so well for this slim volume.

3. Wollstonecraft gives Jemima this sum as her salary for running the madhouse where Maria is locked up; see *Maria or the Wrongs of Woman* (New York: Norton, 1974), p. 69.

4. The exceptions are male apprentices who, by dint of hard labor and, above all, unfailing honesty and attachment to the good of their masters, eventually themselves become businessmen. See, for example, "The Two Shoemakers."

5. It would not prove very easy to get free of this "connection." Eight years later More writes to Mrs. Garrick "I am afraid Mrs. Montagu must

think strangely of me. I told her six weeks ago, we should be immediately delivered from all connesion [*sic*] with that wretched Milkwoman, and yet with all my zeal and industry, I have not been able to accomplish it, to my regret, for after all the trouble I have had, I would not get rid of her but in an honourable and conscientious manner, which I now hope to do." Als Hannah More to Mrs. Garrick, 30 November 1792, Garrick Correspondence, Folger MS, W. b. 487.

6. The Ann Yearsley episode always has elicited a great deal of commentary (see Walpole's discussion below), partially, I suspect, because it so neatly serves as a lightening rod for the commentator's own political views. Certainly political perspective is marked in our own contemporaries' examinations of the More-Yearsley relationship. Although More's "connection" with Yearsley was relatively insignificant in terms of More's extraordinarily long and successful career, critical discussions sometimes magnify the Yearsley controversy quite out of proportion. A sampling of recent work includes Patricia Demers, *The World of Hannah More* (Lexington: Univ. Press of Kentucky, 1996); Moira Ferguson, "Resistance and Power in the Life and Writings of Ann Yearsley, *The Eighteenth-Century: Theory and Interpretation* 27 (1986); Charles Howard Ford, *Hannah More: A Critical Biography* (New York: Peter Lang, 1996); Cheryl Turner, *Living By The Pen* (London: Routledge, 1994). Donna Landry, *The Muses of Resistance* (Cambridge: Cambridge Univ. Press, 1990), presents not only the most thorough discussion of the "milkmaid poet" but the most enlightening. Devoting an entire chapter to Yearsley, Landry within our context is most interesting for showing us the More-Yearsley controversy from the poor woman's perspective: Landry's analysis, suggesting that the differences between the women stemmed from class differences rather than from simple personality clashes, supports my thesis that More simply could not see beyond the templates that her vision of the poor presented. See especially pp. 149ff of Landry's chapter four; for discussion of class as a particular problem between the two women, see "The pleasures of the text—with a vengeance," pp. 152–55.

7. Edward Royle and James Walvin, *English Radicals and Reformers: 1760–1848* (Lexington: Univ. Press of Kentucky, 1982) p. 3.

8. Royle and Walvin, p.36.

9. Royle and Walvin, p.10.

10. Although the Troid edition of the diaries and letters is currently available only up to December, 1779 (Hemlow begins with 1792), entries for Burney's period of court service fortunately are relatively easily available in *The Famous Miss Burney: The Diaries and Letters of Fanny Burney*, ed. Barbara G. Schrank and David J. Supino (New York: John Day Co., 1976). See pp. 156, 157, 169, 173, 215–218, 230.

11. The gesture of providing at a fixed interval a good dinner for the poor, often with some appropriate entertainment, satisfies mid- and late-eighteenth-century social imperatives on a number of levels, for not only does it reflect the social responsibility as well as human empathy of the well-off, it also encourages good behavior and productivity on the part of the poor. More's Cheddar scholars, for example, are being rewarded for having met clearly defined goals. In two of the most popular of eighteenth-century texts, Henry Brooke's *The Fool of Quality* and Thomas Day's *The History of Sandford and Merton*, both of which are intended to teach children and their parents

how to develop into good people and productive citizens, such dinners are described in detail. In *The Fool of Quality* the dinner prepared for the poor by Mr. Fenton is a weekly affair. Every Sunday he invites to dinner the heads of deserving local families. They are treated not only to a fine dinner but the warmth and fellowship of the family: "after a saturating meal and an enlivening cup, they departed, with elevated spirits, with humanized manners [!], and with hearts warmed in affection toward every member of this extraordinary house" (London: Edward Johnson, 1776, vol. 1, p. 176). For an extended discussion of *The Fool of Quality* and *Sandford and Merton* see my *Social Protest in the Eighteenth-Century English Novel* (Columbus: Ohio State Univ. Press, 1985), chapter two, *passim.*

12. Als Hannah More to Mrs. Garrick, 2 Feb. 1793. Garrick Correspondence, Folger MS, W. b. 487.

13. The references in this section of the chapter are to *Horace Walpole's Correspondence with Hannah More, Lady Browne. . . .*, ed. W. S. Lewis, Robert A. Smith, and Charles H. Bennett (New Haven: Yale Univ. Press, 1961), hereafter cited as *Walpole.*

14. *Walpole*, note 16, page 361.

15. Lewis *et al.* (*Walpole*, note 19, p. 361–62) comment that "HW has made two slips: although the crime was committed at Birmingham, the hanging (of two men, not one) took place at Warwick. 'Warwick, Sept. 8. At a quarter past twelve, Francis Field, otherwise Rodney, and John Green, convicted for the offence of being aiding and assisting in the demolishing of the house of Mr Taylor at Ashton, near Birmingham, were . . . executed pursuant to their sentence. The rioters . . . assured the multitude they should not have interrupted the tranquillity of the inhabitants of Birmingham had it not been for the publication of the seditious handbill, and the meeting at the Hotel in Birmingham, on the 14th of July, to celebrate the anniversary of the French Revolution' (*General Evening Post,* 8–10 Sept. 1791). The handbill which was supposed to have helped provoke the Birmingham Riots of 14 July 1791 read in part as follows: "My countrymen, the second year of Gallic Liberty is nearly expired. At the commencement of the third, on the 14th of this month, it is devoutly to be wished that every enemy to civil and religious despotism would give his sanction to the *majestic common cause* by a public celebration of the anniversary. . . . Is it possible to forget that our own Parliament is venal? Your minister hypocritical? Your clergy legal oppressors? The Reigning Family extravagant?. . .' Whether this was actually written by a fanatical republican, as the loyalists claimed, or was merely a Tory hoax to discredit the meeting, was never established."

There is still a great deal that was never established with regard to the causes, and causers, of the Birmingham riots. R. B. Rose in a thoughtful essay argues that the government at the highest levels almost certainly did not directly incite or support the public rioting, although the local government was at best inept at quelling the unrest and probably in fact encouraged it. He concludes that "the disorder . . . was an explosion of latent class hatred and personal lawlessness triggered-off by the fortuitous coming together of old religious animosities and new social and political grievances which the attack on such men as Joseph Priestley symbolised." See his "The Priestley Riots of 1791," *Past and Present,* vol 18, Nov. 1960, pp. 68–88 *passim.*

16. More's account of how the letters to and from Walpole are collected

and published is interesting: it is clear that she is quite aware that her letters very well may be published and that she takes it for granted that letters which are made available in a public context should be carefully edited to remove any personal references. Recall her angry response to Mrs. Piozzi's publication of Johnson's negative comments about Garrick, the argument there being the same one that personal comments are not meant for the public and should not be made part of the public record. Thus in May of 1797 More writes to her sister Martha that Walpole's "executors, Mrs. Damer, and Lord Frederick Campbell, have sent me word they will return all my letters, which they have found carefully preserved. I am also applied to in form to consent to give up such of his letters to me as are fit for publication. I have told them how extremely careful I am as to the publication of letters, and that I cannot make any positive engagement; but if when I get to Cowslip Green, I should find on looking them over, that any are quite disencumbered of private history, private characters, &c,—I probably shall not withhold those in my possession; but I am persuaded that after they are reduced as much as will be necessary, there will be little left for publication" (*Memoirs* lll, 22–23).

17. G. H. Spinney, "Cheap Repository Tracts: Hazard and Marshall Edition," *The Library* 20 (1939–40), p. 310.

18. *The Works of Hannah More. A New Edition, with Additions and Corrections, in Eleven Volumes.* (London: T. Cadell, 1830), vol. III, p. 43.

## Five. Two Sides of a Question

1. Hannah More, *Memoirs of the Life and Correspondence of Mrs. Hannah More,* 4 vol., ed. William Roberts (London: R.B. Seeley, 1834), ll, 345. All further references to the *Memoirs* are to this edition.

2. Als Hannah More to Mrs. Garrick, 8 Jan. 1793. Garrick Correspondence, Folger MS, W. b. 487.

3. Henry Thompson, *The Life of Hannah More: With Notices of Her Sisters* (Philadelphia: E. L. Carey & A. Hart, 1838), vol. 1, pp. 151–52, discusses the inception of *Village Politics* at some length:

long before the darkest features of the [French] revolution had attained their full proportion, England did not number among her sons or her daughters a more ardent antagonist of the revolutionary party than Hannah More.

Accordingly, in the year 1792, when violence and rapine, under the names of liberty and equality,—and atheism and blasphemy, called, by a like perversion, philosophy and reason, were preached and published among the peasantry of England through the agency of clubs and emissaries,—universal, almost, became the call on Mrs. More to arm in the most holy cause of religion and order. But the most importunate, perhaps, of her suitors was her friend Bishop Porteus, who urged her acquaintance with the habits and feelings of the lower orders, and her clear and vigorous style, as an irresistible call on her pen for some production, calculated to dispel the delusions so assiduously propagated among the vulgar. . . . [S]he published anonymously her admirable dialogue called "Village Politics; by Will. Chip, a Country Carpenter;" in which, by plain and irresistible arguments, expressed

in language pure but universally intelligible, she exposes the folly and
atrocity of the revolutionary doctrines. The better to disguise the authorship, she employed Mr. Rivington, instead of her usual publisher
Mr. Cadell, to introduce her pamphlet to the public. . . . But long con-
cealment was impractical; and while all were praising the work, the
more discerning began to congratulate the authoress. Its circulation
was incalculable; some thousands were purchased by Government for
distribution: it was reprinted by societies and individuals; it was trans-
lated into French, and even into Italian, with such accommodations as
suited the Papal government; and there is every reason to believe that
this clear, concise, and sensible statement of a question which was then
perplexing and insnaring thousands had a very considerable effect in
reclaiming the deluded, and fore-arming the sound.

4. Hannah More, *The Works of Hannah More. A New Edition, with Additions and Corrections, in Eleven Volumes*, vol. lll (London: T. Cadell, 1830), p.
365. All further references to *Village Politics* are to this edition. Because *Village
Politics* is relatively short, and finding the context for specific quotations would
not present a problem to a reader, I omit page numbers for the quotations I
cite in this chapter.

5. More often uses phrases or situations in her stories that come from
her own informal correspondence with friends. We shall see in the next chapter
how much of the tone and detail in "The Shepherd of Salisbury Plain" seems
to come from a letter More received that discussed the "blessings" accorded
a friend's dying wife; similarly, details from a description of servant-mis-
tress relations during the French unpleasantness appear in *Village Politics*. In
this context, this joke about needing a new "constitution" and sending for
the doctor calls to mind a letter More sent to one of her sisters in which More
complains about the state of her own health; she makes a joke very similar to
the one here in Jack's response to Tom. She tells her sister that "I yielded to
the importunity of Mrs. Boscawen, and sent for Dr. Pitcairn. I told him I did
not send for him to cure a cold, but to have a conversation with him about
my general health; that he must *do as they do in France*; that is, discard
palliatives, and give me a new constitution" (*Memoirs*, II, 227).

6. I discuss more fully the criticisms of the legal system in the work of
Godwin and Wollstonecraft in, for Godwin, chapter six of *Social Protest in the
Eighteenth-Century English Novel* (Columbus: Ohio State University Press, 1985)
and, for Wollstonecraft, chapter six of *Her Bread to Earn: Women, Money and
Society from Defoe to Austen* (Lexington: The University Press of Kentucky, 1993).

7. "O the Roast Beef of Old England" is the title of a contemporary
song. It also is the title of one of Hogarth's most famous prints, *O the Roast
Beef of Old England: The Gate of Calais*. Sean Shesgreen, in his discussion of the
print in *Engravings by Hogarth*, ed. Sean Shesgreen (New York: Dover, 1973),
print 72, describes the print and the song from which Hogarth takes its title:
"'O the Roast Beef of Old England,' propagandistic in tendency, depicts the
French as a starved, ragged people oppressed by their religion and exposed
to ridicule by their affectation. The engraved title of the plate comes from a
nationalistic anti-French song popular during the period." The date of the
print is 1748/9.

Thus the song with which More ends her *Village Politics* has a specifically anti-French theme, underscoring yet again the political direction of her pamphlet. The fact that the song had been part of the culture of More's intended audience for so long presumably would have made her argument seem even more comforting to them.

8. E. P. Thompson, *The Making of the English Working Class* (New York: Vintage, 1963), pp. 177–178.

9. Isaac Kramnick, *Republicanism and Bourgeois Radicalism* (Ithaca: Cornell Univ. Press, 1990), p. 100. The following citations to Kramnick are from pages 101–102.

10. Josiah Wedgwood, *An Address to the Workmen in the Pottery, on the Subject of Entering into the Service of Foreign Manufacturers* (Newcastle: J. Smith, 1783). Since the *Address* is a relatively short pamphlet, I omit page citations for quotations in my text.

## Six. Social and Political Circumstances

1. Jonathan Wordsworth, "Introduction" to Hannah More, *Village Politics* (Oxford: Woodstock Books, 1995), p. 4.

2. Hannah More, *The Works of Hannah More. A New Edition, with additions and corrections in Eleven Volumes* (London: T. Cadell, 1830), vol. lll, 363. All further references to More's works are to this edition unless specifically noted.

3. *Works,* vol. lll, 397.

4. See for example Mitzi Myers, "Hannah More's Tracts for the Times: Social Fiction and Female Ideology," especially pp. 264–268 in *Fetter'd or Free? British Women Novelists, 1650–1815,* ed. Mary Anne Schofield and Cecilia Macheski (Athens: Ohio State Univ. Press, 1986) and Elizabeth Kowaleski-Wallace, *Their Fathers' Daughters: Hannah More, Maria Edgeworth, and Patriarchal Complicity* (New York and Oxford: Oxford Univ. Press, 1991). More recent feminist analyses, building on the shaky constructions of earlier politically focused criticism, continue to misinterpret More's work on education for the poor, especially More's philosophy of education for poor women. See for example Jacqueline Pearson, *Women's Reading in Britain, 1750–1835* (Cambridge: Cambridge Univ. Press, 1999), pp. 194–95. Pearson remarks that More is "a female reader and writer centrally concerned with issues of female literacy," but she sees this concern as part of "More's special mission . . . to labouring-class women;" More's "'counter-revolutionary feminism' [a phrase she takes from Kathryn Sutherland] offered women more opportunities to 'enlarge their sphere of activity and influence' than revolutionary feminists like Wollstonecraft." But More saw her "special mission" not as giving women "more opportunities," but, as we have seen, in keeping them at work and away from revolt.

5. The one exception to this rule is the young man who works so hard, either as an apprentice or in his trade, that he eventually manages to rise above his original station; stories that recount such transformations are "The Two Shoemakers" and "The History of Tom White," both of which I discuss in the next chapter. The reasons that More's over-all scheme allows for this particular kind of change will be explored in connection with those stories.

6. The tone of thankful resignation, of appreciation for even the small-

est alleviation of the most painful debilitation as a gift from a benevolent God, is part of the mind-set of More's circle. A letter from one of More's correspondents could (perhaps did) have served as the template for the shepherd's analysis of the blessings of his wife's situation. The letter, from a Mr. Newton to More, dated Dec. 30, 1790, recounts the last illness and the eventual death of his wife. The letter is extraordinarily touching. The couple had been married forty years, and Mr. Newton tells More, "You, perhaps, knew, madam, from what you have read of mine, and possibly from what you have seen in me, that my attachment to my dearest, was great, yea excessive, yea idolatrous! It was so when it began. I think no writer of romances ever imagined more than I realized. It was so when I married. She was to me precisely (how can I write it?) in the place of God. In all places and companies, my thoughts were full of her. I did every thing for her sake." Her illness lasted two years. "This was not a sudden stroke. She did not die by a flash of lightning [sic], by what is called accident, nor by those rapid disorders which break the thread of life in a few days or hours. The Lord gave me time to prepare for it; yea, by the gradual train of his dispensations, he gradually prepared me for it himself." After almost two years, "a total loss of appetite, or rather a loathing of food, . . . took place, which soon reduced her to a state of great weakness. In the beginning of October she took to her bed, and was soon after, I suppose from some defect in the spine, deprived of all locomotive power. She could neither move herself, nor without the greatest difficulty be moved. . . . *But the case was mingled with many merciful alleviations. Her patience was wonderful—her natural spirits as good as when she was in health. Often when my eyes were full of tears, she has constrained me to smile. When she could not move her body, she was thankful that she could move her hands, thankful that the Lord had laid no more upon her than what she could bear. And when I once said, 'You are a great sufferer,' she replied, 'I do suffer, but not greatly'"* (italics mine). The letter appears in *Memoirs of The Life and Correspondence of Hannah More* by William Roberts (London: R. B. Seeley and W. Burnside, 1834), vol. ll, pp. 237–247.

7. Bridget Hill, *Women, Work, and Sexual Politics in Eighteenth-Century England* (Oxford: Basil Blackwell, 1989), p. 82, remarks that servants effectively are expected to work even in the pauses of their larger responsibilities; this is the same expectation that More draws in her stories for all poor people. This view of the poor, which takes in also the servant, apparently does not much change in the course of the century: Hill quotes from a letter of 1737 in which one Elizabeth Purefoy makes inquiries for a servant. Purefoy lists the work to be done by a maid, a list so long that it seems much more than any one person could manage, yet Purefoy adds that "there is very good time to do all this provided she is a servant, & when she has done her worke she sits down to spin." Hill discusses at some length the role of the wife in the economic life of the agricultural family; see pp. 19–35, *passim.*

8. Modern historians make explicit reference to the distinction between goods produced in the home for the use of the family and goods produced by the family in order to earn money to support itself in the purchase of other essentials, a situation that More simply takes for granted. Hill, p. 25, cites Alice Clark's work on the seventeenth-century family in which Clark "notes the distinction between work done by women that contributed solely to the household and that done for sale or exchange. It is the distinction

between work that has 'use value' and that which has 'exchange value.' . . . The first is production directed only at the members of the household, where nothing is sold or exchanged. The second type, while still partly or even largely directed towards the maintenance of the household, produces a surplus which is either sold or exchanged. The money made from marketing such products goes towards the upkeep of the household."

9. It may be useful to point out the similarity between what More shows here as the optimal relation between the poor man and his benefactor and the very similar relationship that William Wordsworth posits as his ideal in "The Old Cumberland Beggar," which precisely documents the same mindset. Throughout the poem, the beggar's stellar function is to serve as a recipient for the narrator's charity: the narrator's life, for many years, has been enriched, *his* character improved, by having the beggar as recipient—as object—of his charity. "Him from my childhood have I known; and then/ He was so old, he seems not older now. . . . While from door to door,/ This old Man creeps, the villagers in him/ Behold a record which together binds/ Past deeds and offices of charity, / Else unremembered." There is no sense in the poem that a desired objective in this situation would be to remove the beggar from his poverty. The beggar has a social function, and that function is to provide an object for freely-given charity and thus a means for the moral and psychological improvement of those with whom he comes in contact.

This vision of the poor had been common in English culture long before Wordsworth used it in his Romantic rendering of the story of the Old Cumberland Beggar. Certainly throughout much of the eighteenth century it was common to view the poor as simply a natural and not-to-be-regretted part of the social order. In fact, for there to *be* a social order, it was necessary for there to be different steps on the social ladder. The "Great Chain of Being" is not much referred to by modern critics, but it does a great deal to help us conceptualize the hierarchical thinking of the period. A more modern formulation, with reference specifically to social class, is Isaac Kramnick's. Kramnick reminds us that, at a time when the middle class in England was steadily becoming more important—and becoming ever more conscious of itself *as* a middle class—it was all the more necessary to have a lower class to be positioned above, for one cannot be "middle" without both "upper" and "lower" to refer to. In *Republicanism and Bourgois Radicalism* (Ithaca: Cornell Univ. Press, 1990), he points to many radical enunciations of middle-class consciousness, such as Priestley's or Wedgewood's, but the view of a necessary poor class is as pronounced on the right as on the left. In this context, the Cheap Repository Tracts of Hannah More provide a mine of documentation.

Wordsworth's own comment on his poem is that it is a response to the "AMENDED poor-law," which he attacks as "heartless" essentially because it changes the giving of charity from a voluntary measure: "The political economists were about that time beginning their war upon mendicity in all its forms, and by implication, if not directly, on alms-giving also. . . . [T]he inhumanity that prevails in this measure is somewhat disguised by the profession that one of its objects is to throw the poor upon the voluntary donations of their neighbours; that is, if rightly interpreted, to force them into a condition between relief in the Union poorhouse, and alms robbed of their Christian grace and spirit, as being *forced* rather from the benevolent than given by them. . . ." This fascinating comment is quoted (unfortunately without precise reference) in John L. Mahoney's *The English Romantics: Major Poetry and Critical Theory* (Lexington: D.C. Heath, 1978), p. 112.

10. Elizabeth Inchbald, *Nature and Art,* 2 vols., 2nd ed. (London: G.G.and J. Robinson, 1797), ll, 197–202.

11. Soame Jenyns, *A Free Inquiry into the Nature and Origin of Evil,* repr. in Richard B. Schwartz, *Samuel Johnson and the Problem of Evil* (Madison: Univ. of Wisconsin Press, 1975). Samuel Johnson in his review of *A Free Inquiry* answered Jenyns with a bitter and poignant rebuke. Those who don't think poverty is hard to bear, he suggests, have not experienced it first hand. It may be true, he says, that the poor are not so sensitive to the small irritations that pain the rich, "but this happiness is like that of a malefactor who ceases to feel the cords that bind him when the pincers are tearing his flesh." Claude Rawson, "Killing the Poor: An Anglo-Irish Theme?" in *Essays in Criticism* XLIX, April, 1999, no. 2, p. 103, notes that a century earlier Swift and Mandeville also are writing "for the preservation or improved functioning of the status quo. Swift wrote a sermon 'On the Poor Man's Contentment,' in which he showed the poor 'that your Condition is really happier than most of you imagine.'"

12. *Works,* iv, 115.

13. J. Paul Hunter, *Before Novels: The Cultural Contexts of Eighteenth-Century English Fiction* (New York: Norton, 1990).

14. More did not herself write all of the tracts for the Cheap Repository, although all the pieces that were published were under her close editorial supervision; for attributions and dates see the still irreplaceable article by G. H. Spinney, "Cheap Repository Tracts: Hazard and Marshall Edition" (*The Library,* vol. 20, 1939–40), pp. 295–340. In this chapter I have chosen to include two of the tales that were not written by More to illustrate the uniformity of the images across the stories. "The Happy Waterman" and "The Lancashire Collier Girl" are not from More's own pen and therefore do not appear in her collected works. The editions and volumes from which I quote for these two stories are, for "The Happy Waterman," *Cheap Repository Tracts; Entertaining, Moral and Religious,* The First Boston Latest Edition, vol. l (Boston: E. Lincoln, 1802), and for "The Lancashire Collier Girl," *Cheap Repository Tracts: Entertaining, Moral, and Religious,* vol. v (New York: The American Tract Society, no date).

15. We know that child labor is common in More's period and long after (see E. P. Thompson, *The Making of the English Working Class* [New York: Vintage, 1963], pp. 247 and 249, for example); it is not the story's recognition of the facts about the likely fate of such children, but its tone of unqualified approbation that I note here.

16. For discussion of More's *Strictures on the Modern System of Female Education,* see my last chapter.

17. *Cheap Repository Tracts: Entertaining, Moral, and Religious,* vol. ll, note, p. 7. The editor is not named.

18. See chapter four, pp. 91–94, for discussion of correspondence on Wollstonecraft between More and Walpole.

19. *Works,* vol. lll, p. 1. "The Death of Mr. Fantom," the sequel to "The History of Mr. Fantom," also appears in vol. lll.

20. Hill, p. 22, suggests that in pre-industrial England the words "family" and "household" were virtually synonymous, and that the servants "were

almost as much members of the 'family' as the children of their masters and mistresses." It seems to me that this sense of the household unit might underlie part of More's insistence that the behavior of the master determines the behavior of the servant; as we see in so many of More's stories in the Cheap Repository series, the master has a moral responsibility for the spiritual as well as lawful behavior of those under his rule.

## Seven. Economic Circumstances

1. The pairing of good and bad apprentices is not a device minted by More, of course. Depictions of contrasting behavior between apprentices have a long history in England: perhaps the most famous illustration of this theme is the set of twelve plates by Hogarth entitled *Industry and Idleness*. The series shows the very different trajectories of Goodchild and Idle; the one, rising quickly and marrying his master's daughter, eventually becomes sheriff of London, alderman, and finally lord mayor, while Idle's career ends at Tyburn. The analysis of these prints in the 1838 *Complete Works of William Hogarth . . . With Some Account of His Life* (London: S. Cornish and Co.), ed. unknown, carries precisely the tone of justice satisfied that we note in More's discussions of "good" and "bad" workers. Hogarth himself seems to have meant the moral to be quite unmistakable, if we are to take as genuine our unknown editor's quotation from Hogarth himself: "Industry and Idleness exemplified in the conduct of two fellow-'prentices; where the one, by taking good courses, and pursuing points for which he was put apprentice, becomes a valuable man, and an ornament to his country; the other, by giving way to idleness, naturally falls into poverty, and ends fatally, as expressed in the last print.—And, lest any print should be mistaken, the description of each print is engraved at top" (3).

Sean Shesgreen, in *Hogarth's Industry and Idleness: A Reading (Eighteenth-Century Studies*, Summer 1976, vol. 9, no. 4) notes that "London was continually threatened by the disorderly conduct of its apprentices in the eighteenth century. . . . [T]ensions mounted in London's most strife-torn neighborhood, building through the 1740s and 1750s to culminate in the final and most violent phase of Spital Fields' history, a lengthy period of intermittent rioting and property destruction of unparalleled dimensions taking place between 1760 and 1773" (590-91). Shesgreen comments that "There are grounds for speculating that *Industry and Idleness* may well represent a parallel effort by Hogarth to contribute to the propaganda campaign by the City's tradesmen and merchants on behalf of order and tranquility among the apprentice and working classes" (592). In other words, Hogarth in his prints as early as the 1740s seems to have been attempting much the same thing More would be doing fifty years later: he is working consciously to try to control a deeply frightening under class. Like More's works directed to the poor, the progress was sold on two grades of paper so that it would be "available to the apprentice class" (Sean Shesgreen, headnote to plate 60, *Engravings by Hogarth* [New York: Dover Publications, 1973] headnote to plate 60).

2. Hannah More, "The Two Shoemakers," in *The Works of Hannah More. A New Edition, with additions and corrections.* 11 Volumes (London: T. Cadell, 1830), vol. lll, p. 440. All further references are to this edition.

3. Olivia Smith, *The Politics of Language: 1791–1819* (Oxford: Clarendon Press, 1986), p. 92, points to the passage in which Jack is described as incapable of concentrating or of taking responsibility for his work as an example of More's "realism;" further, "This is Hannah More at her best, portraying

ordinary work in detail, village life as potentially exciting, and a character who is both specific and familiar. The tracts can bring dignity to labour, unspectacular characters, and ordinary settings by the degree of attention which the author manifestly gives them." But as we can see from the context of Jack's failings here, Smith is misinterpreting More's intention. There is nothing positive about what Jack is doing, nor about the "potentially exciting village life" that distracts him. To underscore More's failings in regard to the "realism" of her portraits of the poor, it suffices, I think, to cast an eye back to the extraordinary realism in this context of Daniel Defoe's depictions of the poor and their poverty in works such as *Moll Flanders* and *Roxana*.

    4. Hannah More, "The St. Giles's Orange Girl," in *Works*, vol. IV, p. 99.

    5. Hannah More, "The History of Tom White the Postboy. In Two Parts," in *Works*, vol. IV, p. 1.

    6. Charles Howard Ford, *Hannah More: A Critical Biography* (New York: Peter Lang, 1996) makes a number of interesting points in his discussion of "Tom White." He reminds us that the boom in eighteenth-century domestic tourism meant that a postboy indeed could do quite well financially; Ford also notes that "irresponsible postboys were obviously a plague to the genteel traveler" (p. 140). Ford comments that More in stories such as "The Two Shoemakers" and "Tom White" is "catering to the materialism of Georgian Britain.... More insisted that juvenile industry developed personal economy which attracted patrons" (p. 141).

    7. Henry Thompson, *The Life of Hannah More: With Notices of Her Sisters,* 2 vol. (Philadelphia: E. L. Carey and A. Hart, 1838), pp. 172–74, comments on the "close resemblance" of Mrs. Jones and Hannah More herself, and notes that "Not the least curious feature of this publication is the complete acquaintance with cottage economy which it exhibits, at a time when the knowledge of that science was chiefly to be gained by experience and reflection. By some it is commonly received as indisputable that a literary woman must be a bad economist; and it may be readily allowed that a *passion* for literature, like a *passion* for dress or dissipation, or any thing else, may estrange a woman from the knowledge of household affairs. Such, however, was not the case in the instance of Hannah More." What Thompson says of "A Cure for Melancholy," the next story to be discussed in this chapter, is equally applicable to the second part of "Tom White:" "In the 'Cure for Melancholy' we have a series of cheap plans for ameliorating the condition of the poor, which must have been the result of careful consideration, and which, in all probability, Mrs. More, to whom her heroine Mrs. Jones bears close resemblance, had actually practiced herself; while in 'The Way to Plenty' the poor are instructed how to make the best of their means, and receipts for cheap dishes are furnished, which Mrs. More must have partly gained by inquiry among the cottagers, or invented and tried herself, although she was, in all probability, indebted for some suggestions to Mrs. Trimmer's 'Economy of Charity,' particularly for the idea of the soup-kitchen." And then he goes on to emphasize the same perspective that More develops in her stories: "Certain it is that the benefits of the Cheap Repository were not exclusively religious and political. By it the poor were taught, during the scarcity of 1795, to economize where they had been accustomed to waste; a lesson of more value than the large sums which Mrs. More actually disbursed in charitable objects; and, doubtless, many an honest labourer had reason to bless the name of Hannah More,

for finding, through the exercise of an economy of which he had before entertained no conception, more comforts in a season of dearth than he had ever been able to enjoy before in years of the greatest abundance."

8. Hannah More, "A Cure for Melancholy," in *Works*, vol. lll, p. 273. "A Cure for Melancholy" appears under different titles in various editions of the Tracts. G. H. Spinney, "Cheap Repository Tracts: Hazard and Marshall Edition," in *The Library* (London: OUP, 1939–40), vol. 20, p. 329, lists "The Cottage Cook, or Mrs. Jones's Cheap dishes, etc" for January, 1797. The title page of the Huntington Library's edition reads "The Cottage Cook, or, Mrs. Jones's Cheap Dishes; Shewing the Way to do much good with little Money." This title page is reproduced in Patricia Demers's *The World of Hannah More* (Lexington: The Univ. Press of Kentucky, 1996), p. 115. Since I am citing the *Works*, I conform to that edition's choice of title. "A Cure for Melancholy" is a three-part story; "The Sunday School," the second in this series of stories, also appears in volume three of the *Works*; "The History of Hester Wilmot," the last in this set of tales, appears in volume four. Like most of the individual stories in the Tracts, this set of stories gets relatively little attention from most critics; Demers, for example, mentions them briefly, omitting entirely "A Cure for Melancholy" and giving just a bit of plot summary for the other two. Her most interesting comment in this context is that More makes a habit of self-reference, "underscor[ing] the effectiveness of lessons inculcated by continuing to advertise intertextually" (114), a tactic I will explore at a number of points in the following discussion.

9. The subsistence the St. Giles Orange Girl ekes out in the best of cases certainly does not bring her to the same economic level that the protagonists of "Tom White" or "The Two Shoemakers" attain.

10. Elizabeth Kowaleski-Wallace in *Their Fathers' Daughters* (New York: Oxford Univ. Press, 1991) discusses "The Cottage Cook" at length (83–86), but rather than attempting to place More's story within eighteenth-century political and social history, Kowaleski-Wallace, as she does so often, insists on forcing More's tale into the template of rather odd feminist concerns: "In an important way, the body remains a central image in 'The Cottage Cook,' as many of Mrs. Jones' reforms serve to alter or control the way the rural poor live their bodies" (85). "Clearly," she tells us, "the point of this tale is to sketch out an important role for the middle classes who are to help the working classes learn the necessary self-discipline allowing for the containment of desire, and Mrs. Jones'actions exemplify a middle-class agency. But what kind of agency is at stake here? . . . It has been argued that such fiction 'encodes reformist aims and reflects *female* cultural bias.' Reading the *Cheap Repository Tracts* as 'a meaty chapter in that bourgeois renovation of manners and morals which marks the transition from the eighteenth to the nineteenth century century,' one critic discovers not so much 'Tory political stasis' as 'a *woman's brand* of bourgeois progressivism—pedagogy, philanthropy, and purification [were More's] cures for the old order's social ills.' Yet three questions implicitly arise from such a perspective. First, what makes the cultural bias identified here distinctly female? Second, in what sense does the kind of progressivism posited here constitute 'a woman's brand' of reform? Is 'a woman's brand' of progressivism different from a male version of the same phenomenon? Third, how 'progressive' is 'a woman's brand' of progressivism? The answers to these questions are important to clarify the argument

and also to illuminate the relation of gender to class issues in Evangelical politics" (83–84). I quote these comments at length because they are typical of much feminist analysis of More (the critic to whom Kowaleski-Wallace alludes is Mitzi Myers), an angle of analysis that seems to me quite far from useful in discussing such issues as these.

11. The fear that educating the poor poses a danger to the upper classes of course does not first present itself in More's time. Claude Rawson, "Killing the Poor: An Anglo-Irish Theme?" in *Essays in Criticism* XLIX, April 1999, no. 2, p. 103 notes that "Mandeville's and Swift's reservations about charity schools were that the poor might be educated away from their station and usefulness, anxieties still active in more nuanced ways a century later, for example in Hannah More." Jacqueline Pearson, *Women's Reading in Britain: 1750–1835* (Cambridge: Cambridge Univ. Press, 1999), p. 179, explores this idea further: "The radical right drew on Mandeville's 'Essay on Charity and Charity Schools' (1773), arguing that society would not benefit from increased lower-class literacy, for reading 'keeps the Poor from Working.' It is not 'the want of Reading and Writing' that causes crime; quite the contrary, for education only produces cleverer criminals." Pearson makes reference to a number of More's contemporaries such as Humphrey Repton, Mary Berry, and Thomas Moore who voiced hesitations along these lines.

12. Thompson, pp. 114–15, notes that More also "encouraged the attendance of farmers' children at her schools, on the payment of small periodical sums." This too, it is clear from his account, is based on a kind of one-upmanship. "Here she met with no opposition. It was to the education of the labourer, not of himself, that the farmer objected. His ignorance prevented his estimating, but not his acknowledging, the value of learning, which it rather led him to exaggerate. Beside, it was now too late to keep his labourer in ignorance, and the only way of maintaining his own superiority was by acquiring superior knowledge. Writing and ciphering, he was well aware, were useful things, and he was willing to spare a trifle to secure these things for his children; and writing and ciphering, Mrs. More very readily allowed, were beneficial and appropriate knowledge for the boy of this class, who had, beside, more time to spare for their acquirement than the child of the day labourer. This addition, therefore, was made in the case of those farmers' children who attended the week-day schools; and the effects fully realized the expectation. The agricultural class became proportionally raised in the scale of spiritual and reasonable beings; and as they associated daily with those who were to be their future servants, the kindly affections of childhood were brought in aid of the commandments of the Gospel."

## Eight. Conclusion

1. Hannah More, *Strictures on the Modern System of Female Education*, 2 vols. (London: A. Strahan, Printers Street, for T. Cadell and W. Davies, Strand, 1799.)

2. The dates of publication relevant here are for *Village Politics* 1792; "The History of Mr. Fantom," 1797 (August); *Strictures on the Modern System of Female Education* 1799.

3. Virtually all modern critics who write about More's ideas on education refer to the fact that More's contemporary, Mary Berry, pointed out

this rather interesting similarity of thought between More and Wollstone-
craft—and noted that More certainly would not be pleased to find herself in
Wollstonecraft's company. See for example Mitzi Myers, "Reform or Ruin: 'A
Revolution in Female Manners,'" *Studies in Eighteenth-Century Culture* II
(Madison: Univ. of Wisconsin Press, 1982), p. 203, as well as Elizabeth
Kowaleski-Wallace, *Their Fathers' Daughters: Hannah More, Maria Edgeworth
& Patriarchal Complicity* (New York and Oxford: Oxford Univ. Press, 1991), p.
214, note 18, and Donna Landry, *The Muses of Resistance* (Cambridge: Cam-
bridge Univ. Press, 1990), p. 313, note 10. Modern discussions of the connections between the thought of More and Wollstonecraft on education, however,
generally focus on parallels between More's *Strictures* and Wollstonecraft's
*Vindication,* as in Landry, pp. 259–60 and Harriet Guest, "The Dream of a
Common Language: Hannah More and Mary Wollstonecraft" in *Textual Practice* 9 (2) 1995, 303–323, *passim.* As I suggest in this chapter, however, it seems
to me that the most suggestive place to look for such parallels in fact is in the
work that each woman produced in the same genre, that is, More's *Strictures*
and Wollstonecraft's *Thoughts.* Of course *Thoughts* represents Wollstonecraft
before she has been radicalized by the debates of the period following the
French Revolution; I will turn to *Wrongs of Woman* later in this chapter.

4. Mary Wollstonecraft, *Thoughts on the Education of Daughters: With
Reflections on Female Conduct in the more important Duties of Life* (Clifton N.J.:
Augustus M. Kelley, 1972, repr. 1787 edition pub. London: J. Johnson), 20–21.

5. The topic of Wollstonecraft and sensibility has received a great deal
of attention, including much discussion of Wollstonecraft's own ambivalence
about sensibility itself over the course of her career. One of the best recent
studies of Wollstonecraft and sensibility is Syndy Conger's *Mary Wollstonecraft
and the Language of Sensibility* (Rutherford, N. J.: Fairleigh Dickinson Univ.
Press, 1994).

6. Moira Ferguson, "Introduction" to *Maria or The Wrongs of Woman* by
Mary Wollstonecraft (New York: Norton, 1975), p. 12.

7. Jemima notes that she was able to stay at table and thus be privy to
these discussions only because she is not a respectable woman, for had she
been wife instead of mistress, the intellectual conversation would take place
only after she had left the table. More makes precisely the same complaint:
"men postpone every thing like instructive discourse till the ladies are with-
drawn; their retreat serving as a kind of signal for the exercise of intellect"
(ll, 46).

8. Barbara M. Benedict, "The 'Beauties' of Literature, 1750–1820: Taste-
ful Prose and Fine Rhyme for Private Consumption" in *1650–1850: Ideas,
Aesthetics, and Inquiries in the Early Modern Era,* ed. Kevin Cope (New York:
AMS Press, 1994), pp. 317–346, presents a graceful overview of the period's
fascination with the concept of the literary compilations known as "Beauties." Her findings support all of More's complaints: these compilations were
widely popular and indeed were used—if not necessarily intended—as short-
cuts to a socially adequate awareness of literature.

# Index

series, 188; "The Way to Plenty;
or The Second Part of Tom
White. Written in 1795, "The
Year of Scarcity," 191-197,
232n6; *Village Politics by Will
Chip*, xii, 4, 12-13, 33, 66-67, 101,
103, 105, 108-124, 126, 135, 164,
170,175, 210, 237n3, 238n5,
238n7, 243n3; hierarchy in, 114-
115; motivation for, 136; religion
in, 115; taxes in, 115, 119, 182;
reprinted as *Village Disputants*,
103; response to, 121-124

More, Martha, 236n16
More, Patti: *Mendip Annals*, 2, 9, 203
More, Sally, 70
Myers, Mitzi, 19, 234n1, 245n10

"O the Roast Beef of Old England,"
67, 120, 238n7
"Old Cumberland Beggar, The," 34
Ordinance of Laborers, 20

Paine, Thomas, 11, 13, 18, 35, 38, 39,
40, 50, 65-66, 83, 92, 108, 114-
115, 119, 126, 136, 207-208,
232n7, 233n11, 233n20, 233n21;
Trial for sedition, 41, 66; *Age of
Reason*, 13, 135, 164; *Common
Sense*, 40, 51, 233n20; *Rights of
Man*, xi, 3-4, 37-66, 69, 85, 118-
119, 121, 135, 164, 195, 208; as
economic treatise, 49, 53-55;
success of, 39; —Topics in:
America, 55-57; America, praise
of, 55-56; aristocracy, 46;
aristocratic succession, 46;
Burke, 48; class, 43; church, 46;
civil government, 59; civil
rights, 43; commerce, 58;
corruption, 49, 57; economics in,
41, 48; English Constitution, 45-
46, 56; empire, 58; equality, 43;
expense of Government, 48;
expense of kings, 48; France, 47,
49; function of government, 55;
hereditary lawmaking body, 59;
hereditary monarchy in, 41, 56-
57, 59; instruction of youth, 59;

legality of kings, 48; military,
cost of, 61-62; monarchy, 46, 48;
monarchy, cost of, 61; natural
rights of man, 41, 43-44;
pamphlet sales, 51-52, 65-66;
parish laws, 45; parish system,
58; pensions, 62-63; Political
Reform, 49; poor, criminality of,
59; poor rates, 62-63; progressive taxation of estates, 64;
Primogeniture in, 41, 46, 53, 61;
publishing history, 51-52;
readers, 51; redistribution of
property, 83, 232n8; revolution,
purpose of, 57-58; riot, 55, 64;
style, 52-53; social costs of
monarchy, 53; Spanish Inquisition, 47; systems of taxation in,
41, 56, 59-60; axes, 48, 60-63;
taxation of commodities, 53;
taxation, history of, 59-62; war,
purpose of, 55, 57
Paley, Archdeacon, 124
Palk, Mrs., 71
pamphlets: designed to make poor
politically inert, 136; dissemination of, 41, 65-66, 94, 100-103,
121-124; sales of *Burke's
Reflections*, 50; Paine's *Rights of
Man*, 65-66; Price's *Observations
of Civil Liberty*, 39
Pamphlet Wars, xi, 3-4, 13, 37, 103-
105, 207
Parish support: More, 117, 129, 159,
175, 233n9; Parish hospitals, 128
Pearson, Jacqueline, 239n4, 246n11
Penny Papers. *See* Pamphlet Wars
Phillips, Richard, 66
Piozzi, Hester Thrale, 80, 89, 236n16
Pitcairn, Dr., 238n5
Pitt, William the Younger, 38, 41, 86,
125
Place, Francis, 125
poaching, 147-149
poor: attitudes toward situation in
life, and blessings, 140-41;
availability of work, 29-30;
barbarous nature of, 97-99;
character of, 33, 59; child labor,
82-83, 117, 145, 156-163, 17-178,

September Massacres, 125
Sheffield, 65
Shesgreen, Sean, 238n7, 243n1
slavery, 83-84
Smith, Olivia, 232n2, 243n3
social hierarchy, 26-28, 34, 114-115
Spence, Thomas, 38
Lady Spencer,      75
Spinney, G.H., 242n14, 245n8
Spital Fields, 243n1
Stonehouse, Sir James, 8, 102, 229n4
*The Stranger*, 215
Sunday schools, 10, 87, 149, 169
Swift, Jonathan, 242n11, 246n11

taxation: More on 111, 113-114, 115,
   119; Paine on 48-49, 53-54, 58-63
Thelwell, John, 38
Thompson, E.P., 27, 38-40, 65-66,
   124-125
Thompson, Henry, 2, 5-7, 13, 234n2,
   237n3, 244n7
Thrale, Mr. and Mrs., 73
Tooke, Horne, 41, 92
Townsend, Robert, 89, 233n9, *A
   Dissertation on the Poor Laws* 4,
   11, 21, 22-35, 63, 231n6
Trimmer, Sarah, 10, 80-83; "The
   Economy of Charity," 10, 244n7;
   *Fabulous Histories*, 80; *Sacred
   Histories*, 81
Turner, Mr., 7-8, 229n4
Turner, Cheryl, 235n6
Two Acts (Sedition Bills), 38, 232n5

Vesey, Elizabeth, 79
Voltaire, 257

Walker, Thomas, 84
Walpole, Horace, 6, 70, 74, 80, 84,
   88, 165; correspondence with
   More, 89-97; 234n1, 237n16

Walvin, James, 184
Washington, George, 233n20
Wedgwood, Josiah, 4-5, 178, 241n9;
   level of language, 134; An
   Address to the Workmen in the
   Pottery on the Subject of
   Entering into the Service of
   Foreign Manufacturers, 118,
   125-134
Wickham, Rev. Hill Dawe, 6
Wilberforce, William, 10-11, 38, 84,
   98
Willis, Dr., 85
Wilkinson, John, 125
Wollstonecraft, Mary, 5, 11, 40, 50,
   54, 91-92, 94, 110, 114, 165, 207-
   208, 213, 215, 234,n3, 238n6,
   246n3, 247n5: Works: *Maria, or
   the Wrongs of Woman* 110-111,
   213, 215; *Thoughts on the
   Education of Daughters, With
   Reflections on Female Conduct in
   the More Important duties of Life*
   216-219, 246n3; —topics in:
   Bible, 219; education of servants, 221-222; education of
   women, 247n7; education of
   young ladies, 218; "improper
   books," 218; masters and
   religious education of servants,
   217; sensibility, 218; woman's
   intellectual ability, 219-222
Wordsworth, Jonathan, 37-38, 135
Wordsworth, William, 34, 241n9
Wyvill, Christopher, 39

Yearsley, Ann, 9, 11, 74-79, 89, 95-
   97, 98, 108, 222, 234n5, 235n6
York family, 74
Yorkshire anti-sedition bill meetings, 38